Recursive Neural Networks for Associative Memory

WILEY-INTERSCIENCE SERIES IN SYSTEMS AND OPTIMIZATION

Advisory Editors

Peter Whittle
Statistical Laboratory, University of Cambridge, 16 Mill Lane, Cambridge CB2 1SB, UK

Sheldon Ross
Department of Industrial Engineering and Operations Research, University of California, Berkeley, CA 94720, USA

GITTINS—Multi-armed Bandit Allocation Indices

WHITTLE—Risk-sensitive Optimal Control

KAMP and HASLER—Recursive Neural Networks for Associative Memory

Recursive Neural Networks for Associative Memory

YVES KAMP
Philips Research Laboratory, Louvain-la-Neuve, Belgium

MARTIN HASLER
Ecole Polytechnique Fédérale de Lausanne, Switzerland

JOHN WILEY & SONS
Chichester · New York · Brisbane · Toronto · Singapore

Other Wiley Editorial Offices

John Wiley & Sons, Inc., 605 Third Avenue,
New York, NY 10158-0012, USA

Jacaranda Wiley Ltd, G.P.O. Box 859, Brisbane,
Queensland 4001, Australia

John Wiley & Sons (Canada) Ltd, 22 Worcester Road,
Rexdale, Ontario M9W 1L1, Canada

John Wiley & Sons (SEA) Pte Ltd, 37 Jalan Pemimpin   05-04,
Block B, Union Industrial Building, Singapore 2057

Library of Congress Cataloging-in-Publication Data:

Kamp, Yves.
  Recursive neural networks for associative memory / Yves Kamp,
Martin Hasler.
    p. cm. — (Wiley-Interscience series in systems and
optimization)
  Includes bibliographical references and index.
  ISBN 0 471 92866 6
  1. Neural networks (Computer Science) 2. Associative storage.
I. Hasler, Martin. II. Title. III. Series.
QA76.87.K36 1990
006.3—dc20   90-42923
                                              CIP

British Library Cataloguing in Publication Data:

Kamp, Yves
Recursive neural networks for associative memory. – (Wiley-
Interscience series in systems and optimization)
1. Artificial intelligence
I. Title II. Hasler
006.3

ISBN 0 471 92866 6

Printed in Great Britain by Biddle Ltd., Guildford

Contents

Contents

Preface

Recent results have stirred considerable interest in a class of electronic circuits, called neural networks, that provide a promising way of looking at some data processing problems. Neural networks are systems made of a large number of simple computational elements operating in parallel; these elements are called "neurons" or "formal neurons". The function of these networks is primarily determined by the connection topology between the neurons, by the connection strengths and the type of processing performed at the computing elements. Although the processing performed by each individual element is often quite elementary, the complete system however is capable of high level functions such as classification, optimization and associative memory. Neural networks can be looked upon from two different viewpoints. On the one hand, they provide strongly idealized models for elucidating the basic properties and the type of processing performed in biological nervous systems. On the other hand, these models can be implemented as electronic circuits in order to perform some specific data processing task without any reference to the biological systems which originally inspired these models. This book will essentially deal with the second type of network.

The interest in neural networks can be traced back to the first half of this century and the paper by McCulloch and Pitts published in 1943 can certainly be considered as one of the milestones in the mathematical analysis of networks of formal neurons [McCulloch and Pitts 43]. In the McCulloch and Pitts model, each processing unit or formal neuron computes a weighted sum of the signals produced by the other units and compares this result with some threshold. If the threshold value is exceeded, the neuron is activated and its activity level is then propagated through the network for subsequent processing steps. In this very simplified form, networks of formal neurons behave as discrete time, discrete valued systems. The contribution of McCulloch and Pitts triggered much interest at the time because it showed that any logical expression satisfying some conditions could be realized by a network of formal neurons. The general conclusion was that very simple processing elements were capable of generating complex behaviour provided they are combined and integrated into a network having the appropriate connectivity pattern.

When compared with sequential systems, neural networks stand out in sharp contrast. They are densely interconnected structures with a high degree of parallelism in which the information processing is widely distributed across the whole structure. One of the reasons for renewed interest in neural networks is that recent technological progress in large scale integrated circuits makes it much easier to build massively parallel machines and one can therefore consider that the hardware implementation of neural networks is now within reach.

Parallel structures allowing high speed computations with elementary processing elements is not the only feature which makes neural networks so attractive. A second advantage is that the information processing is distributed over the whole structure and that the network therefore exhibits better robustness to faulty elements and lower sensitivity to small discrepancies in the performance of the individual computational units.

The type of function realized by the network is mainly defined by its connectivity pattern. All the long-term knowledge required to perform this function is encoded in the connection strengths by means of the weights applied to the signal which is transmitted. This makes it possible to store a large amount of knowledge in a network with a moderate number of computational elements. A common feature of a large majority of neural networks is that this encoding of the knowledge sources can be realized by adaptive learning techniques instead of imposing a priori values to the connection strengths. This feature is especially attractive when complicated tasks have to be performed where the decision rules are difficult to formulate explicitly, as for example in speech recognition or for certain problems in image processing. In contrast, the short-term knowledge, which results from the processing of the input data, is encoded by the activity levels of the network units.

The field of neural networks has considerably expanded in the last ten years and a wide variety of networks have been proposed which all share the basic properties mentioned above. They can be distinguished from each other, either by the particular function performed, by the topology of the connections and the type of learning used to determine the parameter values. A classification can be found in references [Lippmann 87], [Pearson and Lippmann 88]. Here, we will concentrate on a single neural architecture, known as an "associative memory" [Kohonen 77] or a "Hopfield network" [Hopfield 82]. These networks are "recursive" systems because, at each clock period, the output signals of the units are fed back collectively to the inputs.

Recursive networks for associative memories are able to reconstruct exact and complete information from incomplete and degraded data. One assumes first that the network has stored a number of prototype vectors in its internal structure, i.e. in the weights applied by the links connecting the different units. The initial state of these units represents a corrupted or incompletely specified vector of data and the activity level of the units is then updated according to some specific scheme until the network stabilizes on one of the memorized prototypes. The typical application field for such networks is thus the realization of content-addressable memories. It is well known that the performance of traditional address-based memories is limited; on the one hand, because of the serial nature of the processing where each piece of information must be handled sequentially, and, on the other hand, because an important part of the resources is involved merely to calculate the effective address of the necessary data word. In contrast, content-addressable memories are considerably more efficient since all hypotheses are explored in parallel and because the information storage and retrieval is based on the data itself and not on its arbitrary storage location.

Hopfield was among the first to show that, under certain conditions, the dynamic behaviour of recursive networks was ruled by an energy function which decreases monotonically along the system trajectory [Hopfield 82], [Hopfield 84]. This implies that the network converges to a local energy minimum and one concludes therefore that recursive networks can be used, not only as associative memories, but also to solve certain optimization problems.

In this book, we shall discuss the different problems which arise in the analysis and design of discrete time, discrete valued recursive networks. It turns out that, compared with many other types of neural systems, these networks form a special class. For one thing, they exhibit surprisingly complex behaviour, in spite of their simple architecture and dynamic rules. Quite naturally therefore, there exists no unique approach which is capable of describing and explaining all their properties. Instead, the present state of knowledge is the result of a collection of rather different but complementary points of view. The natural consequence is that the results are scattered over different scientific disciplines, each using its own methodology. On the other hand, these networks have experienced an upsurge of interest from broad sectors of the scientific community, witnessed by an increasing flow of publications. The conjunction of these two factors makes this field difficult to access for uninitiated readers. The purpose of this book is to give a simple and structured introduction to this new domain and to provide a guideline through a wealth of material which is not always easy to classify or to put in perspective. With this aim in view, the authors have tried to give a coherent presentation by classifying the most relevant results according to the approach followed. This organization of the book leads inevitably to some arbitrariness, not only in the selection of the contributions, but also in the simplifications required to arrive at a reasonably simple ordering of the material. In particular, some quite interesting results have not been incorporated because they would have obscured the general perspective. It is hoped that this drawback has, to some extent, been remedied by the provision of an extensive list of bibliographical references for more advanced developments. In any case, no claim is made that the selection made is the best or the only possible one : it rather reflects the authors' personal preferences, for which they take full responsibility.

Acknowledgements

The authors are grateful to all those who contributed to the realization of this book.

Yves Bernard made his "NeWSillustrator" software available for the production of the figures.

Marc Vauclair skilfully adapted the LaTeX styles to meet the required page layout.

Several discussions with Philippe Piret helped to clarify some technical questions.

Chapter 1

Principles, problems and approaches

1.1 Principles

1.1.1 Basic definitions

A recursive neural network is a discrete time, discrete valued dynamic system which, at any given instant of time, is characterized by a binary state vector. More precisely, for a recursive network with n units, the *state vector* at time t is of the general form

$$x(t) = [x_1(t), x_2(t), \ldots, x_n(t)]^T \in \{-1, 1\}^n, \tag{1.1}$$

where T denotes transposition. That is, $x(t)$ is a column n-vector whose elements take the values ± 1. The network *dimension* is n.

Let $W = [w_{ij} : 1 \leq i, j \leq n]$ be a real $n \times n$ matrix and θ a real n-vector. The behaviour of the system along the time axis is described by a *dynamic equation* of the type

$$x_i(t+1) = \text{Sgn}\,[\sum_{j=1}^{n} w_{ij}\, x_j(t) - \theta_i], \qquad i = 1, 2, \ldots, n, \tag{1.2}$$

with the convention

$$\sum_{j=1}^{n} w_{ij}\, x_j(t) - \theta_i = 0, \qquad \Rightarrow \quad x_i(t+1) = x_i(t). \tag{1.3}$$

The matrix W and the vector θ are the *parameters* of the network. One observes that there are 2^n possible state vectors, represented by the vertices of the n-dimensional hypercube C^n. In the course of time, the successive state vectors generated by the dynamic equations (1.2) run through the vertices of the hypercube and the network thus performs a mapping of C^n, the space $\{-1, 1\}^n$, into itself. On the other hand, for fixed i, the right hand side of (1.2) can be considered as a *threshold function* in n variables since it performs

1

a mapping of C^n into $\{-1,1\}$. From this point of view, a recursive neural network consists of a set of n threshold functions which are recursively applied to linear functions of their outputs.

A recursive network can be considered as an extremely simplified model of the human brain. In the framework of such a neurobiological interpretation, each element of the state vector corresponds to a neuron and w_{ij} is then the *synaptic weight* of the link connecting neuron j to neuron i. The quantity

$$h_i(x(t)) = \sum_{j=1}^{n} w_{ij}\, x_j(t) \tag{1.4}$$

represents the *synaptic potential* applied to neuron i; if this potential exceeds some given *threshold* θ_i, neuron i is activated. The *vector of synaptic potentials* is defined as

$$h(x) = [h_1(x), h_2(x), \ldots, h_n(x)]^T. \tag{1.5}$$

Usually, the connections between neurons are supposed to be symmetrical, i.e. $w_{ij} = w_{ji}$, which implies that the *synaptic matrix* W itself is symmetric. This hypothesis might be explained by the fact that the popular Hebb law, described in Subsection 1.2.2, automatically leads to symmetric synaptic matrices. In addition, the symmetry of W also guarantees some useful properties, as we shall see in Chapter 2. From a biological point of view however, this symmetry assumption is not justified since physiological measurements have shown that the excitatory ($w_{ij} > 0$) or inhibitory ($w_{ij} < 0$) attribute of a synapse is exclusively determined by the emitting neuron j [Eccles 77], [Kuffler et al. 84]. Unfortunately, asymmetric networks are much more difficult to analyze, which explains why much less is known about this type of network. Therefore, we shall almost always restrict the analysis to symmetric synaptic matrices; exceptions to this rule will be made in Subsection 3.3.4 and in Chapter 6 because some learning techniques used for determining the synaptic matrix are unable to take the symmetry requirement into account. On the other hand, one usually puts $w_{ii} = 0$, supposing that a neuron has no selfconnection. Consequently, the synaptic matrix should have a zero diagonal, but this constraint will not systematically be taken into account in the sequel. Let us also observe that, without loss of generality, the synaptic matrix can be normalized so that $|w_{ij}| \leq 1, (i,j = 1,2,\ldots,n)$. As for the *threshold vector* θ, it will be assumed to be zero, whenever this hypothesis in not critical for the results we wish to establish. The choice of θ is not completely immaterial however since, for example, $\theta = 0$ implies $\mathrm{Sgn}(Wx) = -\mathrm{Sgn}(Wy)$ for each pair of vectors such that $x = -y$. However, it is possible to simulate a threshold by extending the state vector by one unit whose activity level is permanently equal to -1 and by defining an extended synaptic matrix $[W\ \theta]$ of dimension $n \times (n+1)$.

Remark • Sometimes the state vectors are assumed to belong to the space $\{0,1\}^n$ instead of $\{-1,1\}^n$. This is the convention adopted in, for example, [Hopfield 82], [Goles and Olivos 81], [Goles 82], [Goles et al. 85], [Weisbuch and Fogelman-Soulie 85], [Fogelman-Soulie and Weisbuch 87]. The dynamic equation (1.2) is then replaced by

$$u_i(t+1) = H[\sum_{j=1}^{n} w_{ij}\, u_j(t) - \theta_i'], \qquad i = 1, 2, \ldots, n, \tag{1.6}$$

where $u_i \in \{0,1\}$, H is the Heaviside unit step function defined by

$$
\begin{aligned}
H(y) &= 0 \qquad \text{if } y < 0, \\
     &= 1 \qquad \text{if } y > 0,
\end{aligned}
\tag{1.7}
$$

with the convention $u_i(t+1) = u_i(t)$ if $y = 0$. The change of variable $x_i = 2u_i - 1$ achieves the transformation from the domain $\{0,1\}$ to the domain $\{-1,1\}$ and equation (1.6) becomes then

$$x_i(t+1) = 2H[\frac{1}{2}\sum_{j=1}^{n} w_{ij}\, x_j(t) + \frac{1}{2}(\sum_{j=1}^{n} w_{ij} - 2\theta_i')] - 1. \tag{1.8}$$

Since the factor $1/2$ plays no rôle in the argument of the unit step function, one finally obtains

$$x_i(t+1) = \text{Sgn}\,[\sum_{j=1}^{n} w_{ij}\, x_j(t) + \sum_{j=1}^{n} w_{ij} - 2\theta_i']. \tag{1.9}$$

Comparison with equation (1.2) shows that the values of the threshold vectors in the domains $\{-1,1\}^n$ and $\{0,1\}^n$ are not independent. If one chooses $\theta = 0$ for a network in the domain $\{-1,1\}^n$, then the equivalent network in the domain $\{0,1\}^n$ should have as threshold values $\theta_i' = \frac{1}{2}\sum_{j=1}^{n} w_{ij}, (i = 1, 2, \ldots, n)$. This observation will be further commented upon in Chapter 3 (§ 3.3.1) where it will become apparent that an inappropriate choice for the threshold vector can adversely affect the network performance.

1.1.2 Synchronous, asynchronous and block-sequential dynamics

With the fundamental equation (1.2) as starting point, the elements of the state vector can be updated in different ways.

• *Synchronous operation*

In this case, all components of the state vector are updated simultaneously. The dynamic equation (1.2) can then be written in the more compact form

$$x(t+1) = \text{Sgn}\,[Wx(t) - \theta], \tag{1.10}$$

where the sign function is applied to each component of its argument. This operation mode is thus similar to a Jacobi iteration for the solution of linear equations [Golub and Van Loan 83].

- *Asynchronous operation*

Here, each element of the state vector is updated separately, while taking into account the most recent values for the components which have already been updated. Along this line, several variants are still possible, but the most usual one is *sequential updating* where the new element values are computed in the order in which they appear in the state vector. Thus, when updating element x_i, use will be made of the fact that new values have already been computed for the elements x_1 up to x_{i-1} according to the formula

$$x_i(t+1) = \text{Sgn}\,[\sum_{j=1}^{i-1} w_{ij}\, x_j(t+1) + \sum_{j=i}^{n} w_{ij}\, x_j(t) - \theta_i]. \tag{1.11}$$

This scheme is reminiscent of a Gauss-Seidel iteration in linear algebra [Golub and Van Loan 83]. Starting from the state vector $x(t) = [x_1(t), x_2(t), \dots, x_n(t)]^T$, one complete *sequential iteration* consists in updating successively each of the n components according to equations similar to (1.11) until one obtains the new state vector $[x_1(t+1),\ x_2(t+1), \dots, x_n(t+1)]^T$. Of course the components of the state vector can be updated in some different order, e.g. according to a fixed permutation of the natural order or at random but in such a way that each element is at least updated once in a given interval of time. Since these variants are of little interest, only sequential updating will be considered in the sequel for asynchronous operation mode.

- *Block-sequential operation*

This type of operation is a mixture of the preceding two [Goles 82], [Goles et al. 85]. The state vector is divided in subvectors which are sequentially updated; the elements within each subvector are however updated synchronously. More precisely, one defines an ordered partition $\mathcal{I} = \{I_1, I_2, \dots, I_K\}$ on the set $\{1, 2, \dots, n\}$ such that

$$\forall x \in I_i,\ \forall y \in I_j,\ i < j\ \Rightarrow\ x < y. \tag{1.12}$$

The block-sequential updating scheme associated with $\mathcal{I}$ is then defined as follows. For each $i \in I_k\ (k = 1, 2, \dots, K)$

$$x_i(t+1) = \text{Sgn}\,[\sum_{j=1}^{n} w_{ij}\, z_j - \theta_i], \tag{1.13}$$

where

$$z_j = x_j(t+1) \quad \text{if } j \in I_1 \cup I_2 \cdots \cup I_{k-1},$$
$$z_j = x_j(t) \qquad \text{otherwise.}$$

One can of course consider that the block-sequential mode is the most general one, from which all others can be derived as particular cases. For $K = 1$, namely when $I_1 = \{1, 2, \ldots, n\}$ one obtains the synchronous mode, while $K = n$ corresponds to the asynchronous sequential mode.

1.1.3 Associative memory

Up to now, a particular type of recursive network has been defined and it remains to be shown how such a network can operate as an associative memory. Let us assume that by some means a copy of p binary vectors $\xi^{(1)}$, $\xi^{(2)}, \ldots, \xi^{(p)}$ has been integrated into the structure of a system. The system will behave as an associative memory if it reproduces at its output one of the vectors, say $\xi^{(r)}$, when triggered at the input by a vector $x(0)$ which is sufficiently close to $\xi^{(r)}$. This type of memory has an obvious field of application in classification and pattern recognition problems. In this case, $\xi^{(r)}$ will be selected as a typical representative, hence called *prototype vector*, of class r. Depending on the particular application envisaged, the prototype vector can either be defined a priori, or be selected as the centre of gravity in a collection of samples of the class. Let us point out that it would be more appropriate to call memories of this type *autoassociative memories* as opposed to *heteroassociative memories*. The latter store p *pairs* of vectors $(z^{(r)}, \xi^{(r)})$, $(r = 1, 2, \ldots, p)$ and produce vector $\xi^{(r)}$ at the output when the input is presented with a vector close enough to $z^{(r)}$. In the following, we will mainly deal with the autoassociative case.

Let us now see how a recursive network characterized by the dynamic equations (1.2) could exhibit associative memory properties. One should first observe that a recursive network has, strictly speaking, neither input nor output. The solution consists in using the initialization vector as input. As for the output vector, it will be the vertex of the hypercube on which the state vector finally stabilizes. In order to clarify what stabilization means, it should be noted that two situations can occur in view of the fact that the number of state vectors is finite. Starting from an initial vector $x(0)$, the network can reach :

- either a *cycle*, which means that there exists a natural number $T > 1$, called the *period*, such that $x(t + T) = x(t)$ for sufficiently large t.

- or a *fixed point*, defined by the fact that $x(t + 1) = x(t)$ when t is large enough.

As a consequence of these definitions, it is seen that, if y is a fixed point, then this holds true whatever the operation mode of the network, be it synchronous, asynchronous or block-sequential updating. In order for a network to operate as an associative memory, one should first of all be able to impose the prototype vectors $\xi^{(1)}, \xi^{(2)}, \ldots, \xi^{(p)}$ as fixed points. Next, an initial vector $x(0)$, close enough to $\xi^{(r)}$ should converge to it by repeated application of the dynamic equations (1.10) or (1.11), depending on whether the network operates in synchronous or asynchronous mode.

1.1.4   Basins and radii of attraction

In order to measure the dissimilarity between two binary vectors x and y $\in \{-1, 1\}^n$, we shall use the *Hamming distance* $d(x, y)$ defined by

$$d(x, y) = \frac{1}{2} \sum_{i=1}^{n} |x_i - y_i|. \tag{1.14}$$

We shall denote by $N_r(y)$, the *neighbourhood* of y with radius r, namely, the set of binary vectors located at most at distance r from y. Thus

$$N_r(y) = \{x \in \{-1, 1\}^n \mid d(x, y) \leq r\}. \tag{1.15}$$

The *basin of direct attraction* $B_1(\xi)$ of a fixed point ξ is the largest neighbourhood of ξ such that any vector in this neighbourhood is attracted by the fixed point in a *single* iteration :

$$B_1(\xi) = \text{Max}_r\{N_r(\xi) \mid x(0) \in N_r(\xi) \Rightarrow x(1) = \xi\}. \tag{1.16}$$

The *radius of direct attraction* $R_1(\xi)$ is the radius of $B_1(\xi)$.

Remarks • One should distinguish between the basin of direct attraction as defined above and the *domain of direct attraction* $D_1(\xi)$ which is the set of all points in $\{-1, 1\}^n$ which are attracted by ξ in a single iteration :

$$D_1(\xi) = \{x(0) \in \{-1, 1\}^n \mid x(1) = \xi\}. \tag{1.17}$$

Indeed, the domain of attraction can include points which lie outside the basin $B_1(\xi)$ and consequently $B_1(\xi) \subseteq D_1(\xi)$. For example, the network of dimension $n = 2$ and with the parameters

$$W = \begin{bmatrix} 2 & 1 \\ 1 & 1/2 \end{bmatrix}, \qquad \theta = 0,$$

has two fixed points $\xi = [1, 1]^T$ and $\eta = [-1, -1]^T$. The vectors $[1, -1]^T$ and $[-1, 1]^T$ are attracted in a single iteration by ξ and η respectively. Hence, $B_1(\xi) = \{\xi\}$, $B_1(\eta) = \{\eta\}$ but $D_1(\xi) = \{\xi, [1, -1]^T\}$ and $D_1(\eta) = \{\eta, [-1, 1]^T\}$.

• Attraction in asynchronous operation mode will, in general, depend on the order in which the elements are updated. For instance, the network with parameters

$$W = \begin{bmatrix} 1 & -2 \\ -2 & 1 \end{bmatrix}, \qquad \theta = 0,$$

has two fixed points, $\xi = [1, -1]^T$ and $\eta = [-1, 1]^T$. If the elements are updated sequentially, i.e. in the order x_1, x_2, then vector $[-1, -1]^T$ is attracted by ξ and vector $[1, 1]^T$ by η, while the opposite is true if the updating order is x_2, x_1. In view of the intricacies resulting from this type of phenomenon, it will be understood in the following that attraction in asynchronous operation mode will mean that attraction holds whatever the updating order of the elements is. As a consequence of this convention, one easily verifies the following property.

Theorem 1.1 *The basin of direct attraction is independent of the particular operation mode, be it synchronous, asynchronous or block-sequential.*

In the following, we will also be interested in examining the dynamics by which a vector is attracted by a fixed point after *several* iterations. One defines the *basin of attraction of order k*, denoted by $B_k(\xi)$, as the largest neighbourhood of ξ such that any vector in this neighbourhood converges to ξ in k iterations at most :

$$B_k(\xi) = \text{Max}_r\{N_r(\xi) \mid x(0) \in N_r(\xi) \Rightarrow x(k) = \xi\}. \tag{1.18}$$

The *basin of long-term attraction* $B(\xi)$ is defined as the largest neighbourhood of a fixed point in which attraction takes place in a finite number of iterations :

$$B(\xi) = \text{Max}_r\{N_r(\xi) \mid x(0) \in N_r(\xi) \Rightarrow \exists k \quad \text{such that} \quad x(t) = \xi$$
$$\text{if} \qquad t \geq k\}. \tag{1.19}$$

The *radius of attraction of order k*, $R_k(\xi)$ and the *radius of long-term attraction*, $R(\xi)$ of a fixed point ξ are the radii of the neighbourhoods $B_k(\xi)$ and $B(\xi)$ respectively.

1.2 Problems

1.2.1 Introduction

In the preceding section, the concept of fixed points has been introduced in an intuitive way. More precisely, a binary n-vector y is a fixed point if

$$y = \text{Sgn}(Wy - \theta), \tag{1.20}$$

where the sign function is applied componentwise. As we have seen above, one of the first problems to be considered is how to impose prescribed prototype vectors as fixed points of the network. This should in principle be achieved by an appropriate choice of the network parameters, namely the synaptic matrix W and the threshold vector θ. In fact, the threshold vector turns out to be of little practical use for this purpose. Indeed, we shall see in Chapters 2, 3 and 4 that the number p of fixed points is usually smaller than the dimension n of the network. Let us then assume that W' and θ' are the parameters of a recursive network such that prototypes $\xi^{(1)}, \xi^{(2)}, \ldots, \xi^{(p)}$ with $p \leq n$ are fixed points. If these prototype vectors are linearly independent, then the matrix

$$X = [\xi^{(1)}, \xi^{(2)}, \ldots, \xi^{(p)}], \tag{1.21}$$

has full column rank and one can always find a matrix W of order n satisfying the equation $WX = W'X - \theta'\mathbf{1}^T$, where $\mathbf{1}$ is a p-vector of "ones". This implies that there exists a network with zero threshold vector and having the same prototype vectors as fixed points. A simple solution for this equation is given by

$$W = (W'X - \theta'\mathbf{1}^T)(X^T X)^{-1} X^T. \tag{1.22}$$

Consequently, one can define a fixed point by the relation

$$y = \mathrm{Sgn}\,(Wy). \tag{1.23}$$

The general problem of constructing a synaptic matrix so as to impose some vectors as fixed points is far from completely solved, the more so as this problem interferes with other questions which will be examined hereafter. Let us observe by the way that a trivial solution would consist in taking for W the unit matrix or, more generally, a diagonally dominant matrix, i.e. such that $w_{ii} \geq \sum_{j \neq i} |w_{ij}|$ for $(i = 1, 2, \ldots, n)$. This type of solution has to be discarded of course, because it implies that every vector is a fixed point, but with zero radius of attraction.

In the course of time, two rules have emerged as classical solutions to impose fixed points by means of the synaptic matrix W. These are *Hebb's law* and the *projection rule*, also called the *pseudo-inverse rule*. In view of their importance, these solutions will be presented separately below. Other methods to determine W rely essentially on some learning techniques and will be examined in Chapter 6.

1.2.2   Hebb's law and its variants

Based on Hebb's work, the most widely accepted hypothesis explaining the learning mechanism achieved by associative memories is that some functional modification takes place in the synaptic links between the neurons. In partic- ular, it is assumed that correlated neuron activities increase the strength of the synaptic link [Hebb 49]. Usually, this hypothesis of synaptic plasticity is quantitatively expressed by stating that the synaptic weight w_{ij} should increase whenever neurons i and j have simultaneously the same activity level and that it should decrease in the opposite case. Consequently, in order to store a proto- type ξ according to Hebb's hypothesis, the synaptic weight should be modified by an amount $\Delta w_{ij} = \Delta w_{ji} = \eta\, \xi_i\, \xi_j$ where η is a positive learning factor [Anderson and Hinton 81]. For the complete synaptic matrix the modification will thus be

$$\Delta W = \eta \xi \xi^T. \tag{1.24}$$

If several prototype vectors $\xi^{(1)}, \xi^{(2)}, \ldots, \xi^{(p)}$, have to be stored, one considers that the resulting synaptic matrix is given by *Hebb's law*

$$W = \frac{1}{p} \sum_{k=1}^{p} \xi^{(k)} \xi^{(k)T} = \frac{1}{p}\, X\, X^T, \tag{1.25}$$

where X is the matrix (1.21) of the prototype vectors and the normalization factor $1/p$ ensures that $|w_{ij}| \leq 1$. For convenience, other normalizations will occasionally be considered in the sequel. Let us observe in passing that Hebb's law is sometimes referred to as the *sum of outer products* of the prototypes and that, according to (1.25), W has the form of an autocorrelation matrix. When the prototypes are orthogonal, i.e. if $\xi^{(k)T}\xi^{(l)} = n\delta_{kl}$ where δ_{kl} is the Kronecker symbol, they can be retrieved exactly since, in view of (1.25), one has

$$W\xi^{(k)} = \frac{n}{p}\, \xi^{(k)}, \qquad k = 1, 2, \ldots, p, \tag{1.26}$$

which obviously satisfies the definition (1.23) of fixed points. However, if the prototypes are not orthogonal, the correlations between them may prevent exact retrieval and it is to be expected that the number of vectors which can be stored will be reduced if the Hamming distance between these vectors becomes smaller. An interesting result in this respect was derived in [Dembo 89] : if ρn denotes the minimum Hamming distance between prototypes, then one can construct p-tuples of prototypes which cannot be stored as soon as $p > 1/(1 - 2\rho)$. On the other hand, this problem of correlated prototypes is unavoidable since, for most applications, the selection of these prototypes is not free but is imposed by the patterns to be stored. Since orthogonality is in any case an important property, the natural question to ask is what the maximum number of mutually orthogonal vectors is in a binary n-dimensional space. Let us first observe that this question only makes sense if n is even and that, in addition,

n is an upper bound. The conjecture is that this upper bound can indeed be reached but no general proof for this assertion exists so far. Among the many special cases where such a proof can be given, one should mention the case where n is a power of 2. Under the latter hypothesis, the vectors are the columns of the Hadamard matrix of order n for which recursive construction procedures are known [Hall 67].

The expression

$$W = \frac{1}{p}[XX^T - pI_n],\tag{1.27}$$

where I_n is the unit matrix of order n, corresponds to the *Hebbian law with zero diagonal*. In case of orthogonal prototype vectors, retrieval is still exact. Indeed, one has

$$W\xi^{(k)} = (\frac{n}{p} - 1)\xi^{(k)}\tag{1.28}$$

and since in practice $p \leq n$, the right hand side has still the same sign as $\xi^{(k)}$ in view of convention (1.3). Definition (1.23) of the fixed point is thus satisfied.

Since Hebb's rule does not always provide perfect retrieval, a modification has been proposed which allows to give variable weightings to the prototypes in order to reinforce those which are more difficult to memorize [Amari 72]. This *weighted Hebbian rule* is defined by

$$W = \sum_{k=1}^{p} \lambda_k\, \xi^{(k)}\, \xi^{(k)T}, \qquad \lambda_k \geq 0 \text{ and } \sum_{k=1}^{p} \lambda_k = 1,\tag{1.29}$$

or in more compact form

$$W = X\Lambda X^T, \qquad \Lambda = \mathrm{diag}(\lambda_1, \lambda_2, \ldots, \lambda_p).\tag{1.30}$$

In the particular case where the λ_k's are identical and equal to $1/p$, one recovers the classical Hebbian rule (1.25).

Hebb's law together with its variants are said to be *local rules* because the weight of a synapse depends only on the activities of the neurons i and j at both ends. This local character of the Hebbian law is of course important in the framework of a neurobiological interpretation, but it is still considered to be of importance outside this field, even for pattern recognition applications for example, where its real significance is far less obvious.

We shall see hereafter that the number of prototypes which can be stored by Hebb's law is rather limited and the memory will thus quickly reach saturation if new prototypes are continuously acquired in the course of time. In order to model short-term memory, Hebb's law needs thus to be revised so as to allow new prototypes to be stored at the expense of the older ones. A simple implementation of this idea consists in modifying the learning rule (1.24) to

$$\Delta W = \eta \xi \xi^T - \beta W, \tag{1.31}$$

where β $(0 \leq \beta \leq 1)$ is a *forgetting factor* [Kohonen 84]. More sophisticated approaches to the modelling of short-term memories will be examined in Chapter 6.

Finally, it should be observed that with Hebb's law there is no need to completely recompute the synaptic matrix if the set of prototype vectors is modified. When a prototype is added, the new synaptic matrix W' can be obtained from the old one via the following update formula

$$W' = \frac{1}{p+1}[pW + \xi^{(p+1)} \, \xi^{(p+1)T}]. \tag{1.32}$$

1.2.3   The projection or pseudo-inverse rule

Since Hebb's law cannot guarantee perfect retrieval of the prototypes, a completely different construction rule has been proposed for the synaptic matrix [Kohonen 84], [Kohonen and Ruohonen 73], [Kohonen 77], [Amari 77], [Personnaz et al. 85], [Personnaz et al. 86], [Personnaz et al. 87b]. An obvious way of satisfying definition (1.23) is to look for a matrix W such that

$$W \, X = X, \tag{1.33}$$

where X is the matrix (1.21) of the prototype vectors. This amounts to imposing more stringent constraints on W than strictly necessary since equality of the signs on both sides of (1.33) would be sufficient. Nevertheless, this seemingly simple-minded approach gives rise to interesting results. It will again be assumed that X has full column rank, which is a reasonable assumption, since in general $p \leq n$ and since the prototype vectors are usually linearly independent. Reference [Venkatesh and Psaltis 89] presents essentially the same idea but uses a formulation in terms of the spectrum of a linear operator.

Equation (1.33) has in principle an infinite number of solutions given by

$$W = XX^+ + Z \, (I_n - XX^+), \tag{1.34}$$

where $X^+ = (X^T X)^{-1} X^T$ is the pseudo-inverse of X and where Z is an arbitrary matrix of order n [Penrose 56]. Choosing $Z = I_n$ produces the trivial solution $W = I_n$ which, as we have seen above, is meaningless for associative memories. However, the particular solution obtained with $Z = O_n$, i.e.

$$W = XX^+ = X(X^T X)^{-1} X^T, \tag{1.35}$$

gives the *projection rule* also known as the *pseudo-inverse rule*. Matrix W performs the projection of an arbitrary vector on the subspace $\mathcal{X}$ spanned by the p prototypes to be stored. If the prototype vectors are orthogonal, then the projection rule reduces to Hebb's law within a scaling factor since in that case $X^T X = n I_p$. With this orthogonality hypothesis, the action of W on an arbitrary vector x is simply given by

$$ W x = \sum_{k=1}^{p} \alpha_k \, \xi^{(k)} \text{ with } \alpha_k = \frac{1}{n} \, \xi^{(k)T} x, \qquad (1.36) $$

which is equivalent to decomposing x in its components along the prototype vectors. One should keep in mind that, with W given by (1.35), $W x$ is the best least squares approximation of x by means of a linear combination of the prototypes $\xi^{(1)}, \xi^{(2)}, \dots \xi^{(p)}$. If $p = n$, the subspace $\mathcal{X}$ becomes the entire space $\{-1, 1\}^n$ and the projection becomes ineffective. Indeed, one can verify that in this case, $X^+ = X^{-1}$ and $W = I_n$, which brings us back to the degenerate situation where each of the 2^n binary vectors is a fixed point. Thus, when the number of independent prototype vectors to be stored gets close to n, one should expect that the radii of attraction will shrink dramatically. This point will be examined in more detail in the following chapters.

Before closing this subsection, it will prove useful to list some of the properties of projection operators which will be needed in the sequel. Let us first recall that a real projection operator W is formally defined as an *idempotent* symmetric matrix, i.e. satisfying $W^2 = W$ [Golub and Van Loan 83]. The idempotency property implies, in turn, that W is *positive definite* ($W \geq 0$), namely that $z^T W z \geq 0$ for any n-vector z, and this forces the following identity on the matrix elements

$$ \sum_{j \neq i}^{n} w_{ij}^2 = w_{ii}(1 - w_{ii}), \qquad (i = 1, 2, \dots, n). \qquad (1.37) $$

As a consequence, one has the inequality

$$ 0 \leq w_{ii} \leq 1, \qquad (i = 1, 2, \dots, n), \qquad (1.38) $$

showing, in particular, that the normalization $|w_{ij}| \leq 1$ is satisfied. Finally, for the specific projection operator defined in (1.35), one has

$$ \sum_{i=1}^{n} w_{ii} = \text{Tr } W = \text{Tr}[X (X^T X)^{-1} X^T], \qquad (1.39) $$

where Tr denotes the *trace* operator. Since $\text{Tr}(AB) = \text{Tr}(BA)$ if AB is a square matrix, one finds

$$ \sum_{i=1}^{n} w_{ii} = p. \qquad (1.40) $$

As pointed out above, the synaptic matrix defined in (1.35) satisfies the symmetry assumption which is usually made in most analyses of recursive networks. Along the same line, one can also force a zero diagonal in expression (1.35) without affecting perfect retrieval of the prototypes [Personnaz et al. 86]. Indeed, if we put $W' = W - \text{diag}(w_{11}, w_{22}, \ldots, w_{nn})$, then one can verify by using (1.33), (1.38) and convention (1.3) that the elements of $W'\xi^{(k)}$ and $\xi^{(k)}$ have the same sign.

In contrast with Hebb's law, the projection rule (1.35) is *nonlocal* because the value of a synaptic weight w_{ij} depends on the activity level of *all* neurons in the network. However, there exists an iterative procedure which converges to the projection rule and which is characterized by the fact that it consists in successive *local* corrections. This procedure is based on the following idea. One considers the set of linear equations

$$(X^T X)U = X^T, \tag{1.41}$$

where U is a $p \times n$ matrix. To solve this system, the Gauss-Seidel algorithm is applied [Golub and Van Loan 83] and, at each step, one computes the matrix $V = XU$. Since the matrix $X^T X$ of the system is positive definite, the algorithm converges to the solution $U = (X^T X)^{-1} X^T$ and consequently V converges to the pseudo-inverse (1.35). One can show that this method amounts in fact to an iterative computational scheme of the synaptic weights where each stage consists in local corrections [Diederich and Opper 87].

Let us also observe that, just as for Hebb's law, there is no need to completely recompute the projection operator if a prototype is added or removed from the set of vectors to be memorized. Indeed, Greville's theorem gives an incremental procedure for the calculation of the pseudo-inverse [Greville 60].

Finally, it is worth pointing out that the pseudo-inverse rule is well adapted to storing *sequences* of prototypes where an input $\xi^{(i)}$ is required to evoke an output $\xi^{(i+1)}$ [Personnaz et al. 87b], [Guyon et al. 88a], [Guyon et al. 88b]. This problem is in fact just a particular case of *heteroassociation* mentioned in Subsection 1.1.3. Indeed, in order to store the sequence $\xi^{(1)}, \xi^{(2)}, \ldots, \xi^{(p)}$ one should associate the pair of vectors $(\xi^{(1)}, \xi^{(2)}), (\xi^{(2)}, \xi^{(3)}), \ldots, (\xi^{(p-1)}, \xi^{(p)})$. If one defines the matrices $X' = [\xi^{(1)}, \xi^{(2)}, \ldots, \xi^{(p-1)}]$ and $X'' = [\xi^{(2)}, \xi^{(3)}, \ldots, \xi^{(p)}]$, all that is needed is to find a matrix W which satisfies the equation $WX' = X''$. One solution is

$$W = X''(X'^T X')^{-1} X'^T. \tag{1.42}$$

With this synaptic matrix, the network will start generating the sequence as soon as it is initialized with one of its elements.

The pseudo-inverse rule is however not the only solution for insuring heteroassociativity. Herz and his coauthors show how Hebb's law should be extended in order to memorize sequences and isolated prototypes [Herz et al. 88], [Herz et al. 89].

1.2.4   Analysis and synthesis

Approaches to a scientific field can often be classified in two categories which, roughly speaking, could be labeled as *analysis* and *synthesis*. In analytic studies, one is given a system and the purpose is to investigate its properties and essential limitations. For the synthesis problem, on the other hand, one starts from a given list of performance requirements which the system should meet and the purpose here is to compute the system parameters in order to achieve this goal in an optimal way. A typical example of this *analysis-synthesis* approach can be found in *electrical network theory* [Belevitch 68]. This discipline deals with the networks obtained by interconnection of idealized resistances, capacitances and inductances. Electrical network *analysis* consists in collecting, and where necessary in developing, the tools needed to describe the properties of these networks, such as, for example, the fact that some frequency bands are easily transmitted, while others are strongly attenuated. *Synthesis*, in contrast, is concerned with finding the capacitance and inductance values such as to realize a filter with prescribed pass- and stopband behaviour. From a methodological point of view, analysis comes first since it outlines the field of properties which can reasonably be prescribed as a target for the synthesis stage.

In neural networks and more specifically in recursive network theory, one can also distinguish between analysis and synthesis but, in view of the fast evolution of this field, methods for analysis have progressed at a faster pace than techniques for synthesis.

1.2.5   Analysis problems

The question of analysis is discussed in Chapters 2, 3, 4 and 5. The purpose there is to investigate the properties of recursive networks constructed according to Hebb's law or the projection rule. Indeed, these rules are still the most important ones for the determination of the synaptic matrix. So far, we have only given the basic principles on which recursive networks are based but this is sufficient for pointing out where the most important problems lie.

• *Absence of cycles*

The very principle of associative memories relies on the assumption that, starting from an initial state, the network will converge to the nearest fixed point. Thus, before we examine how to impose fixed points, we should find the conditions under which cycles are excluded. In particular, the merits of synchronous, asynchronous and block-sequential operation will be investigated in this respect.

- *Capacity*

We have seen above that, in principle, Hebb's law and the projection rule are able to impose a set of prototype vectors as fixed points. For Hebb's rule, in fact, this may lead to retrieval errors if the prototypes are not orthogonal. Part of the analysis will thus consist in examining to what extent correlation between prototypes reduces the memorization performance. We shall see that this question is related to the important problem of *capacity*, i.e. the maximum number of prototypes which can be imposed as fixed points of the network. We shall mainly investigate the asymptotic capacity limits when the dimension n of the network becomes very large.

- *Parasitic fixed points*

Considering definition (1.23), one sees that, if y is a fixed point, then so is $-y$, which shows that, when a fixed point is deliberately created, some undesirable ones may appear. This situation would still be acceptable if the parasitic fixed points were restricted to the negative of the prototypes. Unfortunately, both experiment and more detailed analysis show that there probably exists a huge number of parasitic fixed points with uncontrollable location. This can considerably impede the retrieval process since a state vector can get trapped in such a parasitic fixed point during the successive iterations of the network. At present, there are very few effective counter-measures against this problem. However, some information is available, as we shall see, on the nature and the number of parasitic fixed points.

Concerning the nature of parasitic fixed points, we shall see in the following chapters, mainly in Subsections 3.3.4 and 4.3.2, that Hebb's law tends to create parasitic fixed points which are linear combinations of the prototypes.

Reference [Bruck and Roychowdhury 90] gives an estimate of the number of parasitic fixed points in the case of a Hebbian law and orthogonal prototypes. Equality (1.26) implies that any binary vector in the linear subspace $\mathcal{X}$ spanned by the prototypes is automatically a fixed point. The problem is then to compute the number of binary vectors in $\mathcal{X}$. The general conclusion is that the number of parasitic fixed points generated in this way grows exponentially with the dimension of the network. The technique used for the derivation of these results is essentially based on the polynomial representation of Boolean functions. A completely different approach, relying on statistical methods, will be developed in Chapters 3 and 4 and the effect of asymmetric synaptic couplings ($w_{ij} \neq w_{ji}$) will also be examined.

- *Basin of attraction*

Each fixed point has a basin of attraction for which a formal definition was given in the preceding section. It is intuitively plausible that a large capacity and a wide basin of attraction are conflicting targets and we shall estimate hereafter the capacity reduction when the radius of attraction increases. It should be stressed that a large proportion of the results concerning basins of attraction are obtained by assuming that the initial state vector is *directly* attracted by the fixed point through a *single* iteration of the dynamic equations. Although the recursive nature of the network is completely ignored in this way, results obtained with this approach are nevertheless important because they highlight the essential limitations of recursive networks. We shall see that it is possible to discuss to some extent the problem of long-term attraction but the technical difficulties are much higher and the results less precise.

1.2.6   Synthesis problems

As a natural continuation of the preceding comments, it is clear that the central synthesis problem, investigated in Chapter 6, can be decomposed as follows.

1. Given a set of prototypes, is it possible to impose these prototypes as fixed points of a recursive network?

2. Assuming that the answer to this first question is affirmative, how should one construct the synaptic matrix W (and possibly the threshold vector θ) in order to achieve this goal?

3. In addition, is it possible to impose a prescribed radius of attraction for the fixed points?

As we have seen, Hebb's law and the projection rule provide more or less an answer to the first two questions, but Hebb's law does not guarantee exact retrieval, whereas the projection rule goes beyond what is strictly required. For the latter, indeed, the synaptic matrix satisfies (1.33), whereas equality in sign would have been sufficient. In view of these facts, some authors have completely reconsidered the synthesis problem on a new basis. Before giving an introduction to these approaches, some general remarks are in order here. In principle, questions 1 and 2 are independent but, in practice, it turns out that there is no efficient algorithm which can provide an answer for the first question without also solving the second one. In fact, the two questions are coupled and should be considered simultaneously. On the other hand, question 3 is generally solved in an indirect way by incorporating it in an extended version of question 2. In these cases, the third question always concerns the basin of *direct* attraction, i.e. the neighbourhood where all vectors are attracted by the fixed point in a single synchronous or asynchronous iteration. This remark is of importance because it shows that, for synthesis problems, the recursive nature of the network is almost systematically ignored.

One can show that the synthesis problem can be formulated as follows : find a matrix W and a vector θ such that the following equation is satisfied

$$\text{Sgn}\left\{[W\ \theta]\begin{bmatrix} x^{(k)} \\ -1 \end{bmatrix}\right\} = \xi^{(k)}, \qquad k = 1,2,\ldots,p, \tag{1.43}$$

for all binary vectors $x^{(k)}$ which should be attracted by $\xi^{(k)}$. Indeed, in the simplest case, $x^{(k)} = \xi^{(k)}$, and the equation above expresses the fact that the prototypes $\xi^{(1)}, \xi^{(2)}, \ldots, \xi^{(p)}$ are fixed points. If, however, one requires that equation (1.43) should hold for a set of vectors $x^{(k)}$ which are noisy versions of $\xi^{(k)}$, then this amounts to *explicitly* specifying a prescribed basin of attraction around each prototype $\xi^{(k)}$ [Gardner et al. 88]. An *indirect* way of imposing such a basin of attraction consists in requiring that the equality (1.43) should hold with a security margin on the absolute value of the components in the left hand side. More precisely, one requires that

$$\xi_i^{(k)}[(W\xi^{(k)})_i - \theta_i] > b, \quad i = 1,2,\ldots,n, \quad k = 1,2,\ldots,p, \tag{1.44}$$

where b is a prescribed positive quantity [Forrest 88], [Diederich and Opper 87]. It is observed that these variants of equation (1.43) are in fact equivalent to verifying that some well defined sets of binary vectors are linearly separable by affine hyperplanes, the normals of which are given by the rows of W. It is then not surprising that a solution to these problems can be obtained via a suitable adaptation of the perceptron algorithm [Fukanaga 72], [Duda and Hart 73], [Tou and Gonzalez 74]. It is known, however, that this algorithm converges only if the vectors are indeed separable, which shows, incidentally, that questions 1 and 2 above are solved simultaneously. These adaptations of the perceptron algorithm proceed by successive corrections of the synaptic weights and they can thus be interpreted as a particular form of learning. Some authors propose to maximize the security margin b in (1.44) by linear programming or some other techniques [Krauth and Mézard 87], whereas Peretto suggests a relaxation method [Peretto 88].

The preceding considerations have shown that a recursive network limited to direct attraction can in fact be compared to a particular type of linear classifier which should separate by appropriate hyperplanes the different prototypes and the vectors belonging to their basin of attraction. By pushing this analogy somewhat further, one is led to the following generalization of equation (1.43)

$$\text{Sgn}\left\{[W\ \theta]\begin{bmatrix} x^{(k)} \\ -1 \end{bmatrix}\right\} = z^{(k)}, \tag{1.45}$$

where $z(k) \in \{-1,1\}^n$ is not necessarily the prototype vector of class k but some binary code attached to this class. This last formulation reduces the synthesis of recursive networks (at least as far as direct attraction is concerned) to the synthesis of threshold networks [Dertouzos 65], [Singleton 62].

1.3   Approaches

1.3.1   Introduction

Although recursive networks are governed by a very simple dynamic equation, it will turn out that their behaviour is rather complex and it is thus not surprising that there is no unique approach which can describe all their properties. On the contrary, the present state of knowledge concerning these networks results from the combined conclusions derived from different but complementary approaches. Before embarking on a detailed study, it will prove useful to put these approaches in perspective.

1.3.2   The deterministic approach

As pointed out at the beginning of this chapter, a recursive network is a *discrete* time nonlinear dynamic system. There exists an obvious analogy with the field of *continuous* time nonlinear systems, described by ordinary differential equations, where the stability of the solutions plays a central rôle. A classical approach to this stability problem uses "Liapunov's second method" [Barnett and Storey 70]. The idea of this method depends on a generalization of the energy concept associated with autonomous dynamic systems; the energy is a positive valued function which tends to a minimum as the system converges to an equilibrium point. In order to find out whether cycles can appear in a recursive network, we will use a similar idea. In particular, we will show that cycles are excluded and that the network thus necessarily converges to a fixed point if the state vector can be associated with a scalar function which is monotonically decreasing along a trajectory of the network. In view of the analogy referred to above, this function will be called *energy function*.

The rôle of this energy function is not restricted to the problem of guaranteeing the absence of cycles. Indeed, it will serve as starting point for the extension to higher order networks considered in Chapter 5 and it will also be used to estimate the *transient length*, i.e. the number of iterations needed to reach a fixed point. On the other hand, the monotonic decrease of the energy function is of interest in its own right as well as an analytic test. In this sense, a recursive network is no longer used as an associative memory but as a means for the minimization of a cost function which can be expressed as the energy function associated with a recursive network. Precisely, many problems in robotics and pattern recognition amount to an optimization problem which requires the minimization of a function of very many variables, a task of considerable complexity requiring very large computation times on sequential machines. On the other hand, parallel electronic architectures can provide attractive solutions for these problems, since the internal variables are simultaneously adjusted in a consistent way via the dynamic equations. As a consequence, parallel realizations of recursive networks can be considered as extremely well suited to the problem of cost function optimization. This point of view is further developed in references [Hopfield and Tank 85], [Tank and Hopfield 86] but lies outside the scope of this book.

Although the energy function concept provides an extremely useful way of guaranteeing the absence of cycles, it is unable to solve the other problems mentioned in Section 1.2; in particular those concerning capacity and basins of attraction. In order to obtain a rough estimate of capacity limitations, we shall make use of the interpretation which considers recursive networks as being essentially linear threshold functions separating binary vectors into a certain number of classes (see § 1.1.1). A capacity bound can thus be obtained by counting how many different separating hyperplanes can be realized and this turns out to be a classical combinatorial problem.

Finally, we shall establish a simple procedure to compute, for a given network, the *radii of direct and long-term attraction* of a fixed point and we shall apply this method to analyze the properties of the weighted Hebbian rule.

All these methods of analysis share the common feature that they rely exclusively on the fundamental dynamic equation (1.2). Consequently, they have a wide range of validity but, on the other hand, the results are rather limited. The general approach just described is called *deterministic* as opposed to the following two which rely on hypotheses concerning the statistical distribution of the prototype vectors or the synaptic weights in order to derive deeper results.

1.3.3 The statistical approach

It was pointed out above that Hebb's law cannot guarantee exact retrieval of the prototype vectors when they are not mutually orthogonal. This problem becomes even more acute if we consider that the network is initialized with a noisy version $x(0)$ of prototype $\xi^{(1)}$, because $x(0)$ will most probably have nonzero components along the rival prototypes and this may considerably perturb the retrieval process. The weak point in the deterministic approach comes from the fact that it does not have the appropriate tools to deal efficiently with the correlations between the state vectors and the prototype vectors. The interest of the statistical approach lies precisely in the fact that it provides these tools. The different variants of the statistical approach rely on a common basic principle which will be illustrated by treatment of the simplest version. There, the correlation between $x(0)$ and $\xi^{(1)}$ is considered as a *signal* with superimposed *noise* coming from the correlation between $x(0)$ and the remaining prototypes $\xi^{(2)}, \xi^{(3)}, \ldots, \xi^{(p)}$. One can easily conceive that the noise term becomes more important when the number of prototypes increases and when the distance between $x(0)$ and $\xi^{(1)}$ is larger. In both cases, the correlation between $x(0)$ and the other prototypes may become too large for correct retrieval. In order to express quantitatively this effect on the capacity of the network and on the radius of attraction, the noise needs to be modelled in a simple way, for example, as a Gaussian random variable. Since the noise is, in fact, the sum of random projections, this Gaussian hypothesis is justified by the central limit theorem [Feller 66], [Cramér 57]. For correct use of this theorem, two conditions should be satisfied : the individual noise terms should be independent random variables and their number should tend to infinity. In order to satisfy the latter condition, the number of units (neurons) in the network should become infinite, with the consequence that the result will hold asymptotically. The independence of the noise terms is a more delicate question. Indeed, the independence assumption is quite plausible when the dynamic equations are applied for the first time, but it is in fact no longer justified for subsequent iterations in view of the fact that the units are fully interconnected. Hence, the results derived by this simple statistical approach are strictly speaking only valid in the framework of direct attraction. More elaborate techniques will be needed to obtain some results concerning long-term attraction.

If d denotes the Hamming distance between two vectors, then $\rho = d/n$ represents the fraction of the elements in which these vectors disagree. Concerning the attraction of a state vector x by a prototype ξ for large values of n, several viewpoints can be considered. First, if a *residual error rate* is tolerated after convergence, then the capacity of the network is of course larger. Second, the ρn initial errors can be considered as *random* errors but, for worst case analysis, one should consider *all* positions which these ρn errors can occupy in the state vector and convergence is then required to take place for each of the $\binom{n}{\rho n}$ error patterns.

The statistical approach consists first in estimating the probability of residual errors after convergence. Next, one determines the upper limit for the number of prototypes in order for this probability to become vanishingly small when the network dimension goes to infinity : this then yields the capacity bound. A variant of this approach consists in defining a *macroscopic variable* or *macrovariable* which should represent the global state of the network and, if possible, also the vicinity of the state vector with respect to a given prototype. An attractive candidate in this respect is the *overlap* $m = n^{-1}x^T\xi$. One of its obvious advantages is that it can be regarded as estimating a statistical mean if n is large. But, macroscopic variables are really useful only if it is possible to set up a *transition function* $m(t + 1) = \phi(m(t))$ because this allows the time evolution of the network to be tracked and thus results to be established concerning long-term attraction [Kinzel 85], [Amari and Maginu 88].

1.3.4 Thermodynamic extension

Recursive neural networks are of interest, not only because they behave as associative memories, but also because they provide a simple model for the investigation of disordered magnetic systems, as, for example, spin glasses. Most magnetic materials have only a single equilibrium state within a global rotation or reflection. For the special class of spin glasses however, an infinite number of stable or metastable configurations are possible. The properties of spin glasses are accurately represented by a system in which the spins interact according to the model of a recursive neural network with the restriction that the state of a spin is not a deterministic variable but a random variable with a *Gibbs distribution*. This analogy with spin glasses goes far beyond the fact that it provides an interesting interpretation for recursive networks. It also suggests that classical techniques of statistical mechanics could be applied to the investigation of these networks. One of these techniques consists in associating with each state vector x some energy level $H(x)$, similar to the energy function used in the deterministic approach. The main difference is that this energy defines here a Gibbs distribution with a probability density of the form

$$\Pr(x) \sim e^{-\frac{H(x)}{T}} \tag{1.46}$$

where T is a parameter called *temperature*. From this point of view, the state vector is now a random variable with a probability density given by (1.46). States with lower energy have higher probability of being observed but the temperature parameter can either enhance or smooth the effect of the energy on the probability distribution : the higher the temperature, the more the states tend to become equiprobable. Formula (1.46) for the probability density and the general expression for the energy are similar to those used in the description of Boltzmann machines without hidden units [Hinton and Sejnowski 86], [Aarts and Korst 88].

The properties of a recursive network are not easily derived from its Gibbs distribution (1.46); special techniques are used to approximate expectations derived on the basis of this distribution. One is thus led to the *mean field equations* which describe the interactions at equilibrium between the components of the mean state vector $\bar{x}$. For the time being, one can consider that a typical form of these mean field equations is given by

$$\bar{x} = \tanh \beta W \bar{x} \qquad \text{where } \beta = T^{-1}. \tag{1.47}$$

One can see that these equations are similar to the deterministic equation (1.23) of the fixed point, except that the sign function is replaced here by a hyperbolic tangent. Moreover, the slope at the origin becomes steeper as the temperature decreases. Thus, in terms of the *mean* state vector, one recovers a set of *deterministic* equations which, in the zero temperature limit, tend to the fixed point equation (1.23). In this sense, (1.47) can be considered as the thermodynamic extension of equation (1.23).

On the basis of the mean field equations (1.47), the analysis proceeds along the same lines as for the statistical approach. Most often, the network will not be characterized by the state vector but rather by the overlap macrovariable which provides then automatically a statistical mean with respect to the distribution of the prototype vectors. To summarize, in the thermodynamic extension, the results are obtained via a twofold averaging process, with respect to the Gibbs distribution and to the distribution of the prototypes. Finally, it should be pointed out that the thermodynamic extension is not restricted to Hebb's law but that it can also be applied to other derivations of the synaptic matrix, such as e.g. the projection rule.

Chapter 2

The deterministic approach

2.1 Existence of cycles and transient length

2.1.1 Introduction

The purpose of this chapter is mainly to investigate the existence of cycles and the problem of how to impose fixed points with prescribed basins of attraction. As a by-product of this analysis, general bounds will also be derived for the memory capacity and the transient length. In order to establish the conditions under which a recursive network is devoid of cycles, we shall apply a technique which is similar to that used in stability theory of ordinary differential equations. In order to clarify the differences and similarities, let us consider the following set of first order differential equations

$$\frac{dv}{dt} = W\,v - \theta, \tag{2.1}$$

where v is an n-vector whose components are real valued functions of time, W is a real symmetric matrix of order n and θ is a real n-vector. To show that this system has no periodic solutions, it is sufficient to find a scalar function $E(v)$, somewhat inappropriately called *energy function*, which is strictly decreasing on any trajectory of the system as long as $dv/dt \neq 0$. A convenient choice for $E(v)$ in this respect is

$$E(v) = -\frac{1}{2}\,v^T\,W\,v + v^T\,\theta\,, \tag{2.2}$$

since, on any trajectory described by (2.1), one has

$$dE/dt = -\parallel dv/dt \parallel^2, \tag{2.3}$$

where the notation $\parallel \cdot \parallel$ stands for the Euclidean vector norm. This last relation shows indeed that the energy is strictly decreasing on any finite interval of time, as long as v is not a constant vector. This is precisely the type of argument which will be used in this section, in a form adapted to the discrete systems under consideration here. It is virtually identical to Liapunov's second method [Barnett and Storey 70] for investigating the stability of the solution $v = 0$ for the system of differential equations

$$\frac{dv}{dt} = W\,v. \tag{2.4}$$

The origin is asymptotically stable if and only if there exists a strictly positive definite matrix P which is the unique solution of the Liapunov equation

$$W^T P + P W = -Q\,, \tag{2.5}$$

for any given strictly positive definite matrix Q. Indeed, the energy function $E' = v^T P\,v$, which is strictly positive for all $v \neq 0$, is, on the other hand, also strictly decreasing on any trajectory of the system since, in view of (2.4) and (2.5), one has

$$\frac{dE'}{dt} = -v^T Q\,v < 0 \qquad \forall v \neq 0\,. \tag{2.6}$$

The analogy between these approaches does not hold beyond the fact that, in both cases, some energy functions E and E' are defined which are decreasing along the system trajectories. First, E is not required to be a sign definite form, with the consequence that one can dispense with the solution of Liapunov's equation and that matrix W of system (2.1) can directly be used to define E, even if W is not strictly positive definite. In addition, the purpose here is not to investigate the stability of a solution but rather the absence of cycles, which is a much more limited goal.

2.1.2   Asynchronous dynamics

By analogy with (2.2), we shall define the energy associated with some state vector x as

$$E(x) = -\frac{1}{2}\,x^T W\,x + x^T \theta\,. \tag{2.7}$$

Theorem 2.1 [Hopfield 82], [Fogelman-Soulie et al. 83] *If the synaptic matrix is symmetric with nonnegative diagonal elements, then the asynchronous operation mode of a recursive network is devoid of cycles.*

Proof Without loss of generality, the analysis can be restricted to the case where the first element of the state vector is updated according to the dynamic equations (1.11). Consequently, the state vectors at times t and $t+1$ will be written as

$$x(t) = \begin{bmatrix} x_1(t) \\ x'(t) \end{bmatrix}, \quad x(t+1) = \begin{bmatrix} x_1(t+1) \\ x'(t) \end{bmatrix}, \tag{2.8}$$

where $x'(t) = [x_2(t), x_3(t), \ldots, x_n(t)]^T$. Conformable partition of the vector θ and matrix W gives

$$\theta = \begin{bmatrix} \theta_1 \\ \theta' \end{bmatrix}, \quad W = \begin{bmatrix} w_{11} & w_1^T \\ w_1 & W' \end{bmatrix}, \tag{2.9}$$

and the energy at time t can then be expressed as :

$$E(x(t)) = -\frac{1}{2} \left[w_{11} x_1^2(t) + 2x_1(t) w_1^T x'(t) + x'^T(t) W' x'(t) \right]$$
$$+ \theta_1 x_1(t) + x^T(t) \theta'. \tag{2.10}$$

Subtraction of a similar expression for $E(x(t+1))$ yields then

$$E(x(t+1)) - E(x(t)) = -\frac{1}{2} w_{11} x_1^2(t+1) - x_1(t+1) w_1^T x'(t)$$

$$+ \theta_1 x_1(t+1) + \frac{1}{2} w_{11} x_1^2(t) + x_1(t) w_1^T x'(t) - \theta_1 x_1(t). \tag{2.11}$$

By adding and subtracting in the right hand sides the terms $w_{11} x_1^2(t)$ and $x_1(t+1) w_{11} x_1(t)$, the energy variation resulting from the update of element x_1 can be expressed as

$$E(x(t+1)) \quad - \quad E(x(t)) = -\frac{1}{2} w_{11}(x_1(t+1) - x_1(t))^2$$

$$- \quad [x_1(t+1) - x_1(t)] \left[\sum_{j=1}^n w_{1j} x_j(t) - \theta_1 \right]. \tag{2.12}$$

In virtue of the dynamic equations (1.11), one observes that the factor $\sum_{j=1}^n w_{1j} x_j(t) - \theta_1$ has the same sign as $x_1(t+1)$ which shows that $x_1(t+1) \neq x_1(t)$ implies $E(x(t+1)) < E(x(t))$ if $w_{11} \geq 0$. $\qquad\square$

Since Hebb's law, the projection rule and their variants satisfy the hypotheses of Theorem 2.1, (see Section 1.2), the following property holds.

Corollary 2.2 *The different forms of the Hebbian law (weighted Hebb rule, with or without zero diagonal) and of the projection rule (with or without zero diagonal) are devoid of cycles for asynchronous updating.*

Remarks • Simple counterexamples show that the hypotheses of Theorem 2.1 are critical for cycle-free operation in asynchronous updating mode. Let us first weaken the symmetry assumption for the synaptic matrix by considering a network of dimension $n = 2$ with zero threshold vector and with the following skew symmetric synaptic matrix

$$W = \begin{bmatrix} 0 & 1 \\ -1 & 0 \end{bmatrix}. \tag{2.13}$$

The elements are assumed to be updated sequentially, i.e. in the order in which they appear in the state vector. Starting from the initial vector $x(0) = [1, -1]^T$, the dynamic equations (1.11) yield successively :

$$x_1(1) = \text{Sgn}\,([0,1]\,x(0)) = -1 \;\Rightarrow\; x(1) = [-1,\,-1]^T,$$

$$x_2(2) = \text{Sgn}\,([-1,0]\,x(1)) = 1 \;\Rightarrow\; x(2) = [-1,\,1]^T,$$

$$x_1(3) = \text{Sgn}\,([0,1]\,x(2)) = 1 \;\Rightarrow\; x(3) = [1,\,1]^T,$$

$$x_2(4) = \text{Sgn}\,([-1,0]\,x(3)) = -1 \;\Rightarrow\; x(4) = [1,\,-1]^T.$$

Since $x(4) = x(0)$, we have thus a cycle of length 4. On the other hand, negative diagonal elements w_{ii} can also induce cycles, even when the synaptic matrix is symmetric. To see this, replace the synaptic matrix (2.13) of the previous example by

$$W = \begin{bmatrix} -1 & 0 \\ 0 & 1 \end{bmatrix}.$$

Starting from the same initialization, the sequential update of the elements gives the following state vectors :

$$\begin{aligned} x(1) &= [-1,\,-1]^T, & x(2) &= [-1,\,-1]^T, \\ x(3) &= [1,\,-1]^T, & x(4) &= [1,\,-1]^T = x(0), \end{aligned}$$

and thus a cycle of length 4, as shown in Figure 2.1.

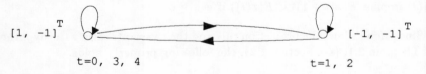

$$[1,\,-1]^T \qquad\qquad\qquad\qquad\qquad\qquad\qquad [-1,\,-1]^T$$

$$t=0,\;3,\;4 \qquad\qquad\qquad\qquad t=1,\;2$$

Figure 2.1 : Example of a cycle generated by negative diagonal elements.

• The proof given above shows that a recursive network operating in asynchronous mode and satisfying the hypotheses of Theorem 2.1, converges spontaneously towards a local minimum of the associated energy function. This conclusion reveals that there may exist two dual descriptions for the asynchronous dynamics of a recursive network. The first of these is the approach used so far, which describes the time evolution of the system by means of the dynamic equation (1.11). In the second, one can define an "energy function" characterizing the state of the network and the state value will move from one vertex of the hypercube to the next if this induces an energy reduction.

The interest of the latter formulation is twofold. From a theoretical point of view, this approach will be used several times in the sequel and especially as a natural extension to higher order networks as shown in Chapter 5. From the application point of view, this dual approach also shows that the interest of recursive networks is not limited to the realization of associative memories but that they can also be considered as devices capable of automatically finding a minimum for a cost function, provided that the latter can be expressed in the form (2.7) of an energy function associated with a recursive network. On the other hand, the minimization of a cost function in a discrete space of high dimensionality is a problem of combinatorial complexity, for which these recursive networks may thus provide an attractive solution. Applications of recursive networks to the solution of travelling salesman problems, analog to digital conversion, linear programming and image coding can be found in [Hopfield 84], [Hopfield and Tank 85], [Tank and Hopfield 86], [Chua and Lin 88].

• In expression (2.7) for the energy, one can of course replace by a single constant θ_0, the sum of the terms $w_{kk} x_k^2$ whose contribution is anyway independent of the state vector since $x_k \in \{-1, 1\}$. An equivalent expression of the energy function is thus given by

$$E(x) = -\sum_{i=1}^{n} \sum_{j>i} w_{ij} x_i x_j + \sum_{i=1}^{n} \theta_i x_i + \theta_0. \tag{2.14}$$

It is the sum of three homogeneous forms, respectively of degree two, one and zero in the state variables. This kind of expression of the energy will be convenient for the higher order extensions considered in Chapter 5.

As we shall see now, the energy function introduced above can also be used to estimate the transient length τ, i.e. the number of iterations of the dynamic equations (1.11) which are required to reach a fixed point. The idea is as follows : an estimate is made, on the one hand, of the difference Δ between the highest and lowest possible energy levels in the space $\{-1, 1\}^n$ and, on the other hand, of the smallest energy reduction δ resulting from a modification of the state vector according to the dynamic equations. An upper bound on the transient length is thus given by the ratio Δ/δ. Most results concerning this question were obtained in references [Fogelman-Soulie et al. 83], [Goles et al. 85]. The presentation given below is slightly different in that the binary space considered here is $\{-1, 1\}^n$ instead of $\{0, 1\}^n$ and because of minor differences in the computation of Δ. The estimation of the transient length will first be performed for the asynchronous case and will be continued in the next subsection for the synchronous mode. In the following, the notation $\lfloor a \rfloor$ will be used to designate the integer part of a positive real number a.

Theorem 2.3 [Fogelman-Soulie et al. 83] *In the case of a symmetric synaptic matrix W with nonnegative diagonal elements, one can assert the following upper bounds for the transient length τ of asynchronous updating.*

- *If the diagonal of W is nonzero*

$$\tau \leq \frac{M + \sum_{i=1}^n |\theta_i|}{w}, \tag{2.15}$$

where M is the sum of the $\lfloor \frac{n^2}{4} \rfloor$ largest coefficients $|w_{ij}|$ $(j \neq i)$ and where $w = \text{Min}_{1 \leq i \leq n} w_{ii}$.

- *If $w_{ij} \in \mathbf{Z}$ $(i, j = 1, 2, \ldots, n)$*

$$\tau \leq \frac{2(M + \sum_{i=1}^n |\theta_i|)}{1 + 2w}. \tag{2.16}$$

- *If $|w_{ij}| \in \{0, 1\}$ $(i, j = 1, 2, \ldots, n)$*

$$\tau \leq \frac{5}{2} n^2. \tag{2.17}$$

Proof Expression (2.14) for the energy yields the inequality

$$-\sum_{i=1}^n \sum_{j>i}^n |w_{ij}| - \sum_{i=1}^n |\theta_i| \quad + \quad \theta_0 \leq E(x)$$

$$\leq \sum_{i=1}^n \sum_{j>i}^n |w_{ij}| + \sum_{i=1}^n |\theta_i| + \theta_0, \tag{2.18}$$

and so the obvious bound

$$\Delta < 2 \left[\sum_{i=1}^n \sum_{j>i}^n |w_{ij}| + \sum_{i=1}^n |\theta_i| \right]. \tag{2.19}$$

But this estimate of Δ may be too crude because it relies on the assumption that, by modifying the signs of the state vector components, one can achieve arbitrary sign patterns for the $n(n-1)/2$ products $x_i x_j$ $(j \neq i)$ in expression (2.14) of the energy. In fact, the change of k signs in the state vector, induces $k(n-k)$ sign changes for the products $x_i x_j$ $(j \neq i)$, and the maximum is reached when $k = \lfloor \frac{n}{2} \rfloor$. Hence, at most $\lfloor \frac{n^2}{4} \rfloor$ sign modifications are realizable for the products $x_i x_j$ $(j \neq i)$ and the maximum energy variation on the binary space $\{-1, 1\}^n$ is thus bounded by

$$\Delta \leq 2(M + \sum_{i=1}^n |\theta_i|), \tag{2.20}$$

where M is the sum of the $\lfloor \frac{n^2}{4} \rfloor$ largest absolute values among the off-diagonal elements of W.

Let us now estimate δ. The energy variation resulting from flipping an element of the state vector is given by (2.12). The contribution of the second term is difficult to estimate but, when $w_{11} \neq 0$, the first term gives $\delta > 2\,w_{11}$ and one has thus in general $\delta \geq 2\,\mathrm{Min}_{1 \leq i \leq n}\,w_{ii}$. This, together with (2.20), leads to the bound (2.15).

On the other hand, if the elements of W are integers, one can, without affecting the network dynamics, adjust the threshold values θ_i in such a way that

$$|\sum_{j=1}^{n} w_{ij}\,x_j - \theta_i| \geq \frac{1}{2} \qquad \forall x \in \{-1,1\}^n, \quad i = 1, 2, \ldots, n, \qquad (2.21)$$

and the contribution of the second term in (2.12) is then greater than or equal to one. Hence, $\delta \geq 1 + 2w$, which leads to the bound (2.16) on the transient length but one should keep in mind that adjusting the thresholds θ_i as explained above will in principle also affect the value of the numerator of (2.16).

Finally, if all elements of W have absolute values equal to zero or one, then $M \leq n^2/4$. On the other hand, when $|\theta_i| > n$ then $|\theta_i| > |\sum_{j=1}^{n} w_{ij}\,x_j|$ and the sign of x_i is then determined in a single iteration ($x_i = -\,\mathrm{Sgn}\,\theta_i$). Consequently, in the estimation of Δ, one can assume that $\sum_{i=1}^{n} |\theta_i| \leq n^2$, and this yields the result (2.17).   □

2.1.3   Synchronous dynamics

We keep for the energy the same expressions (2.7) and (2.14) as for asynchronous operation.

Theorem 2.4 [Goles et al. 85] *If the synaptic matrix is positive definite on the set $\{-1, 0, 1\}^n$, then the recursive network is free of cycles for synchronous updating.*

Proof With expression (2.7) for the energy and taking into account the symmetry of W, one finds that the energy variation resulting from the state vector update is given by

$$E(x(t+1)) - E(x(t)) = -[x^T(t+1) - x^T(t)][W\,x(t) - \theta]$$

$$-\frac{1}{2}[x^T(t+1) - x^T(t)]\,W[x(t+1) - x(t)]. \qquad (2.22)$$

In view of equations (1.10) for synchronous operation, each component in $W x(t) - \theta$ has the same sign as the corresponding component in $x(t+1)$.

Hence, if $x(t+1) \neq x(t)$, the first term gives a strictly negative contribution and this effect is possibly enhanced by the second term since W is positive definite on the set of values which can be assumed by the difference $\frac{1}{2}[x(t+1) - x(t)]$. Let us recall that a symmetric diagonally dominant matrix is necessarily positive definite, but that this type of synaptic matrix is of no practical interest as pointed out in Section 1.2.   □

Corollary 2.5 *Hebb's law (with or without weighting) as well as the projection rule guarantee the absence of cycles for synchronous operation.*

Definitions (1.25), (1.30) and (1.35) show that W is indeed positive definite in all these cases.

It is seen that the sufficient condition for cycle-free operation is more stringent for synchronous than for asynchronous operation (respectively : $W \geq 0$ and W symmetric; $w_{ii} \geq 0$). In particular, the Hebbian law and the projection rule with zero diagonal may lead to cycles in synchronous dynamics, but the cycles are then at most of length 2 as shown below [Goles et al. 85].

Theorem 2.6 *When W is symmetric, a recursive network in synchronous updating mode converges either to a fixed point or to a cycle of period $T = 2$.*

Proof Here, we will define an energy function which depends not only on the current state vector, but also on the preceding one, namely

$$G(t) = -x^T(t) W x(t-1) + [x^T(t) + x^T(t-1)] \theta . \qquad (2.23)$$

By subtraction, one immediately obtains

$$G(t+1) - G(t) = -[x^T(t+1) - x^T(t-1)][W x(t) - \theta] . \qquad (2.24)$$

Since, in view of (1.10), each component of the second factor has the same sign as the corresponding component of $x(t+1)$, one concludes that $x(t+1) \neq x(t-1)$ implies $G(t+1) < G(t)$, which allows either fixed points or cycles of length 2.   □

Corollary 2.7 *The zero diagonal Hebb law and zero diagonal projection rule lead to cycles of at most length 2 in synchronous operation mode.*

Example The synaptic matrix

$$W = \begin{bmatrix} 0 & 1 \\ 1 & 0 \end{bmatrix}$$

with the initialization $x(0) = [1, -1]^T$ produces a cycle of length 2.

Remarks • Here too, the symmetry of the synaptic matrix is a critical condition as shown by the example with the skew symmetric matrix (2.13) and zero threshold vector. Starting from the initialization $x(0) = [1, -1]^T$, the synchronous updating mode produces the sequence of state vectors :

$$x(1) = \text{Sgn} \left(\begin{bmatrix} 0 & 1 \\ -1 & 0 \end{bmatrix} \begin{bmatrix} 1 \\ -1 \end{bmatrix} \right) = \begin{bmatrix} -1 \\ -1 \end{bmatrix};$$

$$x(2) = \text{Sgn} \left(\begin{bmatrix} 0 & 1 \\ -1 & 0 \end{bmatrix} \begin{bmatrix} -1 \\ -1 \end{bmatrix} \right) = \begin{bmatrix} -1 \\ 1 \end{bmatrix};$$

$$x(3) = \text{Sgn} \left(\begin{bmatrix} 0 & 1 \\ -1 & 0 \end{bmatrix} \begin{bmatrix} -1 \\ 1 \end{bmatrix} \right) = \begin{bmatrix} 1 \\ 1 \end{bmatrix};$$

$$x(4) = \text{Sgn} \left(\begin{bmatrix} 0 & 1 \\ -1 & 0 \end{bmatrix} \begin{bmatrix} 1 \\ 1 \end{bmatrix} \right) = \begin{bmatrix} 1 \\ -1 \end{bmatrix} = x(0),$$

and hence a cycle of period $T = 4$.

• A separate proof can be given for Theorem 2.4 for the special case where the synaptic matrix is obtained by the projection rule [Personnaz et al. 86]. It should be recalled that the projection rule is usually applied with a zero threshold vector and we shall therefore set $\theta = 0$ in expression (2.7) for the energy. Since W is a projection operator, it follows that $W x(t+1)$ is the best least squares approximation of $x(t+1)$ in the linear subspace $\mathcal{X}$ spanned by the prototype vectors $\xi^{(1)}, \xi^{(2)}, \ldots, \xi^{(p)}$. Hence,

$$\| x(t+1) - W x(t+1) \| \leq \| x(t+1) - W x(t) \| . \tag{2.25}$$

On the other hand, $x(t+1)$ is, in view of the dynamic equations (1.10), the *sign approximation* of $W x(t)$ or, more precisely, the best approximation of $W x(t)$ in $\{-1, 1\}^n$. Moreover, if $x_i(t+1) \neq x_i(t)$, then, in view of (1.3), $\sum_j w_{ij} x_j(t) \neq 0$ and thus $x(t+1) \neq x(t)$ implies

$$\| x(t+1) - W x(t) \| < \| x(t) - W x(t) \| . \tag{2.26}$$

This inequality, in turn, implies that $E(x(t+1)) < E(x(t))$ if one takes into account the facts that $\| x(t+1) \| = \| x(t) \| = n^{1/2}$ and that W is idempotent. □

• A unified proof for Theorems 2.1 and 2.6 can be found in [Bruck and Goodman 88].

Just as in the preceding subsection, we shall now estimate for synchronous dynamics, the length of the transient τ before a fixed point or cycle of length 2 is reached [Goles et al. 85].

Theorem 2.8 *For synchronous dynamics one can assert the following upper bounds for the transient length.*

• *If $W > 0$ over $\{-1, 0, 1\}^n$,*

$$\tau \leq \frac{M + \sum_{i=1}^n |\theta_i|}{\lambda_{\min}}, \tag{2.27}$$

where, similarly to Theorem 2.3, M is the sum of the $\lfloor \frac{n^2}{4} \rfloor$ largest coefficients $|w_{ij}|$ ($j \neq i$) and where $\lambda_{\min}$ is the smallest eigenvalue of W.

• *If W is symmetric and if $w_{ij} \in \mathbf{Z}$ ($i, j = 1, 2, \ldots, n$),*

$$\tau \leq 4 \sum_{i=1}^n \sum_{j>i} |w_{ij}| + 2 \sum_{i=1}^n |w_{ii}| + 4 \sum_{i=1}^n |\theta_i|. \tag{2.28}$$

• *If W is symmetric and if $|w_{ij}| \in \{0, 1\}$ ($i, j = 1, 2, \ldots n$),*

$$\tau \leq 6n^2. \tag{2.29}$$

Proof In Theorem 2.3 we have already obtained an estimate $\Delta \leq 2(M + \sum_{i=1}^n |\theta_i|)$ of the largest energy variation over the space $\{-1, 1\}^n$. The minimum energy reduction δ which results from a synchronous update remains to be computed. If W is strictly positive definite, i.e. if $v^T W v > 0$ for all $v \neq 0$, then the absolute value of the second term in (2.22) is at least equal to $2\lambda_{\min}$ where $\lambda_{\min}$ is the smallest eigenvalue of W [Golub and Van Loan 83]. One has thus, $\delta \geq 2\lambda_{\min}$, which yields the bound (2.27). When matrix W is not positive definite, but merely symmetric, then the relevant expression to be considered for the energy is not (2.7) but (2.23), which can be written more explicitly as

$$\begin{aligned} G(t) = \quad & - \sum_{i=1}^n \sum_{j>i} w_{ij}[x_i(t)x_j(t-1) + x_j(t)x_i(t-1)] \\ & - \sum_{i=1}^n w_{ii}\, x_i(t)\, x_i(t-1) \\ & + \sum_{i=1}^n \theta_i \left[x_i(t) + x_i(t-1) \right]. \end{aligned} \tag{2.30}$$

Let us first estimate the maximum variation Δ of the energy function G. During synchronous update of the state vector, the coefficient of w_{ij} or that of θ_i in (2.30) can change by at most 4 units, while the maximum variation for the coefficient of w_{ii} is at most 2 units. One has thus

$$\Delta \le 4 \sum_{i=1}^{n} \sum_{j>i} |w_{ij}| + 2 \sum_{i=1}^{n} |w_{ii}| + 4 \sum_{i=1}^{n} |\theta_i| . \tag{2.31}$$

If the elements of W are integers, the threshold value θ_i can be adapted in order to satisfy (2.21), just as in Theorem 2.3. Consequently, expression (2.24) yields as minimum energy variation $\delta \ge 1$ and the ratio Δ/δ gives then bound (2.28) for the transient length. Finally, if all elements of W have absolute values equal to 0 or 1, the analysis can again be restricted to the case where $|\theta_i| \le n$, whence the bound (2.29). $\quad\square$

Theorem 2.9 *When the synaptic matrix W is a strictly positive definite projection operator, and when the threshold vector is zero, then the transient length is bounded by*

$$\tau \le \frac{n\sqrt{n-1}}{2m}, \tag{2.32}$$

where $m = \mathrm{Min}_{1 \le i \le n} w_{ii}$ for asynchronous update and $m = \lambda_{\min}(W)$ for synchronous operation.

Proof If $W > 0$, then it is easily verified by means of (1.37) and (1.38) that all diagonal elements, and hence m, are strictly positive. Next the specific properties of the projection operator can be used to obtain a more precise estimate of the quantity Δ in the numerator of the inequality $\tau \le \Delta/\delta$. Indeed, from (1.37) one readily derives

$$\sum_{j \ne i} w_{ij}^2 \le 1/4, \qquad (i = 1, 2, \dots, n) , \tag{2.33}$$

and the Cauchy-Schwartz inequality shows then that

$$\sum_{j \ne i} |w_{ij}| \le \frac{\sqrt{n-1}}{2} . \tag{2.34}$$

Making use of this inequality in the bound (2.19) on Δ, and assuming that $\theta = 0$, one obtains the upper bound (2.32), just as in Theorems 2.3 and 2.8. Here, use of the sharper bound (2.20) for Δ has only a minor influence on the upper bound for τ. $\quad\square$

2.1.4 Block-sequential dynamics

First, one should remember that, for block-sequential updating (§ 1.1.2), one defines a partition $\mathcal{I}$ of the state vector in K subvectors

$$x^T = [x^{(1)T}, x^{(2)T}, \dots, x^{(K)T}], \tag{2.35}$$

which, in turn, induces the following conformable partition of the synaptic matrix and of the threshold vector

$$
W = \begin{bmatrix} W_{11} & W_{12} & \cdots & W_{1K} \\ W_{21} & W_{22} & \cdots & W_{2K} \\ \vdots & & & \\ W_{K1} & W_{K2} & \cdots & W_{KK} \end{bmatrix}, \quad \theta = \begin{bmatrix} \theta^{(1)} \\ \theta^{(2)} \\ \vdots \\ \theta^{K} \end{bmatrix}. \tag{2.36}
$$

At a given iteration of the network, the components of $x^{(k)}$ are synchronously updated while taking into account the most recent values already computed for the subvectors $x^{(k-1)}, x^{(k-2)}, \ldots, x^{(1)}$ at the preceding iterations. Thus,

$$
x^{(k)}(t+1) = \mathrm{Sgn}\left[\sum_{j=1}^{k-1} W_{kj} x^{(j)}(t+1) + \sum_{j=k}^{K} W_{kj} x^{(j)}(t) - \theta^{(k)}\right]. \tag{2.37}
$$

Theorem 2.10 [Goles et al. 85] *If the synaptic matrix W is symmetric and if the diagonal blocks W_{kk} ($k = 1, 2, \ldots, K$) corresponding to the partition $\mathcal{I}$ are all positive definite over the space $\{-1, 0, 1\}^{n_k}$ where n_k is the order of W_{kk}, then the block-sequential operation defined by $\mathcal{I}$ is devoid of cycles.*

Proof The argument is quite similar to that of Theorem 2.1. We shall take definition (2.7) for the energy function and, to simplify the notations, we shall assume that subvector $x^{(1)}$ is to be updated. For the state vectors at times t and $t + 1$ we shall thus write

$$
x(t) = \begin{bmatrix} x^{(1)}(t) \\ x'(t) \end{bmatrix}, \quad x(t+1) = \begin{bmatrix} x^{(1)}(t+1) \\ x'(t) \end{bmatrix},
$$

and for the synaptic matrix and the threshold vector

$$
W = \begin{bmatrix} W_{11} & V^T \\ V & W' \end{bmatrix}, \quad \theta = \begin{bmatrix} \theta^{(1)} \\ \theta' \end{bmatrix}.
$$

The synchronous update of the first subvector will be performed according to the following equation

$$
x^{(1)}(t+1) = \mathrm{Sgn}\left[W_{11} x^{(1)}(t) + V^T x'(t) - \theta^{(1)}\right]. \tag{2.38}
$$

If one computes the expressions of $E(x(t+1))$ and $E(x(t))$, then the energy variation can be written in the form

$$
\begin{aligned}
E(x(t+1)) &- E(x(t)) = \\
&- \left[x^{(1)T}(t+1) - x^{(1)T}(t)\right]\left[W_{11}x^{(1)}(t) + V^T x'(t) - \theta^{(1)}\right] \\
&- \frac{1}{2}\left[x^{(1)T}(t+1) - x^{(1)T}(t)\right] W_{11} \left[x^{(1)}(t+1) - x^{(1)}(t)\right].
\end{aligned} \tag{2.39}
$$

If $x^{(1)}(t+1) \neq x^{(1)}(t)$, the first term in the right hand side of formula (2.39) gives a negative contribution and the situation $x^{(k)}(t+1) \neq x^{(k)}(t)$ should necessarily occur for at least one value of k because otherwise $x(t)$ would be a fixed point. On the other hand, the second term in (2.39) is negative or zero in view of the assumption concerning the diagonal blocks W_{kk}. Consequently, as long as a fixed point has not been reached, the energy is strictly decreasing and cycles are thus excluded.   □

Corollary 2.11 *The Hebbian law (with or without weighting) as well as the projection rule lead exclusively to fixed points for recursive networks operating in block-sequential mode.*

Table 2.2 gives a summary of the results obtained so far concerning the existence of cycles for the different updating modes.

	Asynchronous	Synchronous	Block-sequential
symmetric W	cycles are possible		
symmetric W and $w_{ii} \geq 0 \ (i=1,2,\ldots,n)$		cycle ≤ 2	cycles are possible
(Hebb, zero diagonal Hebb, weighted Hebb, Projection, zero diagonal Projection)	fixed points only	only	
$W \geq 0$ (Hebb, weighted Hebb, Projection)		fixed points only	fixed points only

Table 2.2 : Fixed points and cycles for different operation modes.

2.2 Capacity, fixed points and radius of direct attraction

2.2.1 General bounds on the capacity

Abu-Mostafa and St. Jacques give an upper bound on the memory capacity p of a network if one makes the strong requirement that *any* subset of p binary vectors should be retrievable for a choice of the network parameters adapted to that particular set [Abu-Mostafa and St. Jacques 85].

Theorem 2.12 *If, for all possible sets of p binary n-vectors, one can find a corresponding zero diagonal synaptic matrix and a threshold vector such that these vectors are fixed points of the network, then one necessarily has $p \leq n$.*

Proof Consider the matrix $X = [\xi^{(1)}, \xi^{(2)}, \ldots, \xi^{(p)}]$ formed by the p prototype vectors. By assumption, there exists a matrix W and a threshold vector θ such that these prototypes are fixed points, i.e.

$$\text{Sgn}\,(WX - \theta) = X\,. \tag{2.40}$$

The first of these equations can be written explicitly as

$$\text{Sgn}\left\{\ [0\ w_{12} \cdots w_{1n}\ \theta_1]\ \begin{bmatrix} \xi_1^{(1)} & \xi_1^{(2)} & \cdots & \xi_1^{(p)} \\ & X' & \\ -1 & -1 & \cdots & -1 \end{bmatrix}\ \right\}$$

$$= [\xi_1^{(1)}\ \xi_1^{(2)} \cdots \xi_1^{(p)}], \tag{2.41}$$

where the columns of X' are formed by the p prototype vectors with the first element suppressed. The right hand side is precisely defined by these first elements whereas the left hand side is independent of it since $w_{11} = 0$. For each fixed X' and for each of the 2^p possible right hand sides there exists, by assumption, a suitable threshold function, i.e. suitable values for $[w_{12} \cdots w_{1n}\ \theta_1]$ such that equation (2.41) is satisfied. This means that one has to find 2^p threshold functions in n variables and defined in p points of $\{-1,1\}^n$. Denoting by B_n^p the number of such threshold functions, one should thus have $B_n^p \geq 2^p$. This is however impossible if $p > n$. Indeed, it is shown in references [Cover 65] and [Abu-Mostafa and St. Jacques 85] that the maximum number of such threshold functions is given by the inequality

$$B_n^p \leq 2 \sum_{i=0}^{n-1} \binom{p-1}{i}, \tag{2.42}$$

and from there one derives $B_n^p < 2^p$ if $p > n$ since, in this case,

$$B_n^p \leq 2 \sum_{i=0}^{n-1} \binom{p-1}{i} < 2 \sum_{i=0}^{p-1} \binom{p-1}{i} = 2^p\,. \tag{2.43}$$

$\square$

Remarks • Under the assumptions of Theorem 2.12, the memory capacity p is thus bounded by n. It should be stressed that this bound is a pessimistic one, precisely because it is required that *any* p-tuple of binary vectors in $\{-1,1\}^n$ should be retrievable. Besides, Theorem 3.1 will show that asymptotically, i.e. when n tends to infinity, the capacity can get within a small fraction of $2n$.

• The bound $p \leq n$ is completely general in the sense that no assumptions have been made concerning the way in which the synaptic matrix W is obtained : thus it holds true for the Hebbian law, the projection rule, or any other way of constructing W. No hypotheses were made either concerning the structure of W such as symmetry or positive definiteness. The only actual restriction concerns the zero diagonal because one should avoid the trivial solution where W is the unit matrix or a diagonally dominant matrix (see Section 1.2). This capacity limit also holds irrespective of the updating mode used, be it synchronous, asynchronous or block-sequential, since definition (1.20) is independent of any particular operation mode.

• The projection rule has the particular feature that it attains the upper bound since the matrix X of the prototype vectors has, in general, full column rank when $p \leq n$. In other cases, this upper bound is far from tight since the asymptotic capacity estimates derived in Chapters 3 and 4 are much lower.

As a complement to the upper bound obtained above, one can also derive an obvious lower bound on the number of realizable fixed points [Baldi 88b].

Theorem 2.13 *If the synaptic matrix is symmetric and if the set of p vectors to be memorized is nondegenerate, then a lower bound on the capacity is given by*

$$p \geq \frac{n}{2} \, . \tag{2.44}$$

Proof It was pointed out that, as a consequence of Theorem 2.1, the fixed points of any asynchronous network are local minima of the energy function (2.14). In order to impose a vector as a fixed point, it is thus *sufficient* to require that the energy should take in this particular vertex of the hypercube a given value a and some higher value $b > a$ in the n neighbouring vertices which are located at unit Hamming distance (N_1 neighbourhood). Proceeding in this way for the p vectors, one has thus $p(n + 1)$ linear equations in the $n(n-1)/2$ coefficients w_{ij}, the n threshold values θ_i and the constant θ_0 in expression (2.14) of the energy. The set of p vectors is said to be *nondegenerate* if this system of equations is solvable when $p(n+1) \leq n(n-1)/2 + n + 1$ and when their N_1 neighbourhoods are disjoint. The minimum value of p satisfying this inequality yields the lower bound (2.44).   □

2.2.2 The weighted Hebbian law

We have seen in Subsection 1.2.2 that Hebb's rule is unable to guarantee exact retrieval of the prototypes, except for the special case where they are mutually orthogonal. One should remember in this context that binary vector p-tuples exist which cannot be stored as fixed points by the Hebbian law as soon as $p > 1/(1-2\rho)$ where ρn is the minimum Hamming distance between prototypes

[Dembo 89]. This limitation is of course ineffective for orthogonal prototypes since ρ is then equal to $1/2$.

As a remedy to this problem, Amari has proposed a weighted Hebbian law defined in (1.29) and (1.30) [Amari 72] . Hereafter, we examine which conditions the weight factors should satisfy in order to insure exact retrieval and at the same time we shall also obtain an estimate of the radius of direct attraction.

Theorem 2.14 *A sufficient condition, that the weighted Hebbian rule should guarantee perfect retrieval of the prototypes in case of zero threshold vector, is given by the following set of inequalities*

$$\lambda_k \geq \sum_{m \neq k}^{p} \lambda_m \left| \cos(k, m) \right| \quad k = 1, 2, \ldots, p, \tag{2.45}$$

where $\cos(k, m) = n^{-1} \xi^{(k)T} \xi^{(m)}$.

Proof Let us consider prototype $\xi^{(k)}$. With W defined by (1.29), one has

$$W \xi^{(k)} = n \left[\lambda_k \xi^{(k)} + \sum_{m \neq k}^{p} \lambda_m \xi^{(m)} \cos(k, m) \right]. \tag{2.46}$$

Vector $\xi^{(k)}$ is a fixed point provided the elements of $W \xi^{(k)}$ have the same sign as those of $\xi^{(k)}$. This will indeed be the case if condition (2.45) is satisfied. $\square$

Remark • One observes that the inequalities (2.45) may be incompatible. This is especially apparent when the angles between the prototype vectors are all equal. Indeed, putting $c = \cos(k, m)$ and adding together the inequalities (2.45), one obtains, in view of the fact that $\sum \lambda_k = 1$,

$$1 - (p - 1) |c| \geq 0, \tag{2.47}$$

which cannot be satisfied when $|c| > 1/(p-1)$. Consequently, the introduction of weighting factors is not a panacea for imposing fixed points by Hebbian rules. For example, in a network of dimension $n = 9$, weighting factors are of no help if one tries to impose the three vectors

$$\xi^{(1)} = [1, 1, 1, 1, 1, 1, 1, 1, 1]^T,$$

$$\xi^{(2)} = [-1, -1, 1, 1, 1, 1, 1, 1, 1]^T,$$

$$\xi^{(3)} = [-1, 1, -1, 1, 1, 1, 1, 1, 1]^T,$$

as fixed points, since $|c| = 5/9 > 1/2$.

Theorem 2.15 *For the weighted Hebbian rule, a lower bound on the radius of direct attraction of a prototype $\xi^{(k)}$ is given by*

$$R_1(\xi^{(k)}) \geq \lfloor \frac{n}{2}(\lambda_k - \sum_{m \neq k}^{p} \lambda_m |\cos(k,m)|) \rfloor .$$

(2.48)

If the prototypes are orthogonal, this bound becomes

$$R_1(\xi^{(k)}) \geq \lfloor \frac{n}{2}\lambda_k \rfloor,$$

(2.49)

whence, in the case of uniform weighting $\lambda_k = 1/p$,

$$R_1 \geq \lfloor \frac{n}{2p} \rfloor .$$

(2.50)

Proof If $\xi^{(k)}$ is a fixed point, then the synaptic potential $h_i(\xi^{(k)}) = \sum_{j=1}^{n} w_{ij} \xi_j^{(k)}$ has the same sign as $\xi_i^{(k)}$ for $i = 1, 2, \ldots, n$ and the absolute value $|h_i(\xi^{(k)})|$ can be considered as a measure of the robustness of component i against perturbations. In particular, if the state vector x is moved away to a Hamming distance d from the prototype, then this incurs a modification of at most $2d$ in the synaptic potentials, since it was assumed that the synaptic weights are so normalized that $|w_{ij}| \leq 1$. Consequently, as long as

$$2d(\xi^{(k)}, x) \leq \text{Min}_{1 \leq i \leq n} |h_i(\xi^{(k)})|,$$

(2.51)

$h_i(x)$ will have the same sign as $h_i(\xi^{(k)})$ and hence each component of x will be moved back to the prototype value in a single iteration. In the case of a weighted Hebbian rule, the values of the synaptic potential at a fixed point are given by (2.46) and, if λ_k satisfies (2.45), one has in particular,

$$\text{Min}_{1 \leq i \leq n} |h_i(\xi^{(k)})| \geq n \left[\lambda_k - \sum_{m \neq k}^{p} \lambda_m |\cos(k,m)| \right],$$

(2.52)

which, combined with inequality (2.51), yields the desired result (2.48). If the prototypes are orthogonal, weighting is useless for the purpose of imposing these vectors as fixed points but weighting can help in modifying the relative width of the basins of direct attraction. Indeed, with $\cos(k,m) = 0$ for ($k \neq m$), the bound (2.48) reduces to (2.49). If, in addition, weighting factors are identical, then the Hebbian rule becomes identical to the projection rule and one finds then the bound (2.50) already derived in [Personnaz et al. 86].   □

Remarks • The actual basins of direct attraction can in fact be wider than indicated in Theorem 2.15 above. Indeed, we have considered the extreme situation where any deviation from the fixed point is counted with a maximum contribution equal to 1, in the evaluation of the synaptic potential.

• Bound (2.50) would imply that the number of stored prototypes should not exceed $n/2$ if one is to have a radius of direct attraction at least equal to one, i.e. a basin of direct attraction covering at least the N_1 neighbourhood of the prototypes.

Reference [Amari 72] examines the situation where the synaptic matrix has to be constructed from noisy observations of the prototypes. This is often the case in pattern recognition, when the intrinsic variability of the observations prevents direct access to the prototypes. In speech recognition for example, variability of pronunciation is completely unavoidable, even if the experiment is restricted to a single speaker. Consequently, there are no phoneme prototypes available and one has exclusively to rely on a number of realizations of the phonemes.

In practice, we shall assume that we have at our disposal a large number of independent realizations ξ' of prototype ξ and that the matrix $\xi\,\xi^T$ which occurs in the Hebbian law will be estimated from the samples $\xi'\xi'^T$. Let $(1-\nu)$ be the probability that $\xi'_i = \xi_i$ and ν the probability that $\xi'_i = -\xi_i$. We shall also assume that these probabilities are independent for the different elements $i = 1, 2, \ldots, n$ of the state vector. By the law of large numbers [Feller 66], the arithmetic mean of the samples $\xi'\xi'^T$ will converge to $(1-\sigma^2)\xi\,\xi^T + \sigma^2 I_n$ where $1 - \sigma^2 = (1-2\nu)^2$. If we proceed in the same way for all p classes or prototypes and if each class k is weighted by a factor λ_k, then, by analogy with (1.29), we obtain the following expression for the synaptic matrix

$$W = \sum_{m=1}^{p} \lambda_m (1 - \sigma_m^2)\, \xi^{(m)}\xi^{(m)T} + \sum_{m=1}^{p} \lambda_m \sigma_m^2 I_n, \tag{2.53}$$

where $\sum \lambda_m = 1$.

Theorem 2.16 [Amari 72] *In the case of noisy prototypes, the weighted Hebbian rule guarantees that prototype $\xi^{(k)}$ is a fixed point if the weight factors satisfy the following condition* :

$$\lambda_k(1 - \sigma_k^2) + \frac{1}{n} \sum_{m=1}^{p} \lambda_m \sigma_m^2 \geq \sum_{m \neq k} \lambda_m (1 - \sigma_m^2)|\cos(k, m)|, \tag{2.54}$$

and, if the prototypes are orthogonal, a bound for the radius of direct attraction is given by

$$R_1(\xi^{(k)}) \geq \lfloor \frac{n}{2}(\lambda_k(1 - \sigma_k^2) + \frac{1}{2} \sum_{m=1}^{p} \lambda_m \sigma_m^2) \rfloor . \tag{2.55}$$

Proof As for the preceding two theorems, one computes the expression $W\,\xi^{(k)}$, which, in view of (2.53), is given by

$$W\xi^{(k)} = n \left[\lambda_k(1 - \sigma_k^2)\xi^{(k)} + \frac{1}{n}\xi^{(k)} \sum_{m=1}^{p} \lambda_m \sigma_m^2 \right.$$

$$+ \sum_{m \neq k} \lambda_m \, \xi^{(m)} \, (1 - \sigma_m^2) \cos(k, m) \Bigg], \tag{2.56}$$

and it is easily seen that each component of $W \xi^{(k)}$ will have the same sign as the corresponding component in $\xi^{(k)}$ provided λ_k satisfies condition (2.54). For orthogonal prototypes, the minimum synaptic potential is given by

$$\text{Min}_{1 \leq i \leq n} |h_i(\xi^{(k)})| \geq n \left[\lambda_k (1 - \sigma_k^2) + \frac{1}{n} \sum_{m=1}^{p} \lambda_m \, \sigma_m^2 \right], \tag{2.57}$$

and, by appeal to (2.51), the bound (2.55) follows. $\quad\square$

Remark • It is seen that the noise on a prototype, in this case $\xi^{(k)}$, makes its storage more difficult (since the weight factor λ_k has to be larger) and that it reduces the basin of direct attraction. In contrast, the noise on the other prototypes, represented in the formula above by σ_m^2 ($m \neq k$), has a positive effect since it tends to reduce the weight λ_k and to increase the basin of attraction of $\xi^{(k)}$.

2.2.3 The projection rule

Let us first recall that, for orthogonal prototypes, the projection rule and the Hebbian law are identical to within a scaling factor. For this case one recovers the bound (2.50) for the radius of direct attraction derived in [Personnaz et al. 86]. This result tends to corroborate the restriction indicated in Subsection 1.2.3 concerning the projection rule : although it allows one, in principle, a number of prototypes equal to the dimension of the network to be stored, the basin of attraction of these fixed points may shrink considerably as this upper limit is approached.

Another interesting property of the projection operator should also be pointed out. It has been shown in Section 2.1 that the convergence of a network towards a fixed point is characterized by a monotonically decreasing energy function, and this holds for synchronous as well as asynchronous operation. Let δ denote the Euclidean distance between a state vector x and its projection $W x$ on the linear subspace $\mathcal{X}$ spanned by the prototype vectors $\xi^{(1)}, \xi^{(2)}, \ldots, \xi^{(p)}$. By expanding the expression $\delta^2 = (x^T - x^T W) (x - W x)$ one obtains, in view of formula (2.7) for the energy function and with $\theta = 0$, the following result

$$E(x) = -\frac{1}{2} (n - \delta^2). \tag{2.58}$$

This shows that any vector belonging to $\mathcal{X}$, achieves an absolute minimum of the energy, since $\delta = 0$ in that case [Personnaz et al. 86], [Kanter and Sompolinsky 87]. This holds in particular for each prototype and its negative.

But this property is unfortunately not sufficient in order to discriminate between parasitic fixed points and those corresponding to prototypes. Indeed, the example below shows that there exist binary vectors which are linear combinations of prototypes. Since they belong to $\mathcal{X}$, they are fixed points for the projection operator and the energy is equal to its absolute minimum value.

Example

$$\xi^{(1)} = [-1, 1, 1, -1, -1, 1]^T,$$

$$\xi^{(2)} = [1, -1, 1, -1, 1, -1]^T,$$

$$\xi^{(3)} = [1, 1, -1, 1, -1, -1]^T,$$

$$\xi^{(1)} + \xi^{(2)} + \xi^{(3)} = [1, 1, 1, -1, -1, -1]^T.$$

The special problem related to the parasitic fixed points obtained by linear combinations of prototypes will be examined in more detail in Chapters 3 and 4 via statistical methods.

2.3　Long-term attraction

In the preceding two sections, the analysis has been limited to the basins of direct attraction, i.e. the neighbourhoods of the fixed points where all vectors converge to the fixed point in a single synchronous or asynchronous iteration. We shall now consider the problem of long-term attraction, where several iterations may be needed before a fixed point is reached. For simplicity, the analysis will be restricted to synchronous operation and a zero threshold vector. One will quickly realize that the answers which can be obtained for this problem are limited, even though the statistical approach of Chapter 3 will shed some additional light on this question.

The analysis given below is rather general in the sense that it does not make any assumptions concerning a particular construction rule for the synaptic matrix.

The method of analysis of long-term attraction due to Amari amounts essentially to the argument developed in the proof of Theorem 2.15 [Amari 72]. There, we observed that, if ξ is a fixed point, then the absolute value of the synaptic potentials $h_i(\xi) = \sum_j w_{ij} \xi_j$ can be used as a measure of the robustness of the fixed point against perturbations. To simplify notation, we shall assume that the components of the state vector have been ordered by increasing absolute value of the synaptic potential, i.e.

$$|h_1(\xi)| \leq |h_2(\xi)| \leq \cdots \leq |h_n(\xi)| . \tag{2.59}$$

As we have seen above, the radius of direct attraction of a fixed point is given by

$$R_1(\xi) = \lfloor \frac{1}{2} |h_1(\xi)| \rfloor .$$ (2.60)

Indeed, if $x(0) \in N_{R_1}(\xi)$, the vector $x(0)$ deviates from ξ in at most R_1 components, and in view of the normalization $|w_{ij}| \leq 1$, this implies that the synaptic potentials are modified by at most $2R_1$. In view of (2.59) and (2.60), the signs of all synaptic potentials will remain unchanged and consequently,

$$x(1) = \text{Sgn}[W x(0)] = \text{Sgn}[h(\xi)] = \xi .$$ (2.61)

Let us now continue along this line and consider the quantity

$$R_2(\xi) = \lfloor \frac{1}{2} |h_{R_1+1}(\xi)| \rfloor$$ (2.62)

which, in view of (2.59), is larger than or equal to $R_1(\xi)$. If $R_2(\xi) > R_1(\xi)$, then $R_2(\xi)$ is the attraction radius of ξ in two iterations. Indeed, if $x(0) \in N_{R_2}(\xi)$, then $h_i(x(0))$ will have the same sign as $h_i(\xi)$ for $i \geq R_1 + 1$ and thus $x(1) = \text{Sgn}[W x(0)]$ will differ from ξ in at most R_1 components, which means that $x(1) \in N_{R_1}(\xi)$. Taking into account the definition (2.60) of R_1, this implies in turn that $x(2) = \text{Sgn}[W x(1)] = \xi$. By a similar argument, we can construct the sequence

$$
\begin{aligned}
R_1 &= \lfloor \frac{1}{2}|h_1(\xi)| \rfloor \leq R_2 = \lfloor \frac{1}{2}|h_{R_1+1}(\xi)| \rfloor \leq R_3 \cdots \\
&\leq R_{k-1} \leq R_k = \lfloor \frac{1}{2}|h_{R_{k-1}+1}(\xi)| \rfloor \leq \cdots .
\end{aligned}
$$ (2.63)

If all inequalities hold strictly, then R_k is the attraction radius of ξ in k iterations. This construction of nested attraction radii necessarily converges since the sequence R_k is a subset of the finite set of values $\lfloor \frac{1}{2}|h_i(\xi)| \rfloor$. We are now in a position to state the following result [Amari 72].

Theorem 2.17 *Let the components of a fixed point ξ be ordered according to (2.59). If the sequence of R_k's, with the initialization (2.60) and recursively defined by*

$$R_k(\xi) = \lfloor \frac{1}{2}|h_{R_{k-1}+1}(\xi)| \rfloor, \qquad 1 \leq k \leq K,$$ (2.64)

is strictly increasing, then R_k is the radius of attraction in k iterations.

Remarks • The construction of the sequence R_k can terminate in two different ways. The first possibility is that the sequence is strictly increasing, and then

$$R_1 < R_2 < \cdots R_{K-1} < R_K = \lfloor \frac{1}{2}|h_n(\xi)| \rfloor, \tag{2.65}$$

where $n = R_{K-1} + 1$. Since $|h_i(\xi)| \leq \sum_j |w_{ij}| \leq n$, one has $R_K \leq \lfloor \frac{n}{2} \rfloor$ and thus $K \leq \lfloor \frac{n}{2} \rfloor$ in view of the strict inequalities in (2.65). In other words, the largest radius of attraction obtained by Amari's approach is bounded by $\lfloor \frac{n}{2} \rfloor$. This was to be expected since, if $d(x, \xi) > \lfloor \frac{n}{2} \rfloor$ then $d(x, -\xi) \leq \lfloor \frac{n}{2} \rfloor$ and it is known that $-\xi$ is a fixed point together with ξ when the threshold vector θ is zero. Similarly, the number of iterations required to move a vector back to the fixed point is at most $\lfloor \frac{n}{2} \rfloor$ for synchronous operation.

The second possibility is that the sequence of strict inequalities in (2.63) terminates, so that for some k

$$R_1 < R_2 < \cdots < R_k = R_{k+1} = \lfloor \frac{1}{2}|h_{R_k+1}(\xi)| \rfloor, \tag{2.66}$$

where $R_k + 1 < n$. Even if there exists an index $i > R_k + 1$ such that

$$\lfloor \frac{1}{2}|h_i(\xi)| \rfloor < \lfloor \frac{1}{2}|h_{i+\ell}(\xi)| \rfloor \quad \text{with} \ \ell \geq 1 , \tag{2.67}$$

then R_k is nevertheless the largest radius for which one can guarantee attraction by the fixed point. This does not imply that some vectors lying outside this basin may not be attracted by the fixed point, but it cannot be guaranteed by the theory developed above.

• Theorem 2.17 takes into account the recursivity of the network and, in principle, allows one to compute the radii of attraction when several iterations are required for convergence to a fixed point. In practice, this is possible only when the synaptic matrices are given in numerical form, whereas it is difficult to derive general conclusions, holding for a family of synaptic matrices, such as, for example, those constructed by the Hebbian rule. Indeed, in order to apply Theorem 2.17, the potentials $|h_i(\xi)|$ should be ordered by increasing value and, in practice, this is possible only for synaptic matrices given in numerical form. The final result is that general conclusions can be obtained only for the radius of direct attraction, as is seen from the statements of Theorems 2.15 and 2.16.

Example   Consider a network of dimension $n = 12$ and assume that the synaptic potentials have the following absolute values at the fixed point ξ.

$$
\begin{array}{lll}
|h_1(\xi)| = 4.3 & |h_5(\xi)| = 8.4 & |h_9(\xi)| = 10.7 \\
|h_2(\xi)| = 4.5 & |h_6(\xi)| = 8.5 & |h_{10}(\xi)| = 10.8 \\
|h_3(\xi)| = 6.2 & |h_7(\xi)| = 8.7 & |h_{11}(\xi)| = 11 \\
|h_4(\xi)| = 8.2 & |h_8(\xi)| = 10.5 & |h_{12}(\xi)| = 12
\end{array}
$$

According to the preceding theorem, one finds the following values for the successive radii of attraction

$$R_1 = \lfloor \tfrac{1}{2}|h_1(\xi)| \rfloor = 2, \qquad R_3 = \lfloor \tfrac{1}{2}|h_4(\xi)| \rfloor = 4,$$
$$R_2 = \lfloor \tfrac{1}{2}|h_3(\xi)| \rfloor = 3, \qquad R_4 = \lfloor \tfrac{1}{2}|h_5(\xi)| \rfloor = 4.$$

All vectors in the $N_4(\xi)$ neighbourhood are attracted by ξ in at most 3 iterations.

The results to be derived below concerning long-term attraction are of an even more general nature than the preceding ones [Robert 86]. Here, no assumptions are made concerning the functional relation between the synaptic potential and the current state vector. Instead of (1.10), the dynamic equations for synchronous updating will be written in symbolic form as

$$x(t+1) = F(x(t)), \tag{2.68}$$

where the vector valued threshold function F is a mapping of the space $\{-1,1\}^n$ into itself defined by

$$F(x) = \begin{bmatrix} f_1(x_1, x_2, \ldots, x_n) \\ f_2(x_1, x_2, \ldots, x_n) \\ \vdots \\ f_n(x_1, x_2, \ldots, x_n) \end{bmatrix}. \tag{2.69}$$

In general, $f_i(x)$ is a scalar threshold function, i.e. a mapping of $\{-1,1\}^n$ into $\{-1,1\}$ which, in the special case of recursive networks, can be written as $f_i(x) = \mathrm{Sgn}\left[\sum_j w_{ij} x_j\right]$. A fixed point ξ of F is characterized by $F(\xi) = \xi$.

If x and y denote two elements of $\{-1,1\}^n$, then the *difference vector* $\delta(x, y)$ is defined as

$$\delta(x, y) = \frac{1}{2}[|x_1 - y_1|, |x_2 - y_2|, \ldots, |x_n - y_n|]^T, \tag{2.70}$$

or, equivalently, $\delta(x, y) \in \{0, 1\}^n$ with $\delta_i = 0$ if $x_i = y_i$ and $\delta_i = 1$ if $x_i \neq y_i$. We shall use $\tilde{x}^j$ to denote a binary n-vector which deviates from x only in the j-th component, i.e.

$$\tilde{x}^j = [x_1, \ldots, -x_j, \ldots, x_n]^T \tag{2.71}$$

whence

$$\delta(x, \tilde{x}^j) = [0, \ldots, 0, \; 1, \; 0, \ldots, 0]^T. \tag{2.72}$$
$$\uparrow$$
$$j$$

The *discrete derivative* $F'(x)$ of a threshold function $F(x)$ is an $n \times n$ matrix defined as follows [Robert 86]. The value of $F(x)$ is computed in each of the n neighbours $\tilde{x}^j (j = 1, 2, \ldots, n)$ of x and the corresponding difference vectors $\delta(F(\tilde{x}^j), F(x))$ are the columns of $F'(x)$. One has thus

$$F'(x) = [\delta(F(\tilde{x}^1), F(x)), \delta(F(\tilde{x}^2), F(x)), \ldots$$
$$\ldots, \delta(F(\tilde{x}^n), F(x))]. \tag{2.73}$$

The j-th column of $F'(x)$ is composed of zeros and ones, where the ones indicate the positions in which $F(\tilde{x}^j)$ differs from $F(x)$. It should be remembered that the neighbourhood $N_1(y)$ has exactly $n + 1$ points, namely y itself and the n neighbours $\tilde{y}^1, \tilde{y}^2, \ldots, \tilde{y}^n$.

Theorem 2.18 [Robert 86] *Let ξ be a fixed point of F. The necessary and sufficient conditions that each element $x \in N_1(\xi)$ should converge to ξ along a trajectory in $N_1(\xi)$ are :*

• *each column of $F'(\xi)$ has at most a single 1,*
• *there exists an integer $\nu \leq n$ such that $[F'(\xi)]^\nu = O_n$ or, equivalently, there exists a permutation matrix P such that $P^T[F'(\xi)]P$ is strictly lower triangular.*

Under these two conditions, the length of a transient leading from a point in $N_1(\xi)$ to ξ is at most equal to ν.

Proof : Necessity Since ξ is a fixed point, $F(\xi) = \xi$ and we consider the discrete derivative $F'(\xi)$ which is given by

$$F'(\xi) = [\delta(F(\tilde{\xi}^1), \xi), \delta(F(\tilde{\xi}^2), \xi), \ldots, \delta(F(\tilde{\xi}^n), \xi)] . \tag{2.74}$$

Starting from a point $\tilde{\xi}^j$ in $N_1(\xi)$, the trajectory stays, by assumption, in $N_1(\xi)$, i.e. $F(\tilde{\xi}^j) \in N_1(\xi)$. Hence the j-th column of $F'(\xi)$ has at most a single component equal to 1. Let us now prove the second condition. With $\tilde{\xi}^j$ as initialization vector, one has, in view of (2.72) and (2.74),

$$\delta(F(\tilde{\xi}^j), \xi) = F'(\xi)\delta(\tilde{\xi}^j, \xi) . \tag{2.75}$$

Since the trajectory is assumed to stay in $N_1(\xi)$, one concludes that, if $F(\tilde{\xi}^j) \neq \xi$, then $F(\tilde{\xi}^j) = \tilde{\xi}^i$ for some index i and thus

$$\delta(F^2(\tilde{\xi}^j), \xi) = \delta(F(\tilde{\xi}^i), \xi) = F'(\xi)\delta(\tilde{\xi}^i, \xi) =$$
$$= F'(\xi)\delta(F(\tilde{\xi}^j), \xi) = [F'(\xi)]^2\delta(\tilde{\xi}^j, \xi),$$

or, more generally,

$$\delta(F^k(\tilde{\xi}^j), \xi) = [F'(\xi)]^k\delta(\tilde{\xi}^j, \xi) . \tag{2.76}$$

Starting from $\tilde{\xi}^j$, the state vector can at most run through the n neighbours of ξ, namely, $\tilde{\xi}^1, \tilde{\xi}^2, \ldots, \tilde{\xi}^n$ before it converges to the fixed point. There exists thus an integer $\nu_j \leq n$ such that

$$[F'(\xi)]^{\nu_j} \, \delta(\tilde{\xi}^j, \xi) = 0 \ . \tag{2.77}$$

Since a similar relation should hold whatever the starting point in $N_1(\xi)$, one has

$$[F'(\xi)]^\nu \, \delta(\tilde{\xi}^j, \xi) = 0, \qquad j = 1, 2, \ldots, n, \tag{2.78}$$

where $\nu = \mathrm{Max}_{1 \le j \le n} \nu_j \le n$. Taking into account (2.72), this means that all columns of $[F'(\xi)]^\nu$ are zero vectors.

Sufficiency Since the columns of $F'(\xi)$ have at most a single 1, this implies, in view of (2.74), that $F(\tilde{\xi}^j)$ and ξ differ in at most a single component and thus that $F(\tilde{\xi}^j) \in N_1(\xi)$ for all $j = 1, 2, \ldots, n$. In other words, starting from an initial vector in $N_1(\xi)$, the trajectory of the system stays in $N_1(\xi)$ throughout the successive iterations. With $x(0) = \tilde{\xi}^j$ as initialization, we have, by an argument similar to the one used above,

$$\delta(x(1), \xi) = \quad \delta(F(\tilde{\xi}^j), \xi) = \quad F'(\xi) \, \delta(x(0), \xi)$$
$$\delta(x(2), \xi) = \quad \delta(F(x(1)), \xi) = \quad [F'(\xi)]^2 \delta(x(0), \xi)$$

and thus

$$\delta(x(\nu), \xi) = [F'(\xi)]^\nu \, \delta(x(0), \xi) = 0,$$

which means that $x(\nu) = \xi$. Finally, since the elements of $F'(\xi)$ are nonnegative by definition, the Perron-Frobenius theorem implies that $[F'(\xi)]^\nu = O_n$ is equivalent to the existence of a permutation matrix P such that $P^T[F'(\xi)]P$ is strictly lower triangular [Gantmacher 60]. $\qquad \square$

Example Consider the recursive network of dimension $n = 5$ with the following synaptic matrix

$$W = \begin{bmatrix} 0 & 0 & 0 & 0 & 1 \\ 1 & .5 & 0 & 0 & 0 \\ 0 & 0 & 1 & 1 & .5 \\ 0 & 0 & 1 & .5 & 0 \\ 1 & 1 & 0 & 0 & .5 \end{bmatrix}$$

and for which $\xi = [1,1,1,1,1]^T$ is a fixed point. One computes $F(\tilde{\xi}^j) = \mathrm{Sgn}(W\,\tilde{\xi}^j)$ for $j = 1, 2, \ldots, 5$, obtaining

$$F(\tilde{\xi}^1) = \tilde{\xi}^2, \ F(\tilde{\xi}^2) = \xi, \ F(\tilde{\xi}^3) = \tilde{\xi}^4, \ F(\tilde{\xi}^4) = \xi, \ F(\tilde{\xi}^5) = \tilde{\xi}^1,$$

and the discrete derivative defined in (2.74) is thus given by

$$F'(\xi) = \begin{bmatrix} 0 & 0 & 0 & 0 & 1 \\ 1 & 0 & 0 & 0 & 0 \\ 0 & 0 & 0 & 0 & 0 \\ 0 & 0 & 1 & 0 & 0 \\ 0 & 0 & 0 & 0 & 0 \end{bmatrix}.$$

One observes that $F'(\xi)$ has at most a single 1 in each column and that $[F'(\xi)]^3 = O_5$. Hence all points in $N_1(\xi)$ converge to the fixed point in at most 3 iterations, as illustrated in Figure 2.3.

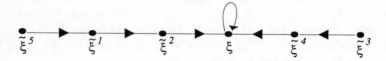

Figure 2.3 : Convergence scheme for the N_1 neighbourhood of ξ.

Here the permutation matrix P which transforms $F'(\xi)$ in a strictly lower triangular form is given by

$$P = \begin{bmatrix} 0 & 1 & 0 & 0 & 0 \\ 0 & 0 & 1 & 0 & 0 \\ 0 & 0 & 0 & 1 & 0 \\ 0 & 0 & 0 & 0 & 1 \\ 1 & 0 & 0 & 0 & 0 \end{bmatrix}.$$

Remarks • The approach followed in reference [Robert 86] consists first in the explicit computation of the new state vectors generated by the threshold function for each possible initialization vector in $N_1(\xi)$. Next, one verifies that the new state vectors still belong to $N_1(\xi)$ and that cycles do not occur. The concept of discrete derivative is indeed the appropriate mathematical tool for efficient verification. An extension of this approach to wider neighbourhoods, such as $N_2(\xi)$, $N_3(\xi)$, ..., is in principle possible [Robert 86] but leads in practice to lengthy computations, among other reasons, because one has to compute the discrete derivative at each point of these neighbourhoods, which, in turn, requires the computation of the threshold function in a large number of points of the space $\{-1, 1\}^n$.

• It seems difficult to draw a comparison between the approaches of Robert and Amari. One can observe however that, in the first case, the lack of precise information on the threshold function F has to be compensated for by an explicit evaluation of the values taken by this function at each point of the N_1 neighbourhood of the fixed point. In the second approach, this evaluation is not necessary since one can consider that it is implicitly contained in the synaptic matrix. Therefore, Amari's approach, although it is more limited in scope since it only deals with recursive networks, can indeed be applied to basins of attraction extending beyond $N_1(\xi)$. For the method followed by Robert, an extension to wider neighbourhoods encounters practical difficulties, especially for networks of large dimension. A second element which makes comparisons difficult is that Amari has to estimate the synaptic potential whereas the approach followed by Robert is an exact one. Finally, in Amari's approach, the hierarchy is clearly organized according to the number of iterations required for convergence, whereas for Robert, the hierarchy follows the sizes of the basins of attraction.

Chapter 3

The statistical approach

3.1 Introduction

The results obtained in the preceding chapter in the framework of the deterministic approach are rather limited, partly because we had to consider extreme and therefore unrealistic situations in order to carry through the analytical developments. This was especially clear for Theorem 2.12 of Subsection 2.2.1 where it was required that *all* subsets of p vectors in $\{-1, 1\}^n$ should be retrievable. Similarly, for the analysis of the basins of attraction in Theorem 2.15 and § 2.2.2, it was assumed that any deviation from a prototype had maximum impact on the value of the synaptic potential.

The statistical approaches presented in this chapter try to remedy this situation. A first very simple result along this line will give a fair idea of the benefit to be expected from a statistical approach to the problem. It concerns the network capacity and it corrects somewhat the pessimistic conclusion of Theorem 2.12. The result obtained there was based on the bound (2.42) for the number B_n^p of realizable threshold functions in n variables and specified at p points. We have seen that, in order to memorize any p-tuple of vectors, B_n^p should be larger or equal to 2^p which, in turn, implied $p \leq n$. This, however, does not mean that the capacity cannot exceed n. Indeed, Cover's result [Cover 65], also presented in a more formal setting in [Venkatesh 86], shows that the capacity can approach $p = 2n$ if some requirements are relaxed. We shall assume here that the p vectors to be stored are in *general position*, which means that any subset of up to n vectors is linearly independent. In this case, the bound (2.42) for B_n^p is attained [Cover 65]. On the other hand, 2^p is the total number of possible threshold functions. Therefore, considering that all threshold functions are equiprobable, the quantity $\Pr(n, p) = B_n^p/2^p$ represents the probability that a random p-tuple of vectors in $\{-1, 1\}^n$ can be memorized. But $B_n^p/2^p$ is just the probability of up to $n-1$ successes in $p-1$ independent trials with success probability $1/2$. Appealing to the law of large numbers for this symmetric distribution one then has for all $\epsilon > 0$

$$\lim_{n \to \infty} \Pr(n, \ 2n(1 - \epsilon)) = 1, \tag{3.1}$$

$$\lim_{n\to\infty} \Pr(n,\, 2n(1+\epsilon)) = 0, \tag{3.2}$$

$$\Pr(n,\, 2n) = 1/2. \tag{3.3}$$

This implies the following assertion [Cover 65].

Theorem 3.1 *For prototype vectors in general position, the capacity p can approach 2n, in the sense that, for all $\epsilon > 0$, the probability of retrieving a fraction $(1 - \epsilon)$ of any set of 2n vectors, tends to unity when the dimension of the network tends to infinity.*

Remarks • At first sight, Theorems 2.12 (§ 2.2.1) and 3.1 may seem to contradict each other but on closer examination this is not so. Indeed, the first one holds for finite n but requires that *all* p-tuples of prototypes should be retrievable without exception. In contrast, the second one only holds asymptotically ($n \to \infty$) and tolerates that a small fraction ϵ of the $2n$ vectors are irretrievable. In other words, for $p < 2n$, "almost" all p-tuples of vectors in general position can "almost" surely be memorized as fixed points of the network. This result expresses the fact that for large n, the probability of exact retrieval varies abruptly as p approaches $2n$ as qualitatively illustrated in Figure 3.1.

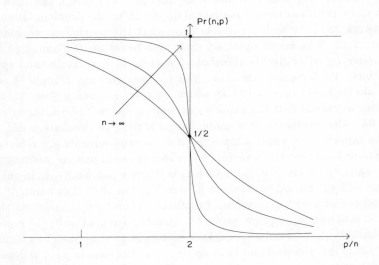

Figure 3.1 : A sketch graph of $\Pr(n, p)$, the probability of exact retrieval of p prototypes as a function of n.

• The range of applicability of Theorem 3.1 is at least as general as that of Theorem 2.12 because it holds true irrespective of the structure of the synaptic matrix, the particular construction rule used for this matrix or the updating mode of the network (synchronous or asynchronous).

In most statistical approaches, a recursive network is considered as a *random* system in the sense that the parameters of the network, namely the synaptic matrix and the threshold vector, are random variables with given probability distributions. The purpose is to establish certain properties which do not depend on the particular values of the parameters, but only on their statistical distribution. Proceeding in this way, one is able to derive statistical conclusions for networks of prescribed parameter distribution [Rozonoer 69a], [Rozonoer 69b], [Rozonoer 69c]. The statistical distribution of the synaptic matrix can be specified in two different ways, either directly for the elements w_{ij} of the matrix (see e.g. [Amari 71], [Amari 74]), or, indirectly, for the components of the prototype vectors which are used to construct this matrix (see e.g. [McEliece et al. 87]). In practice, only the Hebbian law will be considered, because its expression is simple enough that the statistical properties of the synaptic matrix can easily be derived from those of the prototypes. The projection rule is often too difficult to handle in this respect and, for this reason, is almost never considered in the framework of statistical approaches.

One can recognize two principal techniques for the statistical approach. Section 3.2 deals mainly with the evolution of the network as a result of the successive iterations of the dynamic equations. It is easily seen that this evolution would be difficult to follow by the detailed equations (1.2). Hence, a more global approach will be adopted in which we will keep track of the time evolution of the network via a *macrovariable*. This macrovariable is selected in such a way that its evolution as a function of time depends only on the statistical properties of a family of *random* networks and not on the specific parameter values of a particular sample network [Rozonoer 69a], [Rozonoer 69b], [Rozonoer 69c]. Section 3.3 on the other hand, starts from a given distribution of the network parameters and computes the probability of correcting noisy versions of the prototypes in a *single* iteration. This will yield interesting estimates of the capacity, the radius of direct attraction and the transient length required to reach a fixed point.

In this chapter, we shall almost exclusively consider the synchronous updating mode, but many results, especially those concerning capacity and the basins of direct attraction will also hold for asynchronous updating.

3.2   Macrovariables and evolution equations

The dynamic behaviour of a network in a synchronous operation mode is exactly described by equation (1.10) but we shall not need such a detailed description here. On the contrary, we wish to define a *macrovariable* $s(t) = S(x(t))$ which depends on the state vector $x(t)$ at time t and which describes the *global* time evolution of the network. Since this macrovariable should be representative for the whole set of networks having the same parameter distribution, it will essentially be defined as a statistical mean with respect to this distribution. The reader will find in references [Amari 71], [Amari 74] a more precise definition of the concept of a macrovariable and in references [Rozonoer 69a], [Rozonoer 69b], [Rozonoer 69c] a discussion concerning the stochastic hypotheses underlying the theory of random networks and methods yielding macro-descriptions.

If $s(t+1) = S(x(t+1))$ is the macrovariable at the next instant of time $t+1$, we wish to establish an *evolution equation*

$$s(t+1) = \phi(s(t)) \tag{3.4}$$

which then partially describes the dynamic behaviour of the random network. The function ϕ is called the *transition function*. In the sequel, we shall essentially consider two types of macrovariables : the *activity level* and the *overlap*.

The evolution equation defines a discrete time dynamic system and the equilibrium points are solutions of

$$s = \phi(s). \tag{3.5}$$

An equilibrium point s^* is stable if

$$|\phi'(s^*)| < 1. \tag{3.6}$$

Before continuing with the investigation of the network dynamics via macrovariables and evolution equations, we should observe that this approach is in fact not completely rigorous. Indeed, it relies on the validity of some version of the law of large numbers and on the central limit theorem, yet to be established rigorously.

3.2.1   Evolution equation for the activity level

The *activity level* of a network is a function of the state vector defined by

$$a(t) = \frac{1}{n} \sum_{i=1}^{n} x_i(t). \tag{3.7}$$

The use of the activity level as macrovariable for the analysis of recursive networks is due to Amari [Amari 71], [Amari 74] and the most important results obtained along this line are summarized in this subsection.

If the state vector components are independent and identically distributed (i.i.d.) random variables then, according to the law of large numbers [Kendall and Stuart 63], the activity level tends in probability to the statistical mean of the state variables when n is sufficiently large. For simplicity, we shall use the following convention to denote this type of convergence

$$a(t) \overset{\text{P}}{=} \mathcal{E}[x_i(t)], \tag{3.8}$$

where $\mathcal{E}$ is the expectation operator.

We consider now a random network where the synaptic weights w_{ij} ($i, j = 1, 2, \ldots, n$) are i.i.d. random variables with mean $\overline{w}$ and variance σ_w^2. The threshold values θ_i ($i = 1, 2, \ldots, n$) are also assumed to be i.i.d. random variables characterized by a mean $\overline{\theta}$ and a variance σ_θ^2.

Theorem 3.2 [Amari 71], [Amari 74] *For a random network whose parameters are independent random variables, the synaptic weights being identically distributed and likewise the threshold values, the transition function ϕ for the activity level is given by*

$$\phi(a(t)) = 2 \operatorname{erf}(Va(t) - \Theta) = \frac{2}{\sqrt{2\pi}} \int_0^{Va(t) - \Theta} e^{-y^2/2} \, dy, \tag{3.9}$$

where

$$V = n\overline{w}/\sqrt{n\sigma_w^2 + \sigma_\theta^2}, \tag{3.10}$$

$$\Theta = \overline{\theta}/\sqrt{n\sigma_w^2 + \sigma_\theta^2}. \tag{3.11}$$

Proof We have $x_i(t+1) = \operatorname{Sgn}[h_i(x(t))]$, where

$$h_i(x(t)) = \sum_{j=1}^n w_{ij} x_j(t) - \theta_i. \tag{3.12}$$

The synaptic potential h_i is thus written as a weighted sum of $n+1$ independent random variables w_{ij} ($j = 1, 2, \ldots, n$) and θ_i. Assuming that the weights $x_j(t)$ in this sum are independent of the w_{ij} (see the remark below), one finds, in view of the central limit theorem [Cramér 57] that, for sufficiently large n, the distribution of h_i tends to a normal distribution with density

$$f(h_i) = \frac{1}{\sqrt{2\pi}\,\sigma_h} \exp\left(-\frac{(h_i - \overline{h})^2}{2\sigma_h^2}\right), \tag{3.13}$$

where, by (3.7) and (3.12), the mean and the variance are given by

$$\overline{h} = n \, \overline{w} \, a(t) - \overline{\theta} \, , \tag{3.14}$$

$$\sigma_h^2 = n \, \sigma_w^2 + \sigma_\theta^2 . \tag{3.15}$$

Since $x_i(t+1)$ is obtained by applying the sign function to $h_i(x(t))$, one has

$$\begin{aligned} a(t+1) \;\; &\stackrel{\text{P}}{=}\;\; \mathcal{E}[x_i(t+1)] = \Pr\left(h_i(t) > 0\right) - \Pr\left(h_i(t) < 0\right), \\[4pt] &\stackrel{\text{P}}{=}\;\; 2 \int_0^\infty f(h_i) \, dh_i - 1 \, . \end{aligned} \tag{3.16}$$

Taking (3.13) into account, one obtains the desired result (3.9). $\square$

Remarks • The transition function (3.9) has the required form, since, the only time-varying quantity on which it depends is $a(t)$.

• Strictly speaking, the application of the central limit theorem is not justified. Indeed, except for the initialization phase of the network at time $t = 0$, the component $x_i(t)$ has in fact been obtained via the equation

$$x_i(t) = \text{Sgn} \left[\sum_{j=1}^n w_{ij} x_j(t-1) - \theta_i \right] , \tag{3.17}$$

and it depends thus effectively on the weights w_{ij} and the threshold θ_i. Consequently, the random variables $w_{ij} x_j(t)$ and θ_i which occur in expression (3.12) of h_i are actually not independent [Amari 71]. The same problem will also occur in the next subsection when the overlap is taken as macrovariable.

• The results of Theorem 3.2 hold asymptotically, i.e. when the dimension n of the network tends to infinity. If $\overline{w}$ and σ_w^2 are independent of n, then expression (3.10) shows that V tends to infinity, which leads to trivial conclusions. Therefore, the synaptic weights and the threshold values should be determined in such a way that V and Θ tend to appropriate limits when n becomes large. Two possibilities in this direction are presented in [Amari 74]. Let us simply observe that, when the number of prototypes is finite, it suffices to modify the definition (1.25) of Hebb's law to $W = n^{-1} X X^T$ in order to satisfy this condition.

Theorem 3.3 [Amari 71], [Amari 74] *The evolution equation (3.4), (3.9) implies that the activity level will approach either an equilibrium point or a cycle of period 2. If $V > 0$, it necessarily tends to a stable equilibrium point.*

Proof Form (3.4) of the evolution equation yields

$$a(t+2) - a(t+1) = \phi'(a)[a(t+1) - a(t)] \tag{3.18}$$

where $\phi'(a)$ denotes the derivative of the transition function at a point a of the interval $[a(t+1), a(t)]$. It follows from (3.9) that

$$\phi'(a) = \frac{V}{\sqrt{\pi/2}} \, e^{-\frac{1}{2}(Va-\Theta)^2}. \tag{3.19}$$

Consequently, $V > 0$ implies $\phi'(a) > 0$ for all a, which in turn implies, in view of (3.18), that the sequence of activity levels $a(0), a(1), a(2) \ldots$ is monotonically increasing or decreasing. Since, on the other hand, a is bounded by definition (see (3.7)), this sequence necessarily converges.

Consider next the relation between the activity levels of two consecutive iterations

$$a(t+2) = \psi(a(t)), \tag{3.20}$$

with $\psi(a) = \phi(\phi(a))$. Using the chain rule, it is easily verified that the derivative of ψ has the general form.

$$\psi'(a) = \frac{2V^2}{\pi} \, e^\eta \tag{3.21}$$

where η is a function of a, V and Θ. Since $\psi'(a) > 0$ for all a, an argument similar to the one used above shows that the sequence $a(0), a(2), a(4), \ldots$ converges, which leaves only two possibilities, namely : a stable equilibrium point or a cycle with period 2.   □

Theorem 3.4 [Amari 71], [Amari 74] *The activity level of the random network specified in Theorem 3.2 has the following dynamic behaviour.*

• *if* $|V| \leq \sqrt{\pi/2}$, *there is a single stable equilibrium point.*

• *When* $V > \sqrt{\pi/2}$, *there are two stable equilibrium points and one unstable equilibrium point if* $|\Theta| < g(V)$. *There is a single stable equilibrium point if* $|\Theta| > g(V)$.

• *If* $V < -\sqrt{\pi/2}$, *the activity level (and hence the network) goes through a cycle of period 2 when* $|\Theta| < -g(V)$; *a single stable equilibrium point is reached when* $|\Theta| > -g(V)$.

Here the function $g(V)$ *is given by*

$$g(V) = \frac{V}{\sqrt{\pi/2}} \int_0^y e^{-t^2/2} dt \; - y \; \text{ with } y = \sqrt{\log(2V^2/\pi)}. \tag{3.22}$$

Figure 3.2 shows the domains in the V, Θ plane corresponding to these different dynamic behaviours.

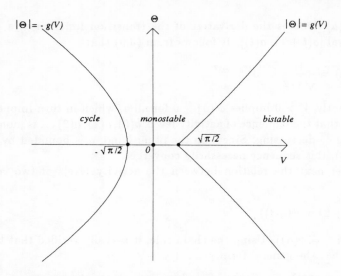

Figure 3.2:   Different dynamic behaviours of the activity level.
(Reprinted by permission of Springer-Verlag ©1974)

Proof Expression (3.19) shows that the transition function ϕ is monotonically increasing (decreasing) if $V > 0$ $(V < 0)$. The absolute value of the slope is maximum and equal to $|V|/\sqrt{\pi/2}$ at $a = \Theta/V$ and decreases monotonically when moving away from this point. Four cases will be examined.

1) $0 < V < \sqrt{\pi/2}$ (Figure 3.3). The slope of the curve $\phi(a)$ is everywhere

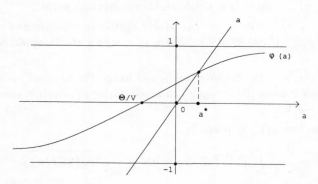

Figure 3.3 : The transition function when $0 < V < \sqrt{\pi/2}$.

smaller than unity and there is a single equilibrium point a^* which, in addition, is stable since $|\phi'(a^*)| < 1$.

2) $V > \sqrt{\pi/2}$ (Figure 3.4). At the point $a = \Theta/V$, the slope of the transition function is larger than one. Hence, there are three equilibrium points

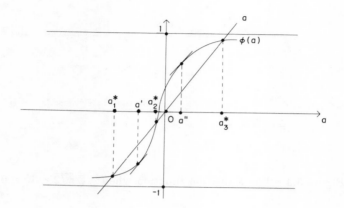

Figure 3.4 : The transition function when $V > \sqrt{\pi/2}$.

a_1^*, a_2^*, a_3^* provided that at the points a' and a'' where the slope equals 1, the inequalities

$$\phi(a') < a' \qquad \text{and} \qquad \phi(a'') > a'' \tag{3.23}$$

hold. Taking (3.19) into account, we see that the points a' and a'' are given by

$$a' = \frac{\Theta}{V} - \frac{1}{V}\sqrt{\log(2V^2/\pi)}, \quad a'' = \frac{\Theta}{V} + \frac{1}{V}\sqrt{\log(2V^2/\pi)} \tag{3.24}$$

and the inequalities (3.23) hold if $|\Theta| < g(V)$ where $g(V)$ is given by (3.22). The equilibrium point a_2^* is unstable because it belongs to the interval $[a', a'']$ where the slope is larger than unity. Points a_1^* and a_3^*, however, are stable since they lie outside this interval and the slope at these points is thus smaller than unity.

3) $-\sqrt{\pi/2} < V < 0$ (Figure 3.5). In this case there is only a single

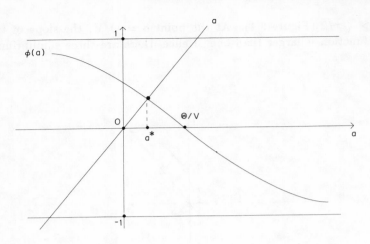

Figure 3.5 : The transition function when $-\sqrt{\pi/2} < V < 0$.

equilibrium point because the absolute value of the slope is everywhere smaller than unity.

4) $V < -\sqrt{\pi/2}$ (Figure 3.6). The absolute value of the slope at $a = \Theta/V$

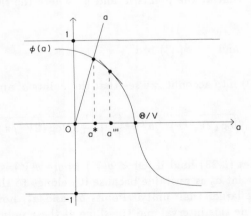

Figure 3.6 : The transition function when $V < -\sqrt{\pi/2}$.

is larger than unity. In order for the equilibrium point a^* to be stable, one should have $|\phi'(a^*)| < 1$, and this indeed holds if, at the point a''', where the slope equals -1, one has $|\phi(a''')| < |a'''|$. Since $a''' = a'$ if $\Theta > 0$ and $a''' = a''$ if $\Theta < 0$, the latter inequality implies that $|\Theta| > -g(V)$ in view of expressions (3.24). When $|\Theta| < -g(V)$, the equilibrium point a^* is unstable and, by Theorem 3.3, the activity level then describes a cycle of period 2. □

Remark • There is a qualitative agreement between this statistical result and Theorems 2.4 and 2.6 (§ 2.1.3) of the deterministic approach which state that, in synchronous operation mode, the period of the cycles is at most 2 and that cycles can only occur if the synaptic matrix is not positive definite. It seems however difficult to establish a precise correspondence between the positive definite property of W and the values of V and Θ for which cycles are excluded.

3.2.2 The evolution equation for the overlap

In the preceding subsection it was assumed that the elements of the synaptic matrix were independent random variables, which led to a rather simple analysis. The main disadvantage of this hypothesis is that it does not hold for synaptic matrices constructed according to Hebb's law. We shall therefore consider hereafter the less stringent hypothesis that the components of the prototypes are independent and identically distributed random variables. In addition, we shall assume that the prototypes are unbiased, i.e., that the values $+1$ and -1 for the elements are equiprobable. The hypotheses are thus

$$\begin{cases} \Pr\left(\xi_i^{(k)} = 1\right) = \Pr\left(\xi_i^{(k)} = -1\right) = 1/2, \\ \xi_i^{(k)} \text{ independent of } \xi_j^{(\ell)} \text{ if } k \neq \ell \text{ or } i \neq j. \end{cases} \tag{3.25}$$

It is interesting to see what these hypotheses actually imply in terms of the synaptic weights computed according to Hebb's law (1.25)

$$w_{ij} = \frac{1}{p} \sum_{k=1}^{p} \xi_i^{(k)} \xi_j^{(k)}, \qquad (j \neq i). \tag{3.26}$$

An element w_{ij} is then expressed as the sum of p independent random variables with zero mean and unit variance. Therefore, if p tends to infinity, the probability distribution of w_{ij} will tend to a normal distribution with zero mean and variance $1/p$ as a consequence of the central limit theorem [Cramér 57]. In contrast with the preceding subsection, the w_{ij} are, however, not independent for finite values of p, because one easily verifies that the mean value of $w_{ij}w_{j\ell}w_{i\ell}$ is not zero, but equals $1/p^2$.

If the state vector $x(t)$ is a corrupted version of a prototype, say $\xi^{(1)}$, we shall select as macrovariable the *overlap*, defined as

$$m(t) = \frac{1}{n} x^T(t)\, \xi^{(1)}, \tag{3.27}$$

and we shall follow the evolution of the network, in particular the convergence of the state vector to $\xi^{(1)}$, by means of $m(t)$. Note that

$$m(t) = 1 - \frac{2}{n}\, d(x(t), \xi^{(1)}) \tag{3.28}$$

where d is the Hamming distance between $x(t)$ and $\xi^{(1)}$. If, for increasing values of time, $m(t)$ tends to unity, then the *error rate* or, equivalently, the relative number of errors $\rho = d/n$ tends to zero.

One assumes that the system is initialized with a random vector $x(0)$, independent of the prototypes $\xi^{(2)}, \dots, \xi^{(p)}$ and which is correlated with $\xi^{(1)}$ to the extent that the overlap $m(0)$ has a fixed value. In a more detailed formulation, one has

$$x_i(0) \text{ independent of } \xi_j^{(k)}, \quad i,j = 1, 2, \dots, n, \quad k = 2, \dots, p,$$

$$x_i(0) \text{ independent of } \xi_j^{(1)}, \quad j \neq i,$$

$$\frac{1}{n} \sum_{i=1}^{n} x_i(0)\xi_i^{(1)} = m(0).$$

We shall now establish the evolution equation of the overlap [Kinzel 85].

Theorem 3.5 *If the components of the prototype vectors are independent random variables with identical and uniform distributions (3.25) and if the synaptic matrix is constructed according to the Hebbian rule, then for $n \to \infty$, the transition function of the overlap is given by*

$$\phi(m(t)) = 2\,\mathrm{erf}\,(m(t)/\sqrt{\alpha}) = \sqrt{\frac{2}{\pi}} \int_0^{m(t)/\sqrt{\alpha}} e^{-y^2/2} dy \tag{3.29}$$

where $\alpha = p/n$.

Proof For the sake of simplicity, we shall assume that the threshold vector and the diagonal of the synaptic matrix are zero. In view of (3.26), the components of the state vector at time $t + 1$ are then given by

$$x_i(t+1) = \mathrm{Sgn}\left[\sum_{j \neq i} x_j(t) \sum_{k=1}^{p} \xi_i^{(k)} \xi_j^{(k)} \right]. \tag{3.30}$$

In the sum on the right hand side we separate the term $k = 1$ and, within the approximation

$$m(t) = \frac{1}{n} \sum_{j \neq i} x_j(t)\, \xi_j^{(1)}, \qquad \text{for } n \to \infty,$$

one obtains

$$x_i(t+1) = \text{Sgn}\left[n\, \xi_i^{(1)}\, m(t) + \sum_{j \neq i} \sum_{k=2}^{p} x_j(t)\, \xi_i^{(k)}\, \xi_j^{(k)} \right].$$

Since $a\, \text{Sgn}\, b = \text{Sgn}\, ab$ if $a = \pm 1$, we conclude that

$$\xi_i^{(1)}\, x_i(t+1) = \text{Sgn}\, [m(t) + N_i(t)] \tag{3.31}$$

where $N_i(t)$ is a noise term defined by

$$N_i(t) = \frac{1}{n} \sum_{j \neq i} x_j(t)\, \xi_i^{(1)} \sum_{k=2}^{p} \xi_i^{(k)}\, \xi_j^{(k)}. \tag{3.32}$$

By adding relations (3.31) for $i = 1, 2, \ldots, n$, we obtain

$$m(t+1) = \frac{1}{n} \sum_{i=1}^{n} \text{Sgn}\, [m(t) + N_i(t)]. \tag{3.33}$$

If the terms $N_i(t)$ are independent random variables, then for $n \to \infty$, the overlap $m(t+1)$ tends to the statistical mean of $\text{Sgn}\, [m(t) + N_i(t)]$. Consequently, with the convention defined in the preceding subsection, we have

$$
\begin{aligned}
m(t+1) \;&\overset{\text{p}}{=}\; \Pr\left(N_i(t) > -m(t) \right) - \Pr\left(N_i(t) < -m(t) \right), \\
&\overset{\text{p}}{=}\; 2\Pr\left(N_i(t) > -m(t) \right) - 1.
\end{aligned}
\tag{3.34}
$$

In order to make proper use of this result, we should find the probability distribution of the random variable $N_i(t)$. If we ignore the correlation between the state vector and the prototypes, then expression (3.32) gives $N_i(t)$ as the sum of $(n-1)(p-1)$ independent random variables $x_j(t)\, \xi_i^{(1)} \xi_i^{(k)}\, \xi_j^{(k)}$ with zero mean and unit variance. In view of the central limit theorem [Cramér 57], $N_i(t)$ tends for large n to a Gaussian distribution with zero mean and variance equal to $(p-1)(n-1)/n^2 \simeq p/n = \alpha$. We can now compute the right hand side of (3.34) which gives

$$m(t+1) = \frac{1}{\sqrt{2\pi}} \int_{-m(t)/\sqrt{\alpha}}^{m(t)/\sqrt{\alpha}} e^{-y^2/2}\, dy, \tag{3.35}$$

and this is the desired result (3.29). The transition function $\phi(m)$ is shown in Figure 3.7 for $m > 0$. $\square$

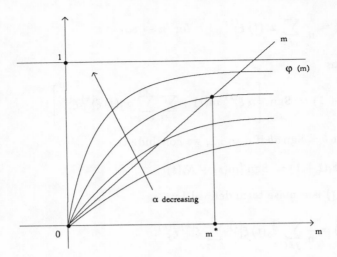

Figure 3.7 : The transition function $\phi(m)$ for the overlap.

The derivative of the transition function is given by

$$\phi'(m) = \sqrt{\frac{2}{\pi\alpha}}\, e^{-\frac{m^2}{2\alpha}} \tag{3.36}$$

and is everywhere positive. By an argument similar to the one used in Theorem 3.3 (§ 3.2.1), the overlap tends necessarily to an equilibrium point m^* satisfying the equation

$$m = \sqrt{\frac{2}{\pi}} \int_0^{m/\sqrt{\alpha}} e^{-y^2/2}\, dy. \tag{3.37}$$

Since the transition function $\phi(m)$ is odd, there are two symmetric solutions with respect to the origin but only the positive solution will be considered in the sequel. Expression (3.36) shows that the slope at the origin equals $\sqrt{2/\pi\alpha}$ so that, if $\alpha = p/n > 2/\pi$, the only equilibrium point is the origin : this means that the initialization vector does not converge to $\xi^{(1)}$ if there are too many prototypes. If $\alpha = p/n < 2/\pi$, the equilibrium point at the origin becomes unstable since the slope $\phi'(0)$ is larger than unity. A second equilibrium point $m^* \neq 0$ appears then which is stable since one can show that $|\phi'(m^*)| < 1$. The smaller α, the closer m^* gets to unity.

Figure 3.8, reproduced from [Kinzel 85], shows the behaviour of m^* as a function of α. As long as $\alpha = p/n < 0.15$, the curve stays almost horizontal and close to unity.

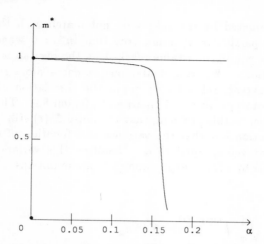

Figure 3.8 : Equilibrium value m^* of the overlap as a function of $\alpha = p/n$.
(Reprinted by permission of Springer-Verlag ©1985)

Consequently, if the number of prototypes does not exceed 15% of the total number of neurons, the network behaves as an associative memory in the sense that a state vector is progressively corrected and converges to a prototype or its negative. The critical value of $\alpha = 0.15$ is in good agreement with the experimental observations [Hopfield 82] and with the theoretical results obtained via some methods of statistical mechanics, as explained in Chapter 4 (Section 4.4). For $\alpha \neq 0$, one has $m^* < 1$ and the state vector does not converge exactly to the prototype. The larger α, the more m^* deviates from unity, which means, in view of (3.28), that the residual error rate increases. In other words, when the number p of prototypes increases proportionally to the size n of the network, then the fixed point reached after convergence does not coincide exactly with a prototype. Some residual error remains which affects $d = \rho n$ components and the fraction $\rho = (1 - m^*)/2$ of corrupted components increases with α. For the critical value $p = 0.15n$, this fraction ρ is still very small and of the order of 0.5 %.

Remark • The result of Theorem 3.5 is not rigorous because $x_i(t)$ is not independent of the prototypes $\xi^{(k)}, (k \geq 2)$, except for the initialization phase at $t = 0$. Indeed, for $t > 1$, $x_i(t)$ is computed via

$$x_i(t) = \text{Sgn} \left[\sum_{j \neq i} x_j(t-1) \sum_{k=1} \xi_i^{(k)} \xi_j^{(k)} \right],$$

and, as a result, the noise term $N_i(t)$ given by (3.32) is not a sum of independent random variables, contrary to the hypothesis made earlier. Consequently, some of the results predicted by the theory do not match with the experimental observations. In particular, it is not true that $m^* = 0$ when $\alpha > 2/\pi$ nor is it true that the equilibrium value reached by the overlap is independent of the initial conditions. Amari and Maginu present a more rigorous analysis which, to some extent, takes into account the correlation existing between $x_i(t)$ and the prototype vectors [Amari and Maginu 88]. They assume as a first approximation to this problem, that the noise $N_i(t)$ still has a zero mean Gaussian distribution but that the variance is a function of time, instead of having a constant value, equal to α. Denoting this variance by $\sigma^2(t)$ and replacing then $\sqrt{\alpha}$ by $\sigma(t)$ in expression (3.29), one obtains

$$m(t+1) = \sqrt{\frac{2}{\pi}} \int_0^{m(t)/\sigma(t)} e^{-y^2/2} \, dy. \tag{3.38}$$

It can be shown that the time evolution of the variance $\sigma^2(t)$ is approximately given by the equation

$$\sigma^2(t+1) = \alpha + 4f^2\left(\frac{m(t)}{\sigma(t)}\right) + 4\alpha\frac{m(t)}{\sigma(t)}f\left(\frac{m(t)}{\sigma(t)}\right)m(t+1) \tag{3.39}$$

where the function $f(u)$ is the normal density

$$f(u) = \frac{1}{\sqrt{2\pi}} e^{-u^2/2}.$$

One can see now that the taking into account of the correlations between the state vector and the prototypes forces one to take the *pair* $(m(t), \sigma(t))$ as macrovariables. Numerical solution of equations (3.38) and (3.39) shows that the overlap at time t now depends on the initial condition $m(0)$ and mainly on whether the initial overlap $m(0)$ is larger or smaller than some threshold value $g(\alpha)$ which in turn is a function of the occupation rate $\alpha = p/n$ of the memory. The results are qualitatively sketched in Figure 3.9.

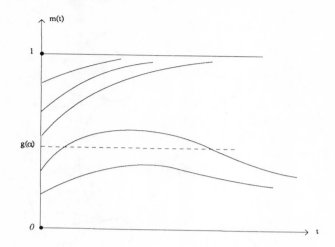

Figure 3.9 : The time evolution of the overlap and its dependence on the initial condition $m(0)$.
(Reprinted by permission of Pergamon Press Ltd. ©1988)

If $m(0) > g(\alpha)$, then the overlap $m(t)$ increases monotonically towards an equilibrium value m^* close to unity, which means that the errors in the initialization state vector are progressively corrected. However, if $m(0) < g(\alpha)$, then $m(t)$ first increases and can possibly exceed the threshold value $g(\alpha)$, but, in the end, it decreases and stabilizes around a small equilibrium value. In the latter case, the network does not behave as an associative memory. This paradoxical phenomenon can be explained if one realizes that the same overlap value can be achieved by different state vectors. Equation (3.28) shows that there is a simple relationship between the overlap and the Hamming distance. Let $d_g = n(1 - g)/2$ be the distance corresponding to the threshold value g of the overlap. The phenomenon described above means that $d = d_g$ does not define a basin of long-term attraction and the explanation proposed by Amari and Maginu is the following [Amari and Maginu 88] : even if most of the vectors at distance d_g are attracted by the prototypes, nevertheless, a small number of these are not, and it is precisely towards these exceptional vectors that the network evolves when it is initialized by a vector at distance $d > d_g$, i.e. $m(0) < g(\alpha)$. Later on, the state vector leaves the basin of radius d_g. A pictorial representation of this situation is given in Figure 3.10.

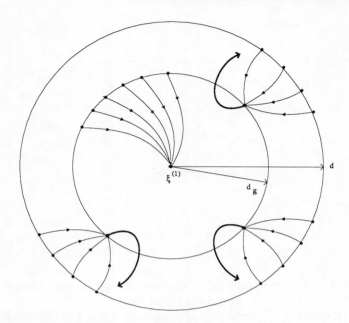

Figure 3.10 : Long-term attraction above and below the overlap threshold.
(Reprinted by permission of Pergamon Press Ltd. ©1988)

3.3   Probabilistic results

In this section we will establish some fundamental results concerning the mech-
anisms of associative memory. These results concern essentially two important
performance criteria : *capacity* on the one hand, and the *basin of attraction* on
the other hand. In addition, we shall also obtain some information on the speed
of convergence or the *transient length* as well as on the nature and the number
of *parasitic fixed points*. This investigation can be developed along different
lines, e.g. according to the updating rule used (synchronous or asynchronous),
according to the type of attraction (direct or long-term) or according to the
final retrieval accuracy (exact convergence or tolerance of some residual error).
Therefore, we can consider that the different problems to be investigated result
from the combination of eight situations :

synchronous mode	asynchronous mode
direct attraction	long-term attraction
exact convergence	residual errors
correction of a random vector	correction of all vectors

Table 3.11

The most important distinction is the residual error rate. If no residual errors are tolerated, then we shall see that the capacity is limited by a bound of the general form $p < n/\log n$, as shown in a number of references [Weisbuch and Fogelman-Soulie 85], [Weisbuch and d'Humières 86], [Peretto and Niez 86], [McEliece et al. 87], [Komlós and Paturi 88]. If some residual error is acceptable, then linear growth of the capacity $p = \alpha n$, becomes possible, even if it appears that the proportionality factor α is rather small, as already suggested by the results of Subsection 3.2.2. This linear growth of the capacity can be examined either by a rigorous statistical analysis [Komlós and Paturi 88], [Newman 88], or by using some techniques borrowed from the field of statistical mechanics [Amit et al. 85b], [Amit et al. 87b], [Amit et al. 87a].

In the left column of Table 3.11 we have listed the cases which will be considered in Subsections 3.3.1 and 3.3.2, while those of the right column will be analyzed in Subsection 3.3.3. In contrast to Section 3.2, the theorems stated in this section are completely rigorous. As far as possible, we shall try to give complete derivations but, we shall refer the reader to the original publications when detailed and highly technical proofs would obscure the fundamental line of arguments. One should notice that throughout this section we shall restrict ourselves to Hebb's law with zero diagonal and zero threshold vector. All the results to be established hold asymptotically, i.e. when the dimension n of the network becomes very large.

Just as in Section 3.2, we shall assume that the components $\xi_i^{(k)}$ of the prototype vectors are random variables distributed according to (3.25). The network is initialized with a vector x at Hamming distance ρn from $\xi^{(1)}$, ($\rho < 1/2$), and we examine conditions under which direct attraction takes place. To simplify notation, we shall assume that ρn is an integer and we shall denote by x' the state vector after a single synchronous iteration, i.e. $x_i' = \mathrm{Sgn}\, h_i(x)$ with

$$h_i(x) = \sum_{j \neq i}^{n} w_{ij}\, x_j \qquad (3.40)$$

where w_{ij} is given by (3.26). Direct attraction will take place if $x_i' = \xi_i^{(1)}$ or, equivalently, if

$$S_i = p\xi_i^{(1)}\, h_i(x) > 0\,, \qquad i = 1, 2, \ldots, n. \qquad (3.41)$$

We see from (3.40) and (3.26) that

$$S_i = \xi_i^{(1)} \sum_{j \neq i}^{n} \sum_{k=1}^{p} \xi_i^{(k)}\, \xi_j^{(k)}\, x_j. \qquad (3.42)$$

If we separate the term for $k = 1$, in the right hand side of the latter expression, then S_i can be rewritten

$$S_i = (1 - 2\rho)n + z_i,$$ (3.43)

with

$$z_i = \xi_i^{(1)} \sum_{j \neq i}^{n} \sum_{k=2}^{p} \xi_i^{(k)} \xi_j^{(k)} x_j.$$ (3.44)

Indeed, since x is at Hamming distance ρn from $\xi^{(1)}$, one has

$$\sum_{j \neq i} \xi_j^{(1)} x_j = n(1 - 2\rho) - 1, \quad \text{or} \quad \sum_{j \neq i} \xi_j^{(1)} x_j = n(1 - 2\rho) + 1,$$

depending on whether the i-th components of the state vector x and the proto-type $\xi^{(1)}$ agree or not. Since in any case we shall take the limit for $n \to \infty$, the difference between the two situations is immaterial and we shall keep in the following the expression $(1 - 2\rho)n$. In view of (3.41) we have thus to examine under which conditions the probability $\Pr(S_i < 0)$ can be made sufficiently small. As shown by (3.43), S_i is composed of a main positive term $(1 - 2\rho)n$ with a superimposed noise term z_i given by (3.44). Component x_i' will coincide with $\xi_i^{(1)}$ if the noise term is smaller than the main term and the acceptable noise intensity decreases as the initialization vector x contains more errors, i.e. as ρ approaches $1/2$. To make the main arguments more transparent, we shall first give a simplified presentation of the results in Subsection 3.3.1 : the ben-efit is that this allows a quick derivation of the conditions under which direct attraction takes place. A rigorous analysis will be performed in Subsection 3.3.2 where the results will be commented upon in more detail.

3.3.1 Direct attraction : heuristic approach

The initialization vector x is a random vector at Hamming distance ρn from $\xi^{(1)}$ and independent of the prototypes $\xi^{(2)}, \ldots, \xi^{(p)}$. More precisely, x_i is inde-pendent of $\xi_j^{(1)}$ for all $i \neq j$ but $\sum_{i=1}^{n} x_i \xi_i^{(1)} = (1 - 2\rho)n$. Expression (3.44) for z_i shows that under these conditions, the noise term is expressed as the sum of $(n-1)(p-1)$ random variables with zero mean and unit variance. Taking into account the distribution (3.25), these variables are moreover independent. By the central limit theorem [Cramér 57], z_i is asymptotically distributed accord-ing to a normal law with zero mean and variance $\sigma_{z_i}^2 = (n-1)(p-1)$ when $n \to \infty$. The probability that $x_i' = \xi_i^{(1)}$ is thus given by

$$1 - \Pr(S_i < 0) = 1 - \Pr(z_i < -(1 - 2\rho)n),$$

$$= 1 - Q\left(\frac{(1 - 2\rho)n}{\sqrt{(n-1)(p-1)}}\right)$$ (3.45)

where

$$Q(u) = \frac{1}{\sqrt{2\pi}} \int_u^\infty e^{-y^2/2} \, dy.$$
(3.46)

If we assume that, after one iteration, the errors on the components of the new state vector x' are independent random variables, then the probability that the initial vector converges directly to the prototype $\xi^{(1)}$ is given by

$$R = \left[1 - Q\left(\frac{(1-2\rho)n}{\sqrt{(n-1)(p-1)}} \right) \right]^n.$$
(3.47)

We should like R to converge to unity with increasing n, which it will do if

$$\lim_{n\to\infty} nQ\left(\frac{(1-2\rho)n}{\sqrt{(n-1)(p-1)}} \right) = 0.$$
(3.48)

If, for the time being, we ignore the fact that the number p of prototypes can also tend to infinity together with n, then we can use the asymptotic approximation [Feller 66],

$$Q(u) \simeq \frac{1}{\sqrt{2\pi}u} e^{-u^2/2} \quad \text{when} \quad u \to \infty.$$
(3.49)

and this shows then that (3.48) is satisfied if, for n large enough,

$$p < \frac{(1-2\rho)^2 n}{2\log n}.$$
(3.50)

This inequality is an upper bound on the capacity if, with probability approaching unity, we want direct attraction without residual error of a *random* vector located at distance ρn from an *arbitrary* prototype. Next, if we want to retrieve exactly *each* of the p prototypes by direct attraction, we should, under the assumption that the errors are independent random variables, replace the exponent n by np in expression (3.47). This leads to the requirement

$$\lim_{n\to\infty} npQ\left(\frac{(1-2\rho)n}{\sqrt{(n-1)(p-1)}} \right) = 0$$
(3.51)

whence the upper bound

$$p < \frac{(1-2\rho)^2 n}{4\log n}.$$
(3.52)

The heuristic derivation above is essentially the one followed in references [Hopfield 82], [Weisbuch and Fogelman-Soulie 85], [Weisbuch and d'Humières 86], [Amari and Maginu 88], [Peretto and Niez 86]. The last of these references considers higher order networks, similar to those examined in Chapter 5.

Remark • According to the formulation (1.25) of Hebb's law, the synaptic matrix W is in fact the autocorrelation matrix of the prototype vectors. Since the synaptic weights are unchanged under a sign reversal of the prototypes, one can consider that Hebb's law is a mapping of the set of n-vectors

$$\mathcal{V} = \{\xi^{(1)}, \xi^{(2)}, \ldots, \xi^{(p)}, -\xi^{(1)}, -\xi^{(2)}, \ldots, -\xi^{(p)}\} \tag{3.53}$$

into the set of symmetric matrices of order n. The question examined by Sussmann [Sussmann 89] is whether this mapping is one-to-one or, in other words, under which conditions the synaptic weight matrix $W(\mathcal{V})$ uniquely determines the prototypes to within the value of the sign. Sussmann shows that, for prototype vectors satisfying the distribution (3.25), the implication

$$W(\mathcal{V}) = W(\mathcal{V}') \Rightarrow \mathcal{V} = \mathcal{V}' \tag{3.54}$$

is essentially correct, when

$$p < \frac{n}{0.7 \log n}. \tag{3.55}$$

One observes immediately that this bound is much looser than (3.52) with $\rho = 0$. This is not surprising since (3.52) guarantees not only that the prototype vectors are uniquely determined by the network parameters but, in addition, that they can effectively be retrieved in a single iteration of some specific dynamic process described by equation (1.2), where the threshold value θ_i has been put equal to zero.

Before going over to a more rigorous analysis, it is interesting to examine some particular situations which show that Hebb's rule should not be applied blindly, but that it needs to be adapted to the specific application in mind, especially when the prototypes have a biased distribution or when the binary vectors are taken in the space $\{0,1\}^n$ instead of $\{-1,1\}^n$.

Let us first consider the case of biased prototypes, i.e. when the components $\xi_i^{(k)}$ are still i.i.d. random variables but where the probabilities of taking on the values $+1$ and -1 are different, namely

$$\left. \begin{array}{l} \Pr(\xi_i^{(k)} = 1) = \tfrac{1}{2}(1 + a) \\ \Pr(\xi_i^{(k)} = -1) = \tfrac{1}{2}(1 - a) \end{array} \right\} \quad \begin{array}{l} i = 1, 2, \ldots, n, \\ k = 1, 2, \ldots, p \end{array} \tag{3.56}$$

for some a in $(-1,1)$. In particular, the mean of a prototype component is given by

$$\mathcal{E}(\xi_i^{(k)}) = a. \tag{3.57}$$

We shall see that the capacity is dramatically reduced if, under these conditions, we keep the usual Hebbian rule (3.26). Indeed, a rough estimate developed later will show that the upper bound for the capacity is then given by an expression of the form

$$p < 1 + \frac{1}{|a^3|}. \tag{3.58}$$

The fact that this bound is now independent of the dimension of the network shows the very powerful reduction in capacity. To simplify the computations, we shall assume that the initialization vector coincides exactly with the prototype $\xi^{(1)}$. The analysis is thus restricted to finding the conditions under which the prototypes can be imposed as fixed points without consideration of the basin of attraction. With $\rho = 0$ and $x_j = \xi_j^{(1)}$, expression (3.42) of S_i now becomes

$$S_i = (n-1)(1 + \zeta_i), \tag{3.59}$$

with

$$\zeta_i = \xi_i^{(1)} \sum_{k=2}^{p} Z_k \tag{3.60}$$

where

$$Z_k = \frac{1}{n-1} \sum_{j \neq i}^{n} \xi_i^{(k)} \xi_j^{(k)} \xi_j^{(1)}. \tag{3.61}$$

Each term on the right hand side of (3.61) has mean value a^3 and, for fixed $\xi_i^{(1)}$, the mean value of ζ_i is thus given by

$$\mathcal{E}(\zeta_i) = \xi_i^{(1)}(p-1)a^3. \tag{3.62}$$

Since S_i should be positive in order for $\xi^{(1)}$ to be a fixed point, the critical situation to be examined is that for which $\xi_i^{(1)} a^3 < 0$ and in this case one should have $(p-1)|a^3| < 1$, which leads to the upper bound (3.58). A simple way to remedy this capacity reduction is to adapt Hebb's law and to replace (3.26) by

$$w_{ij} = \frac{1}{p} \sum_{k=1}^{p} \left(\xi_i^{(k)} - a \right) \left(\xi_j^{(k)} - a \right). \tag{3.63}$$

With $x_j = \xi_j^{(1)}$, expression (3.42) for S_i now becomes

$$S_i = \xi_i^{(1)} \sum_{j \neq i}^{n} \sum_{k=1}^{p} \left(\xi_i^{(k)} - a \right) \left(\xi_j^{(k)} - a \right) \xi_j^{(1)}. \tag{3.64}$$

If we separate the term $k = 1$, then S_i is split into a main term whose mean is equal to or larger than $(n-1)(1-|a|)(1-a^2)$ and a noise term given by

$$z_i = \xi_i^{(1)} \sum_{j \neq i}^{n} \sum_{k=2}^{p} \left(\xi_i^{(k)} - a\right) \left(\xi_j^{(k)} - a\right) \xi_j^{(1)} \qquad (3.65)$$

which is a sum of $(n-1)(p-1)$ random variables with zero mean and variance $(1-a^2)^2$. The probability that $x_i' = \xi_i^{(1)}$ is then given by

$$1 - \Pr(S_i < 0) = 1 - \Pr(z_i < -(n-1)(1-|a|)(1-a^2)). \qquad (3.66)$$

In view of the fact that the distribution (3.56) is biased, it is no longer true that the terms in the right hand side of (3.65) are independent random variables and consequently the central limit theorem does not apply. If, as a first approximation, we nevertheless replace z_i by a Gaussian variable having the same mean and variance, then we derive from (3.66) the upper bound

$$p < \frac{(1-|a|)^2 \, n}{2 \log n}, \qquad (3.67)$$

by means of a similar argument as the one applied above to expression (3.45). This bound is in good agreement with that of reference [Amit et al. 87a] and one observes that the effect of the bias is still to reduce the capacity, but not as strongly as indicated by (3.58) in the case of the usual Hebbian law.

Let us now come back to the case of unbiased prototypes but where the state vectors u and the prototypes $\eta^{(k)}(k = 1, 2, \ldots, p)$ are temporarily taken in the space $\{0, 1\}^n$ and where, accordingly, the sign function has been replaced by the unit step function. Thus, instead of (1.2), the basic dynamic equation to be considered here is

$$u_i(t+1) = H \left(\sum_{j \neq i}^{n} w_{ij} \, u_j(t) \right), \qquad (3.68)$$

where

$$\begin{aligned} H(y) &= 0 \quad \text{if} \quad y < 0, \\ &= 1 \quad \text{if} \quad y > 0. \end{aligned}$$

If, however, we keep the usual Hebbian rule, the synaptic weights are given by

$$w_{ij} = \frac{1}{p} \sum_{k=1}^{p} \xi_i^{(k)} \xi_j^{(k)}, \qquad (3.69)$$

with

$$\xi_i^{(k)} = (2\eta_i^{(k)} - 1), \qquad \in \{-1, 1\}. \tag{3.70}$$

In other words, the dynamic equations of this network are applied on vectors in the space $\{0, 1\}^n$, whereas the synaptic matrix is computed on the corresponding vectors in the space $\{-1, 1\}^n$ [Weisbuch and d'Humières 86], [Weisbuch and Fogelman-Soulie 85]. We shall now briefly examine the consequences of this hybrid approach on the capacity and, for convenience, we shall again assume that the network is initialized with a prototype vector $u = \eta^{(1)}$. In view of (3.69) and (3.70), the synaptic potential can be written as

$$
\begin{aligned}
p\,h_i(u) &= \sum_{j \neq i}^{n} w_{ij}\, u_j, \\
&= \frac{1}{2} \sum_{j \neq i}^{n} \sum_{k=1}^{p} \xi_i^{(k)}\, \xi_j^{(k)} \left(\xi_j^{(1)} + 1 \right)
\end{aligned} \tag{3.71}
$$

and, if we separate the term $k = 1$, we obtain

$$
\begin{aligned}
2p\,h_i(u) &= \xi_i^{(1)} \sum_{j \neq i}^{n} \xi_j^{(1)} \left(\xi_j^{(1)} + 1 \right) \\
&\quad + \sum_{j \neq i}^{n} \sum_{k=2}^{p} \xi_i^{(k)}\, \xi_j^{(k)} \left(\xi_j^{(1)} + 1 \right).
\end{aligned}
$$

If the prototype vectors are unbiased, $\sum_j \xi_j^{(1)} \simeq 0$, and this last expression becomes then

$$2p\,h_i(u) = (n-1)\xi_i^{(1)} + z_i$$

where the noise term is a sum over $(n-1)(p-1)$ independent random variables with zero mean and variance equal to 2 since

$$\mathcal{E}\left[\xi_i^{(k)}\, \xi_j^{(k)} (\xi_j^{(1)} + 1) \right]^2 = \mathcal{E}\left[(\xi_j^{(1)} + 1)^2 \right] = 2.$$

Thus, when n goes to infinity, one can assume that the distribution of z_i tends to a normal distribution with zero mean and variance $\sigma_{z_i}^2 = 2(n-1)(p-1)$. The probability that $h_i(u)$ has the same sign as $\xi_i^{(1)}$ is thus given by

$$1 - \Pr\left(z_i < -(n-1) \right) = 1 - Q\left(\frac{n-1}{\sqrt{2(n-1)(p-1)}} \right)$$

where the function Q is defined in (3.46). If one compares this result with (3.45), one can see that the number of prototypes appears here with a factor 2 and this implies that the bounds (3.50) and (3.52) are to be divided by 2. One can thus conclude that adopting dynamic equations in $\{0, 1\}^n$, on the one hand, and a Hebbian rule defined on vectors in $\{-1, 1\}^n$, on the other hand, finally amounts to a capacity reduction by a factor of 2. In Subsection 1.1.1, we have established the equivalence conditions between networks defined in $\{0, 1\}^n$ and in $\{-1, 1\}^n$. The conclusion here is that the capacity reduction by a factor 2 can be compensated for by an appropriate choice of the threshold vector [Weisbuch and Fogelman-Soulie 85], which amounts to modifying the dynamic equation (3.68) to

$$u_i(t+1) = H \left[\sum_{j \neq i}^{n} w_{ij} \, u_j(t) - \theta'_i \right] , \qquad (3.72)$$

with

$$\theta'_i = \frac{1}{2} \sum_{j \neq i}^{n} w_{ij}. \qquad (3.73)$$

3.3.2   Direct attraction : rigorous approach

We shall now pursue the exact analysis of the conditions required for direct attraction. The application of the central limit theorem in the preceding subsection was not justifiable for several reasons. First, because the noise term z_i was compared with the quantity $(1 - 2\rho)n$ which itself tends to infinity with n and because we ignored the fact that the number of prototypes p also tends to infinity together with n. Next, when one considers several errors, occurring possibly in different prototypes, these errors are in fact not independent (see reference [Kuh and Dickinson 89]), in contradiction with the assumption leading to (3.47) and (3.51). The following three lemmas provide the necessary theoretical framework to meet these difficulties. The first of these lemmas is an adaptation of a "large-deviation" theorem [Feller 66], the second one applies this result to the evaluation of $P = \Pr(S_i < 0)$ via formula (3.49) and the third one shows that the number of erroneous components in the state vector x' is asymptotically Poisson. Theorem 3.9 then concludes the discussion by giving a rigorous proof for the bounds (3.50) and (3.52) on the capacity. The content of this subsection is essentially borrowed from reference [McEliece et al. 87] where one can find the proofs omitted here.

Lemma 3.6 *If ζ is the sum of N independent random variables taking the values $+1$ and -1 with probability $1/2$ and if v tends to infinity such that $v = o(N^{3/4})$, then for $N \to \infty$, one has*

$$\lim_{N \to \infty} \Pr(\zeta \leq -v) = Q\left(\frac{v}{\sqrt{N}}\right) \qquad (3.74)$$

where the function Q is defined in (3.46).

Remark • The notation $v = o(N^{3/4})$ means that $\lim_{N\to\infty} v/N^{3/4} = 0$. Since the limit (3.74) is precisely the result one would obtain by a naïve application of the central limit theorem, the practical meaning of Lemma 3.6 is that this application is essentially correct provided v tends to infinity more slowly than $N^{3/4}$.

Lemma 3.7 *If $0 \leq \rho < \frac{1}{2}$ and if, for $n \to \infty$, p goes to infinity as n^γ with $3/4 < \gamma < 1$ then the probability that, after one synchronous iteration, the component x_i' of the state vector is in error, is given by*

$$P = \Pr(S_i < 0) = \frac{1}{(1-2\rho)\sqrt{2\pi}} \sqrt{\frac{p}{n}} \exp\left(-\frac{n(1-2\rho)^2}{2p}\right) \tag{3.75}$$

when $n \to \infty$.

Proof Taking into account (3.43) and (3.44), we apply the preceding lemma to the variable $\zeta = z_i$ with $N = (n-1)(p-1)$ and $v = (1-2\rho)n$. The constraint $\gamma > 3/4$ concerning the growth of p is critical only for the next lemma but it is sufficient here to satisfy the hypotheses of Lemma 3.6. Consequently, for $n \to \infty$,

$$P = \Pr(S_i < 0) = Q\left(\frac{(1-2\rho)n}{\sqrt{(n-1)(p-1)}}\right). \tag{3.76}$$

The assumption $\gamma < 1$ implies that the ratio n/p tends to infinity with n and so justifies the asymptotic approximation (3.49), which immediately leads to (3.75).   □

Remark • If there are less than ρn errors in the initialization vector, then the main term $(1 - 2\rho)n$ in expression (3.43) of S_i increases and the probability $\Pr(S_i < 0)$ decreases. Expression (3.75) is thus an upper bound for the probability that x_i' is wrong for any initialization vector at Hamming distance equal to or smaller than ρn from prototype $\xi^{(1)}$. One should remember that, as far as direct attraction is concerned, there is no difference between synchronous and asynchronous updating modes (see Theorem 1.1).

Lemma 3.8 *For $n \to \infty$, the probability $P_{[k]}$, that after one synchronous iteration there are exactly k components in error in the state vector x', is given by the Poisson distribution*

$$\lim_{n\to\infty} P_{[k]} \simeq \frac{(nP)^k}{k!} e^{-nP} \tag{3.77}$$

where P is defined by (3.75).

Proof Let $i_1 < i_2 < \cdots < i_k$ be an ordered set of k indices taken in $1, 2, \ldots, n$. One can show that the errors on the different components are asymptotically independent [McEliece et al. 87]. Hence, the probability that the components $x'_{i_1}, x'_{i_2}, \ldots, x'_{i_k}$ are simultaneously in error is given by

$$\Pr(S_{i_1} < 0, S_{i_2} < 0, \cdots, S_{i_k} < 0) = P^k, \quad \text{for } n \to \infty. \tag{3.78}$$

The proof of this result relies on the limitation $\gamma > 3/4$ for the growth of p. Since there are $\binom{n}{k}$ ways of choosing k indices in the set $\{1, 2, \ldots, n\}$, the sum Z_k of these probabilities can be expressed as

$$
\begin{aligned}
Z_k &= \sum_{i_1 < i_2 < \cdots < i_k} P(S_{i_1} < 0, S_{i_2} < 0, \ldots, S_{i_k} < 0) = \binom{n}{k} P^k, \\
&= \frac{(nP)^k}{k!}, \quad \text{for } n \to \infty.
\end{aligned}
\tag{3.79}
$$

The probability $P_{[k]}$ that there are exactly k residual errors, i.e. k erroneous components in the state vector x', is then given by [Feller 66]

$$
\begin{aligned}
P_{[k]} &= Z_k - \binom{k+1}{k} Z_{k+1} + \binom{k+2}{k} Z_{k+2} - \ldots + (-1)^{n-k} \binom{n}{k} Z_n, \\
&= \frac{(nP)^k}{k!} \left[1 - nP + \frac{(nP)^2}{2!} + \cdots \frac{(-nP)^{n-k}}{(n-k)!} \right],
\end{aligned}
\tag{3.80}
$$

and, for $n \to \infty$, this provides the desired result (3.77). $\square$

Theorem 3.9 *If the number of prototypes satisfies the inequality*

$$p < \frac{(1 - 2\rho)^2 n}{2 \log n}, \tag{3.81}$$

with $0 \leq \rho < 1/2$, then the probability that a prototype has a radius of direct attraction at least equal to ρn tends to unity when $n \to \infty$.

Proof In view of Lemma 3.8, the probability that x' coincides exactly with $\xi^{(1)}$ is given by $P_{[0]} = e^{-nP}$ and it is therefore sufficient to show that inequality (3.81) then implies that nP tends to zero when $n \to \infty$. Indeed, taking into account expression (3.75) for P, one verifies that

$$\log(n\,P) = \frac{1}{2} \log n + \frac{1}{2} \log p - \frac{n(1-2\rho)^2}{2p}, \quad \text{for } n \to \infty,$$

and, in view of (3.81), one has

$$\log nP \simeq -\frac{1}{2} \log \log n, \tag{3.82}$$

which concludes the proof. $\square$

Until now we have concentrated on the conditions of direct attraction by a *single* prototype. Next, we shall consider the complete set of p prototypes and the conditions which ensure that *each* of them enjoys the same attraction property.

Theorem 3.10 *If the number of prototypes satisfies the inequality*

$$p < \frac{(1-2\rho)^2 n}{4 \log n}, \tag{3.83}$$

with $0 \le \rho < 1/2$, then the probability that each prototype has a radius of direct attraction at least equal to ρn tends to unity when $n \to \infty$.

Proof By analogy with the notation used in the proof of Lemma 3.8, we shall denote by $\Pr(S_{i_1}^{(\ell_1)} < 0)$ the probability that a vector at distance ρn at most from prototype $\xi^{(\ell_1)}$ has an erroneous component in position i_1 after one synchronous iteration. The network is initialized with random vectors at distance ρn from the prototypes $\xi^{(\ell_1)}, \xi^{(\ell_2)}, \ldots, \xi^{(\ell_k)}$. It is shown in reference [McEliece et al. 87] that the probability of having an error on component i_1 of prototype $\xi^{(\ell_1)}$, component i_2 of prototype $\xi^{(\ell_2)}, \ldots$, and component i_k of prototype $\xi^{(\ell_k)}$ is given by

$$\Pr \left(S_{i_1}^{(\ell_1)} < 0, S_{i_2}^{(\ell_2)} < 0, \ldots, S_{i_k}^{(\ell_k)} < 0 \right) = P^k, \text{ for } n \to \infty \tag{3.84}$$

where P is defined in (3.75). In practice, this means again that the errors on the different components of the different prototypes behave asymptotically as if they were statistically independent. Since there are $\binom{N}{k}$ different ways of choosing k components among the $N = pn$ components of the p prototypes, the sum of the probabilities (3.84) is given by

$$Z'_k = \binom{N}{k} P^k \sim \frac{(NP)^k}{k!}, \quad \text{for } n \to \infty. \tag{3.85}$$

Consequently, the probability $P'_{[k]}$ that there are exactly k errors distributed over the p prototypes can be computed by a formula similar to (3.80) and this yields

$$P'_{[k]} = \frac{(NP)^k}{k!} e^{-NP}, \quad \text{for } n \to \infty. \tag{3.86}$$

Taking into account that $N = np$, one can show as in the preceding theorem that $\lim_{n \to \infty} P'_{[0]} = 1$ if inequality (3.83) is satisfied. $\square$

Remarks • One could ask if the bounds (3.81) and (3.83) are the best possible or, equivalently, how the associative memory performance degrades when the number of prototypes exceeds these bounds. To answer this question, we shall consider expression (3.83) and assume that the number of prototypes is equal to

$$p = (1 - 2\rho)^2 \frac{n}{4 \log n} (1 + \eta),$$

(3.87)

where η is a small positive number. The probability that p prototypes have a radius of direct attraction ρn is, in view of formula (3.86),

$$P'_{[0]} = e^{-NP}.$$

(3.88)

One can interpret (3.88) as an estimate of the fraction of the p memories which have a radius of direct attraction ρn. Taking into account expression (3.75) and the fact that $N = np$, one has asymptotically

$$\log NP = \log n + \log p + \frac{1}{2} \log p - \frac{1}{2} \log n - \frac{n(1 - 2\rho)^2}{2p}.$$

If we replace p by its value (3.87), one finds

$$\log NP \simeq 2\eta \log n.$$

Consequently, the fraction of the p prototypes which has a radius of direct attraction equal to ρn is given by $P'_{[0]} \simeq \exp(-n^{2\eta})$ and, for $\eta > 0$, this fraction tends to zero when $n \to \infty$. Consequently, as long as the number of prototypes does not exceed the bound (3.83), the probability of direct attraction in a radius ρn is arbitrarily close to unity. However, this probability goes to zero as soon as the number of prototypes grows as $n / \log n$ with a coefficient larger than $(1 - 2\rho)^2/4$. This conclusion holds of course for asymptotically large dimensions of the network.

• Kuh and Dickinson propose a different derivation of the bounds (3.81) and (3.83). It is based on a Gaussian approximation for the distribution of the noise term in expression (3.43) [Kuh and Dickinson 89].

• The problem of the synaptic weights defined by

$$w_{ij} = f \left(\sum_{k=1}^{p} \xi_i^{(k)} \xi_j^{(k)} \right),$$

(3.89)

where f is some nonlinear function, has mainly been addressed in the framework of the thermodynamic extension (Chapter 4). The special case where f is the sign function (*clipped Hebb rule*) is particularly interesting and its analysis is relatively simple. It relies essentially on counting techniques as explained in [Piret 88]. When ρ is zero, the inequalities (3.81) and (3.83) become respectively

$$p < \frac{n}{\pi \log n} \quad \text{and} \quad p < \frac{n}{2\pi \log n}. \tag{3.90}$$

Similar results have also been obtained for the case where the initialization vector of the network is close but not identical to a prototype vector.

• The results of Theorems 3.9 and 3.10 hold asymptotically. In reference [Jacyna and Malaret 89], an analysis for *finite* n is presented which precludes any use of the central limit theorem. For direct attraction, explicit expressions are obtained for the probability distribution of the state vector after one synchronous iteration when the number of prototypes is equal to 2 or 3. However, no precise and general upper bound is obtained for the capacity. For long-term attraction, the analysis is restricted to the case where the state vector is close to the fixed point. Simulations show that, for this situation, the components are almost independent of each other. Consequently, during the successive iterations of the network, the error probability on single component satisfies a recurrence formula which is in fact equivalent to the result (3.35) established by Kinzel [Kinzel 85].

3.3.3 Long-term attraction

The preceding subsection provided only a partial analysis of the capacity and the basins of attraction. Indeed, the analysis was restricted to direct attraction and *all* errors had to be corrected or, equivalently, *exact* convergence to the prototype was required. An additional problem considered in this subsection is that the network should be capable of correcting *all* vectors having a given error rate. In order to clarify what this implies, one should remember that we have until now derived the conditions in order to correct errors of a *random* vector at distance ρn of a prototype. In particular, we have computed the probability $P_{[0]}$ that, after one iteration, the new state vector x' is error-free and we have thus required that $\lim_{n \to \infty} (1 - P_{[0]}) = 0$. We shall now require that the network should correct the errors of *all* vectors located at distance ρn of a given prototype. This problem is called "worst case" analysis in reference [Komlós and Paturi 88]. Since the number of vectors at this distance is equal to $\binom{n}{\rho n}$, one can get some idea of the difficulty of this new requirement by considering that it amounts to imposing

$$\lim_{n \to \infty} \binom{n}{\rho n} \left(1 - P_{[0]}\right) = 0, \tag{3.91}$$

in spite of the fact that the events are not independent. It is known that, when n goes to infinity, $\binom{n}{\rho n}$ tends to $e^{n h(\rho)}$ [Feller 66] where $h(\rho) \in [0,1]$ is the entropy function

$$h(\rho) = -\rho \log \rho - (1 - \rho) \log (1 - \rho), \tag{3.92}$$

and condition (3.91) can thus be rewritten as

$$\lim_{n \to \infty} e^{n\,h(\rho)}(1 - P_{[0]}) = 0 \,.   \qquad (3.93)$$

It is easily seen that, for instance, (3.81) is not sufficient to satisfy this last
equation since (3.82) would then imply that

$$1 - P_{[0]} \simeq 1 - e^{-1/\sqrt{\log n}} \,.   \qquad (3.94)$$

It is quite understandable therefore that for worst case analysis the target
of direct attraction should be abandoned and that one should be satisfied
with *long-term attraction* which, in turn, requires that *synchronous* and *asynchronous* updating should be distinguished. Moreover, we shall also examine
the case where the number of prototypes grows linearly with the dimension,
according to $p = \alpha n$ instead of $n/\log n$ as was the case in the preceding two
subsections. It was mentioned at the beginning of this section that in this case
exact convergence could not be guaranteed but that some residual error had
to be tolerated.

The results of this subsection are essentially drawn from the recent contributions by Komlós, Paturi and Newman where detailed proofs can be found
[Komlós and Paturi 88], [Newman 88].

For an initialization vector with error rate ρ (absolute number of errors equal
to ρn), we shall first estimate the error rate ρ' after one synchronous iteration.

Lemma 3.11 [Komlós and Paturi 88] *There exists an upper bound α_s such
that for all $\alpha = p/n < \alpha_s$, one can find an interval $[\epsilon(\alpha), \lambda(\alpha)]$ which holds for
all prototypes and has the following properties.*
• *As α tends to 0, the upper limit of the interval $\lambda(\alpha)$ increases to a constant
ρ_0, while the lower limit $\epsilon(\alpha)$ decreases as $e^{-1/4\alpha}$.*
• *If the initial error rate ρ belongs to the interval $[\epsilon(\alpha), \lambda(\alpha)]$, then, in a single
synchronous iteration, it is reduced to*

$$\rho' = \text{Max} \left\{ e^{-1/4\alpha}, \; c_1 \, \rho h(\rho)(\alpha + h(\rho)) \right\} \,,   \qquad (3.95)$$

*with probability tending to unity, where $h(\rho)$ is the entropy function defined in
(3.92) and where c_1 is a constant.*

Remarks • The interpretation of this lemma is the following. Starting from
a vector located in an annulus centered on a prototype ξ and limited by the
radii $n\epsilon(\alpha)$ and $n\lambda(\alpha)$, the initial error rate is reduced in a single synchronous
iteration to a value $\rho' \simeq \rho^3$ if $\rho > \alpha$ or $\rho' \simeq \alpha \rho^2$ if $\rho < \alpha$. By repeated synchronous iterations, the error rate will undergo a double exponential reduction
until it reaches the value $e^{-1/4\alpha}$ and no further reduction occurs beyond this
point. This evolution is depicted in Figure 3.12.

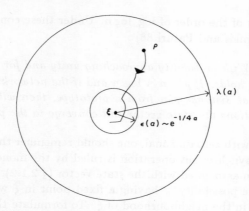

Figure 3.12 : Error rate reduction for synchronous operation.

• After τ synchronous iterations, the error rate is of the order of $\rho^{2^\tau}\ldots\rho^{3^\tau}$ and hence the number of iterations required to reach $\epsilon(\alpha)$ cannot exceed $\tau \sim O(\log \alpha^{-1})$.

• As a consequence of the systematic reduction of the error rate, there are no fixed points as long as $\epsilon(\alpha) < \rho < \lambda(\alpha)$, and this observation produces the following corollary [Komlós and Paturi 88].

Corollary 3.12 *With probability approaching unity and for all $\alpha < \alpha_s$ there are no fixed points in the annuli defined by the radii $n\epsilon(\alpha), n\lambda(\alpha)$ around the prototypes. This property holds true for synchronous as well as for asynchronous operation, since there is no difference between these updating modes as concerns fixed points.*

Repeated application of Lemma 3.11 gives the next two theorems [Komlós and Paturi 88].

Theorem 3.13 *With probability approaching unity and for all prototypes, the following property holds. If $\alpha = p/n < \alpha_s$, and if the network is initialized with a vector at distance $\rho n < n\lambda(\alpha)$ from a prototype, then in $O(\log \alpha^{-1})$ synchronous iterations the state vector will be at most at distance $n\epsilon(\alpha)$ from the prototype and, after that, it will not deviate farther away from the prototype.*

If α tends to 0 faster than $1/4 \log n$ when n tends to infinity, then

$$\lim_{n\to\infty} n\,\epsilon(\alpha) = \lim_{n\to\infty} n\,e^{-1/4\alpha} < \lim_{n\to\infty} n\,e^{-\log n} = 1, \tag{3.96}$$

which means that the state vector converges exactly to the prototype since the absolute number of errors is reduced to zero. On the other hand, the transient length is of the order of $\log \log n$. Under these conditions, Theorem 3.13 becomes [Komlós and Paturi 88] :

Theorem 3.14 *With probability approaching unity and for all prototypes the following property holds. If $p < n/4 \log n$ and if the network is initialized with a vector at most at distance $\rho_0 n$ from a prototype, then within $O(\log \log n)$ synchronous iterations the state vector will converge to the prototype.*

For Hebb's law with zero diagonal, one should remember that convergence to a fixed point in asynchronous operation is ruled by the monotonic decrease of an energy function associated with the state vector (§ 2.1.2). It seems natural, therefore, that the possibility of having a fixed point in ξ will depend on the energy landscape in the neighbourhood of ξ. To formulate this idea in a more precise setting, the concept of *energy barrier* is introduced. Let $S(\xi, \rho)$ denote the set of state vectors at Hamming distance ρn from ξ. In the sequel, S is called the sphere of radius ρn around ξ. To simplify the notation, we shall write ρn, even if, strictly speaking, the notation $\lfloor \rho n \rfloor$ should be used when ρn is not an integer. *The sphere $S(\xi, \rho)$ is an energy barrier for ξ if $E(y) > E(\xi)$ for all $y \in S(\xi, \rho)$.* The practical implication is the following. If such an energy barrier exists around ξ, then there exists a fixed point inside this sphere, even if ξ itself is maybe not a fixed point. Indeed, starting from ξ, successive asynchronous iterations cannot bring the state vector on the sphere S since all points there have higher energy. The theorem below [Newman 88] gives the conditions for which each prototype will be surrounded by an energy barrier and for which thus a fixed point is guaranteed to exist in the vicinity of each prototype.

Theorem 3.15 *There exists a strictly positive α_c such that, if $\alpha = p/n < \alpha_c$, then with probability approaching unity there exists around each prototype $\xi^{(k)}$ $(k = 1, 2, \ldots, p)$ a sphere $S(\xi^{(k)}, \rho)$ with $0 \leq \rho < 1/2$ such that*

$$p\, E(y) > p\, E(\xi^{(k)}) + \epsilon\, n^2, \quad \forall y \in S(\xi^{(k)}, \rho), \quad k = 1, 2, \ldots, p, \qquad (3.97)$$

for some $\epsilon > 0$. Both ρ and ϵ depend on α and the probability of event (3.97) tends to unity exponentially fast when $n \to \infty$.

Proof The energy function $E(x)$ has been defined in (2.7) but, for convenience, we shall use here the function $H(x)$ given by

$$H(x) = 2\, p\, E(x) = -\sum_{k=1}^{p} (x^T\, \xi^{(k)})^2 \qquad (3.98)$$

and which is proportional to $E(x)$ in the case of zero threshold vector. Let us denote by A the following event : for given values of ρ and ϵ, with $0 \leq \rho < 1/2$ and $\epsilon > 0$, the following inequality holds

$$H(y) > H(\xi^{(k)}) + \epsilon n^2 \tag{3.99}$$

for each prototype $\xi^{(k)}$ and all $y \in S(\xi^{(k)}, \rho)$. We wish to show that there exists an α_c such that, if $\alpha < \alpha_c$, one can find $0 \le \rho < 1/2$ and $\epsilon > 0$ for which $\Pr(A) \to 1$ when $n \to \infty$. Let $y^{(k)}(J)$ be a state vector which deviates from $\xi^{(k)}$ on exactly the set J of indices $i_1, i_2, \ldots, i_{\rho n}$. One has

$$
\begin{aligned}
1 - \Pr(A) &= \Pr\left(\cup_J \cup_k \left\{ H(\xi^{(k)}) - H(y^{(k)}(J)) > -\epsilon n^2 \right\}\right) \\
&\le \sum_{k=1}^{p} \sum_J \Pr\left(H(\xi^{(k)}) - H(y^{(k)}(J)) > -\epsilon n^2\right). \tag{3.100}
\end{aligned}
$$

Since $\Pr\left(H(\xi^{(k)}) - H(y^{(k)}(J)) > -\epsilon n^2\right)$ does not depend, either on the prototype index k, or on the set J, and since there are $\binom{n}{\rho n}$ vectors at distance ρn from a given vector, one concludes that

$$1 - \Pr(A) \le p \binom{n}{\rho n} \Pr\left(H(\xi^{(1)}) - H(y) > -\epsilon n^2\right) \tag{3.101}$$

where y is now a vector which differs from $\xi^{(1)}$ exactly on the components $1, 2, \ldots, \rho n$. Let us observe in passing that, in view of the factor $\binom{n}{\rho n}$ on the right hand side of (3.101), the analysis is indeed performed in the framework of a worst case situation. If one defines the quantities

$$
\left.
\begin{aligned}
\tilde{V}_n^{(k)} &= -\sum_{i=1}^{\rho n} \xi_i^{(k)} \xi_i^{(1)} \\
V_n^{(k)} &= \sum_{i=\rho n+1}^{n} \xi_i^{(k)} \xi_i^{(1)}
\end{aligned}
\right\} \quad k = 2, 3, \ldots, p, \tag{3.102}
$$

then, taking (3.98) into account, we see that the energies $H(\xi^{(1)})$ and $H(y)$ can be rewritten as

$$H(\xi^{(1)}) = -n^2 - \sum_{k=2}^{p} \left(V_n^{(k)} - \tilde{V}_n^{(k)}\right)^2, \tag{3.103}$$

$$H(y) = -n^2(1 - 2\rho)^2 - \sum_{k=2}^{p} \left(V_n^{(k)} + \tilde{V}_n^{(k)}\right)^2. \tag{3.104}$$

Using these expressions in inequality (3.101), one obtains

$$
\begin{aligned}
1 - \Pr(A) \le p \binom{n}{\rho n} \Pr\Big(\frac{1}{p} \sum_{k=2}^{p} W_n^{(k)} \ge \\
\left[1 - (1 - 2\rho)^2 - \epsilon\right] \frac{n}{p}\Big), \tag{3.105}
\end{aligned}
$$

with

$$W_n^{(k)} = \frac{4\, V_n^{(k)}\, \tilde{V}_n^{(k)}}{n}. \tag{3.106}$$

The right hand side of (3.105) decreases exponentially fast in n and becomes thus arbitrarily small when $n \to \infty$ provided one can show that asymptotically

$$\Pr\left(\frac{1}{p}\sum_{k=2}^{p} W_n^{(k)} \geq \gamma\right) \leq e^{-Kp} \tag{3.107}$$

for some $K = K(\gamma, \rho)$ with $\gamma = \left[\frac{1-(1-2\rho)^2}{\alpha} - \epsilon'\right]$. Indeed, for large values of n, one has

$$\binom{n}{\rho n} \simeq e^{n\,h(\rho)} \tag{3.108}$$

where $h(\rho)$ is the entropy function (3.92). Inequality (3.107) gives then for the right hand side of (3.105) the following bound

$$p\binom{n}{\rho n}\Pr\left(\frac{1}{p}\sum_{k=2}^{p} W_n^{(k)} \geq \gamma\right) \leq p\, e^{n\,h(\rho)-Kp}. \tag{3.109}$$

One obtains thus the desired result if

$$\alpha K > h(\rho). \tag{3.110}$$

It is shown in [Newman 88] that the latter inequality can be satisfied with $0 \leq \rho < 1/2$ if one takes as definition of $K(\gamma, \rho)$ the expression

$$K(\gamma, \rho) = \Gamma\left(\frac{\gamma}{4\sqrt{\rho(1-\rho)}}\right) \tag{3.111}$$

where the function Γ is defined by

$$\Gamma(u) = \frac{1}{2}\left\{(1 + 4u^2)^{1/2} - 1 + \log\frac{(1+4u^2)^{1/2}-1}{2\,u^2}\right\}. \tag{3.112}$$

One can verify that the right hand side of (3.111) increases when α decreases, which means that the inequality (3.110) is satisfied only if α is sufficiently small. More precisely, for $\alpha < 0.056$, there exists a value $\rho(\alpha)$ such that (3.110) is satisfied, which, in turn, guarantees the existence of an energy barrier according to (3.97). To give an idea of the orders of magnitude, one has $\rho(0.056) = 0.0012$. $\square$

Remarks • The lower bound $\alpha_c = 0.056$ is a pessimistic estimation of the true value which lies, more probably, around 0.14 or 0.15, as suggested by simulations, as well as by the derivations of Subsection 3.2.2 and Section 4.4.

• It can also be shown that the radius $n\rho(\alpha)$ of the energy barrier decreases as $n\,e^{-1/2\alpha}$ when α tends to 0. For a given value of α, one can thus obtain an estimate for the radius of the energy barrier or, equivalently, for the residual error rate after convergence. Conversely, for a prescribed radius $n\rho$ of the energy barrier, one can compute the largest admissible value for α by means of the formula $\alpha(\rho) = 1/(2 \log \rho^{-1})$.

If we wish to use the energy barrier concept, not only to locate fixed points as explained above, but moreover to describe the asynchronous attraction process, we need the following definition : *radius $b_2 n$ is an energy barrier for $b_1 n$ if*, for all prototypes $\xi^{(k)}$, $k = 1, 2, \ldots, p$, the maximum of the energy inside and on the sphere of radius $b_1 n$ around $\xi^{(k)}$ is smaller than the minimum of the energy on the sphere of radius $b_2 n$ (Figure 3.13) :

$$\text{Max}\{E(y) : d(y, \xi) \le b_1 n\} < \text{Min}\{E(y) : d(y, \xi) = b_2 n\}. \tag{3.113}$$

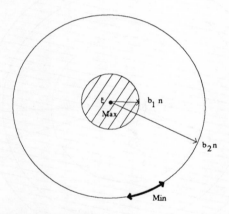

Figure 3.13 : Illustration of the extended concept of energy barrier.

In concrete terms, this definition means that, if a state vector enters the sphere of radius $b_1 n$ in the course of an asynchronous updating process, it will never escape from the sphere of radius $b_2 n$ during the subsequent iterations.

Let us assume that we choose $\alpha_a < \alpha_s$ and such that $n\lambda(\alpha_a)$ is an energy barrier for $n\epsilon(\alpha_a)$. If we select $\alpha < \alpha_a$, we have, in view of Lemma 3.11, that $\lambda(\alpha) > \lambda(\alpha_a)$ and $\epsilon(\alpha) < \epsilon(\alpha_a)$. Since $n\lambda(\alpha_a)$ is, by assumption, an energy barrier for $n\epsilon(\alpha_a)$, we know that no state vector entering the sphere of radius $n\epsilon(\alpha_a)$ can later on escape from the sphere of radius $n\lambda(\alpha_a)$. In addition, taking into account the inequality $\alpha < \alpha_a < \alpha_s$ and Corollary 3.12, we also know that there are no fixed points in the annulus between the spheres of radii

$n\epsilon(\alpha)$ and $n\lambda(\alpha)$. Consequently, if the network is initialized with a vector inside the sphere of radius $n\epsilon(\alpha_a)$, then successive asynchronous iterations will necessarily bring it inside the sphere of radius $n\epsilon(\alpha)$. Indeed, on the one hand, the state vector cannot escape from the sphere of radius $n\lambda(\alpha_a)$ and, on the other hand, there are no fixed points between $n\epsilon(\alpha)$ and $n\lambda(\alpha)$. The precise statement of this result [Komlós and Paturi 88] is given below and a pictorial representation is provided in Figure 3.14.

Theorem 3.16 *If one chooses $\alpha_a < \alpha_s$, then, for $p \leq \alpha_a n$ and for all prototype vectors $\xi^{(k)}$, $k = 1, 2, \ldots, p$, the following property holds. If the initialization vector y is selected such that $d(y, \xi^{(k)}) \leq n\epsilon(\alpha_a)$, then asynchronous iterations will force the state vector to converge with probability approaching unity to a fixed point within a distance $n\epsilon(\alpha) < n\epsilon(\alpha_a)$ from prototype $\xi^{(k)}$.*

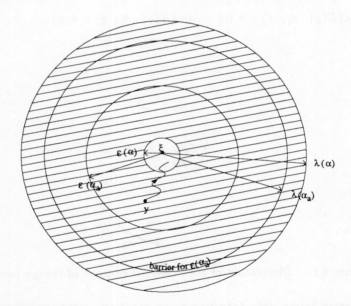

Figure 3.14 : Asynchronous convergence with the energy barrier concept.

If $p < n/4 \log n$, i.e. if α tends to zero faster than $1/4 \log n$ when $n \to \infty$, then, in view of (3.96), the radius $n\epsilon(\alpha)$ tends to zero and, in this case, exact convergence to the prototype is guaranteed. The following property thus holds [Komlós and Paturi 88].

Theorem 3.17 *For $p < n/4 \log n$ and for all prototypes $\xi^{(k)}$, $k = 1, 2, \ldots, p$, if the initialization vector y is such that $d(y, \xi^{(k)}) \leq n\epsilon(\alpha_a)$, then the network will converge exactly to $\xi^{(k)}$ in asynchronous updating mode.*

The main results obtained so far by statistical methods are summarized in Table 3.15.

	Updating Mode	$p \sim \alpha n$ with residual error rate	$p \sim n/\log n$ exact convergence
Direct attraction. Correction of a *random* vector at distance ρn	synchr or asynchr		Th 3.9 & 3.10
Long-term attraction. Correction of *all* vectors at distance ρn	synchr	Th 3.13	Th. 3.14
	asynchr	Th 3.16	Th. 3.17

Table 3.15

3.3.4 Parasitic fixed points

In Chapter 1 we have briefly mentioned the specific problems related to parasitic fixed points, i.e. fixed points which are not prototype vectors. Although the phenomenon is not entirely understood, some information is nevertheless available concerning two aspects of this problem. On the one hand, one can show that a fraction of these parasitic fixed points is formed by linear combinations of prototypes and, on the other hand, one can also get an estimate of the *total* number of fixed points in a recursive network. The conclusion is, however, that there exists a large number of fixed points of unknown origin.

The first type of result lies in the line of the preceding subsection. One considers linear combinations of prototypes of the form

$$\eta = \text{Sgn} \left(\sum_{k=1}^{p} d_k \, \xi^{(k)} \right), \qquad d_k = \pm 1 \,. \tag{3.114}$$

There are in total 2^p such linear combinations and it transpires that, about one half among them, i.e. 2^{p-1}, are indeed fixed points or, at least, that fixed points exist in their close neighbourhood. The concept of *wide sense fixed points* is introduced as follows. A vector x is a fixed point (in the strict sense) if $x = \text{Sgn}(Wx)$; that is, if for each of the n components, $Q_i(x) = x_i h_i(x) > 0$, where $h_i(x)$ is the synaptic potential (1.4) of neuron i. Given the inequalities $0 < \beta < 1$ and $0 \leq \epsilon < 1$, a state vector x is called a *wide sense* (β, ϵ) *fixed point* if $Q_i(x) > \beta n$ for all but at most ϵn indices i. The following result holds [Komlós and Paturi 88].

Theorem 3.18 *For every $\epsilon > 0$, there exists an $\alpha^* = \alpha^*(\epsilon)$ such that, if $p \leq \alpha^* n$, then, with probability approaching unity, more than half of the 2^p*

linear combinations (3.114) of the prototypes are wide sense $(0.5, \epsilon)$ *fixed points and there exists a strict sense fixed point within distance* ϵn *at most.*

These parasitic fixed points enjoy attraction properties in synchronous and asynchronous operation mode, similar to those established above for the prototypes. On the other hand, one can also show that the linear combinations (3.114) can in fact be generalized to *general* real coefficients d_k [Komlós and Paturi 88]. Equivalently, Newman proves that, for α sufficiently small, there exists an energy barrier around each of the linear combinations (3.114) and this result also holds for higher order networks as we shall see in Chapter 5 [Newman 88]. Finally, the analysis of parasitic fixed points obtained by linear combinations of prototypes will be continued in Chapter 4, in the framework of the thermodynamic extension. There, we will show that some of these combinations can be made unstable by adding thermal noise (§ 4.3.2).

As regards the *total* number of fixed points, including those imposed by an appropriate choice of the synaptic matrix as well as the parasitic fixed points, one has the following result [Tanaka and Edwards 80], [McEliece et al. 87].

Theorem 3.19 *If the synaptic matrix is symmetric with zero diagonal and if its elements are independent Gaussian random variables with zero mean and unit variance, then an asymptotic estimate for the number of fixed points is given by*

$$F \simeq (1.0505)\, 2^{0.2874n} . \tag{3.115}$$

Proof Since the distribution of the synaptic weights does not favour any particular state vector, the estimation of the number of fixed points is given by $F = 2^n R$ where R is the probability that an arbitrary vector, e.g. $x = [1, 1, \ldots, 1]^T$, is a fixed point. One has thus

$$R = \Pr(h_1 > 0, h_2 > 0, \ldots, h_n > 0) \tag{3.116}$$

where, in view of the particular choice for x, the synaptic potentials are given by $h_i = \sum_{j \neq i} w_{ij}$ $(i = 1, 2, \ldots, n)$. In view of the central limit theorem [Cramér 57], the distribution of h_i tends, for sufficiently large n, to a Gaussian distribution with zero mean and variance equal to $(n-1)$. On the other hand, h_i and h_j are correlated, because of the symmetry of the synaptic matrix and one has therefore

$$\mathcal{E}(h_i h_j) = \mathcal{E}(w_{ij}^2) = 1. \tag{3.117}$$

To facilitate the evaluation of R, we shall use the method of equivalent Gaussians [Pierce and Posner 80]. Let $Y_0, Y_1, \ldots, Y_n$, be a set of $(n+1)$ independent random variables with identical Gaussian distributions having zero mean and unit variance. On this basis, we construct n new Gaussian variables z_i which have the same statistical properties as the h_i by putting

$$z_i = \alpha Y_i + \beta Y_0, \qquad (i = 1, 2, \ldots, n), \tag{3.118}$$

where $\alpha = (n-2)^{1/2}$ and $\beta = 1$. Indeed, one has $\mathcal{E}(z_i^2) = \alpha^2 + \beta^2 = n - 1$ and $\mathcal{E}(z_i z_j) = \beta^2 = 1$. The advantage of the representation (3.118) is that the variables z_i are conditionally independent for any fixed value of Y_0. Since $z_i > 0$ if $Y_i > -\alpha^{-1}\beta Y_0$, one obtains in this way

$$F = \frac{2^n}{\sqrt{2\pi}} \int_{-\infty}^{+\infty} e^{-t^2/2} \left[Q\left(-\frac{\beta}{\alpha}t\right) \right]^n dt \tag{3.119}$$

where the function Q is defined by formula (3.46). Appealing to the fact that $\alpha^{-1}\beta = (n-2)^{-1/2}$ and performing the change of variable $u = -\alpha^{-1}\beta t$, one obtains

$$F = 2^n \left(\frac{n-2}{2\pi} \right)^{1/2} \int_{-\infty}^{\infty} \{ Q(u) \exp(-u^2/2) \}^n \exp(u^2) \, du. \tag{3.120}$$

When n tends to infinity, this integral can be computed by a saddle point integration as explained in Subsection 4.2.1 (Lemma 4.1) and to this end it is rewritten in more compact form as

$$F = \left(\frac{n-2}{2\pi} \right)^{1/2} \int_{-\infty}^{\infty} \exp\left[n\, h(u) \right] \gamma(u) \, du \tag{3.121}$$

where

$$\exp[h(u)] = 2Q(u) \exp(-u^2/2), \tag{3.122}$$

$$\gamma(u) = \exp u^2.$$

Applying Lemma 4.1, one obtains the asymptotic result

$$F \simeq \frac{\gamma(u_0)}{\sqrt{-h''(u_0)}} \exp\left[n\, h(u_0) \right] \tag{3.123}$$

where u_0 is the maximum of $h(u)$ and so satisfies the equation

$$\exp\left(-u^2/2\right) + (2\pi)^{1/2} u\, Q(u) = 0. \tag{3.124}$$

Numerical solution of (3.124) gives the desired result.   □

Remark • Extension of this result to synaptic weights determined by Hebb's law is not straightforward and the arguments developed above are certainly no longer valid. Indeed, on the one hand, the w_{ij} are now not independent; on the other hand, the purpose of Hebb's law is precisely to impose the prototypes as fixed points and, therefore, the state vectors have not equal probabilities of becoming fixed points. Nevertheless, McEliece and coauthors suggest that, even for Hebb's law, the number of fixed points increases exponentially with n, although probably with a smaller exponent than given in (3.115) [McEliece et al. 87].

Since the existence of parasitic fixed points disturbs the retrieval process, a solution for this problem was sought by modifying the structure of the network and, along this line, networks with *asymmetric* synaptic matrices have been investigated. In order to analyze the effect of asymmetry, the synaptic matrix has been decomposed according to the formula

$$W = U + kV \tag{3.125}$$

where U et V are real matrices of order n with zero diagonal which are respectively symmetric $(U = U^T)$ and skew-symmetric $(V = -V^T)$. The parameter $k \geq 0$ provides a way of controlling the degree of asymmetry. It is assumed that the off-diagonal elements u_{ij} and v_{ij} of these matrices are independent random variables with Gaussian distributions having zero mean and variance equal to $1/(1 + k^2)$. For networks with this structure, Crisanti and Sompolinsky obtain the following estimate of the total number of fixed points [Crisanti and Sompolinsky 88].

Theorem 3.20 *Consider an asymmetric network for which the synaptic matrix W has the structure (3.125) and the elements of W are independent random variables with zero mean and unit variance Gaussian distributions. An asymptotic estimation of the total number of fixed points is given by*

$$F \simeq e^{ng(k)}, \tag{3.126}$$

with

$$g(k) = -\frac{1 - k^2}{(1 + k^2)^2} u_0^2 - \frac{1}{2} \log\left(\frac{\pi u_0^2}{2}\right), \qquad k \leq 1 \tag{3.127}$$

and where u_0 satisfies the equation

$$\frac{1}{2} \log\left(\frac{\pi u_0^2}{2}\right) + \left(\frac{1 - k^2}{1 + k^2} \frac{u_0}{\sqrt{2}}\right)^2$$
$$+ \log\left[2Q\left(\frac{1 - k^2}{1 + k^2} u_0\right)\right] = 0 \tag{3.128}$$

with the function Q defined by (3.46).

Proof The arguments follow very closely those used previously in Theorem 3.19 and we shall therefore only indicate how the different expressions obtained there should be modified. The synaptic potentials are still zero mean Gaussian variables with variance $(n-1)$ but the correlation between them is given by

$$\mathcal{E}(h_i h_j) = \mathcal{E}(w_{ij} w_{ji}) = \mathcal{E}(u_{ij}^2 - k^2 v_{ij}^2) = \frac{1 - k^2}{1 + k^2}. \tag{3.129}$$

The equivalent Gaussian variables are defined as in (3.118) with $\alpha^2 + \beta^2 = n-1$ as before, but where now $\beta^2 = (1 - k^2)/(1 + k^2)$. The estimate of the number of fixed points is given by formula (3.119). Making the change of variable $t = -\sqrt{n}\beta u$ and keeping in mind the fact that $\alpha \simeq n^{1/2}$ when $n \to \infty$, one obtains

$$F = \left(\frac{n(1 - k^2)}{2\pi(1 + k^2)} \right)^{1/2} \int_{-\infty}^{\infty} \left[2\,Q\left(\frac{1 - k^2}{1 + k^2}\,u \right) \right]^n$$

$$\exp\left(-n\,\frac{1 - k^2}{1 + k^2}\,\frac{u^2}{2} \right)\,du. \tag{3.130}$$

This integral can be brought to the form (3.121) by setting $\gamma(u) = 1$ and

$$\exp[h(u)] = 2\,Q\left(\frac{1 - k^2}{1 + k^2}\,u \right) \exp\left(-\frac{1 - k^2}{1 + k^2}\,\frac{u^2}{2} \right). \tag{3.131}$$

Equation (3.128) gives the value u_0 for which $h(u)$ is maximum and by inserting this value in (3.123) one obtains the desired result (3.126). $\qquad \square$

Remarks • Although the proof given here differs from that of Crisanti and Sompolinsky, one can easily verify that the results are identical by observing that

$$2\,Q(-s) = 1 + \text{erf}\left(\frac{s}{\sqrt{2}} \right) \tag{3.132}$$

provided the error function is defined as

$$\text{erf}(x) = \frac{2}{\sqrt{\pi}} \int_0^x e^{-t^2}\,dt. \tag{3.133}$$

• Figure 3.16 shows the function $g(k)$ in the interval $[0,1]$. For $k = 0$, W is symmetric and $g(0) = 0.1992$ which confirms the result of Theorem 3.19. As long as $k < 1$, the function $g(k)$ stays positive and this shows that asymmetry does not destroy the exponential growth of the number of fixed points, but only reduces the exponent. Moreover, this conclusion remains basically unchanged when the elements of the synaptic matrix have nonzero mean distributions [Crisanti and Sompolinsky 88]. For $k > 1$, equations (3.127) and (3.128) are no longer valid but a modified analysis shows that one still arrives at a formula of the general form (3.126) where however $g(k) < 0$, which means that the number of fixed points tends to zero when $n \to \infty$.

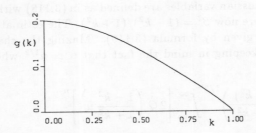

Figure 3.16 : Evolution of the exponent in (3.126) as a function of asymmetry. (Reprinted by permission of The American Physical Society ©1988)

• In practice, one can try to remove the parasitic fixed points by "negative learning". If, during simulations, some parasitic fixed point ξ' is detected, the synaptic weights are modified according to the rule

$$w_{ij} \rightarrow w_{ij} - \epsilon \xi'_i \xi'_j \tag{3.134}$$

where ϵ is a small positive number. The result is that this operation increases the energy associated with ξ' and one observes experimentally that the domains of attraction of the prototypes indeed become larger and are more regularly shaped [Keeler 86], [Kleinfeld and Pendergraft 87].

Chapter 4

Thermodynamic extension

The purpose here is to pursue and to further develop the statistical approach begun in the preceding chapter. Not only will the synaptic weights be considered as random variables via the prototype vectors as was the case before but, in addition, even for a given realization of the prototypes, the equilibrium state of the network will no longer be defined in a deterministic way. More precisely, the equilibrium distribution resulting from the network dynamics is assumed to be a *Gibbs distribution* which, itself, depends on a parameter, called the *temperature*, representing the action of a noise source on the network. The appropriate theoretical framework for this investigation is provided by the theory of statistical mechanics, the basic concepts of which are recalled in Section 4.1. Next, the *mean field equations* are derived which give the mean state vector at equilibrium with respect to the Gibbs distribution and with respect to the distribution of the prototypes. It will become clear that one should distinguish between two cases, according to whether the number p of prototypes is finite (Section 4.2), or grows proportionally to the dimension n of the network (Section 4.4). These mean field equations will be applied mainly to Hebb's law but the projection rule will also be briefly examined.

We shall see that the thermodynamic extension does not give entirely new results compared to those derived by the statistical approach of Chapter 3. In particular, this extension gives no information concerning the basins of attraction since it is essentially restricted to a description of the equilibrium points of the system. Nevertheless, the thermodynamic extension offers some specific advantages. First, it establishes a striking similarity between recursive networks, on the one hand, and spin glasses on the other hand or, more generally, the problems of phase transitions and critical phenomena in physics. Further, it clearly confirms the experimental observation that there exists a critical threshold for the growth of the number of prototypes around $p = 0.14\,n$. Beyond this value, the network loses almost completely its associative memory properties. Finally, the thermodynamic extension emphasizes both the existence of parasitic fixed points formed by linear combinations of prototypes and the fact that some of these can be removed by adding thermal noise to the system.

The results of this chapter are mainly based on the references [Amit et al.

95

85a], [Amit et al. 85b], [Amit et al. 87a], [Amit et al. 87b], [Amit 87], [Kan-
ter and Sompolinsky 87], [van Hemmen 82], [van Hemmen and Kühn 86], [van
Hemmen 87], [Provost and Vallee 83], [Moore 84], [Peretto 84]. For a more
mathematically oriented justification of the approach, the reader is referred
to [Maćkowiak 82] and the references therein. The purpose of this chapter is
rather to interpret and to comment on the different steps of the thermodynamic
extension in order to make it accessible to the uninitiated reader.

4.1   Basic facts of thermodynamics and statistical mechanics

Thermodynamics gives a macroscopic description of physical systems having
a very large number of degrees of freedom. A thermodynamic equilibrium
state is characterized by the values of a small number of *variables* or *thermodynamic functions*. In the typical case of ideal gases, these are the volume
V, the pressure p, the number N of molecules and the intrinsic variable of
thermodynamics, namely the temperature T. These variables are not independent because, at thermodynamic equilibrium, they satisfy the state equation
$pV = NrT$. In this chapter, neural networks will be considered as thermodynamic systems, which implies that the number n of neurons becomes very
large. The thermodynamic variables in this case are the temperature T, the
memory occupation rate $\alpha = p/n$ and the overlaps m_k with the prototype
vectors. These variables are not independent either.

Among the thermodynamic variables, one should distinguish the *extensive*
quantities, which are proportional to the size of the system, and the *intensive* quantities, which are independent of it. The temperature and pressure
are intensive variables, whereas the volume and the number of molecules are
of course extensive quantities. In the case of neural networks, the memory
occupation rate α and the overlaps m_k are intensive variables.

The two principles of thermodynamics rely each on the existence of a state
function, respectively the *internal energy* U and the *entropy* S. Both functions
are extensive quantities.

As a consequence of some external actions, the state of a thermodynamic
system can change. If this modification is slow enough, so that the system
goes through a continuous sequence of equilibrium states, the process is called
reversible, because it can also take place in the opposite direction. If, however, the system changes more rapidly, going through successive nonequilib-
rium states, the process is called *irreversible*.

In the course of a reversible process, the following constraint is always
satisfied :

$$dU = \delta A + TdS \tag{4.1}$$

where δA is the work done by the external forces and where

$$\delta Q = TdS \tag{4.2}$$

is the quantity of heat brought to the system. The symbol δ is used here instead of d to emphasize the fact that it is not the differential of a state function. Indeed, a heat pump, for instance, uses on the average some amount of work although it goes periodically through the same state sequence.

In an isolated system, receiving neither work nor heat, the internal energy stays constant. However, the entropy can increase, but it will never decrease. The entropy increases during the irreversible processes and it reaches a maximum at thermodynamic equilibrium.

If heat is exchanged between a small macroscopic system and a much larger one, then the latter will impose the equilibrium temperature reached by the smaller system. The large system acts as a *heat bath*. The elementary work to be provided to a system in a heat bath during a reversible process is given by the expression

$$\delta A = dU - TdS = d(U - TS).$$

One observes that this elementary work is equal to the differential of the state function

$$F = U - TS, \tag{4.3}$$

which is called the *free energy* of the system. If the reversible process is not isothermal, i.e. if the temperature does not stay constant, one has

$$dF = dU - TdS - SdT = \delta A - SdT. \tag{4.4}$$

The theory of thermodynamics asserts that, in a system without interactions with the external world (except that it is in contact with a heat bath), the free energy must decrease in the course of a reversible process and that it reaches a minimum at thermodynamic equilibrium.

Statistical mechanics establishes a connection between the microscopic laws of mechanics and the macroscopic laws of thermodynamics. One considers dynamical systems with a large number of degrees of freedom. These systems are thus characterized by a state space of high dimensionality. For the neural networks considered here, the space of the macroscopic states x is the domain $\{-1, 1\}^n$ where n is the number of neurons.

We consider the situation where the system is in a heat bath of temperature T. For a neural network, this means that its time evolution does not follow a purely deterministic law but that some noise source interacts with the system.

The precise statistical law which rules the system dynamics will be discussed
later. The stochastic nature of the dynamics means that, at each instant of
time t, we cannot predict exactly the state $x(t)$ of the network but only the
probability $\rho(x,t)$ that the network is in some state x at time t. Starting
at $t = 0$ with some initial probability distribution of the states, the network
converges to an equilibrium distribution

$$\rho(x) = \lim_{t \to \infty} \rho(x,t) . \tag{4.5}$$

According to the theory of statistical mechanics, this limiting distribution is
given by

$$\rho(x) = \frac{e^{-\beta H(x)}}{\sum_y e^{-\beta H(y)}} . \tag{4.6}$$

In this expression, $H(x)$ is the energy of the system in state x and β depends on the temperature of the heat bath via the relation $\beta = 1/kT$ where
k is the Boltzmann constant. Expression (4.6) is called a *Gibbs distribution*
or canonical distribution and the function H is the *Hamiltonian* of the system. Convergence according to equation (4.5) from the initial distribution to
the Gibbs distribution (4.6) will be proved below for some special stochastic
process.

The normalization factor in (4.6),

$$Z = \sum_x e^{-\beta H(x)} , \tag{4.7}$$

is called the *partition function* and the sum extends over the 2^n states of the
domain $\{-1, 1\}^n$. It will also be written as

$$Z = \mathrm{Tr}_x e^{-\beta H(x)} \tag{4.8}$$

where the sum has been replaced by the trace symbol borrowed from statistical
mechanics.

Let us now establish the relationship with the thermodynamical functions U,
S and F. The internal energy should in principle be identical to the function
$H(x)$. But the energy U is a function of the macroscopic state, whereas H
depends on the microscopic state x. Similarly, expression (4.6) leads to a
probability distribution of a random variable H, instead of a single value U.
However, for a system with a large number of degrees of freedom, (in our case,
for large n), this probability density is concentrated around the mean value of
H. Therefore, it is legitimate to identify U with the mean value of H and we
shall thus write

$$U = \mathrm{Tr}_x H(x)\rho(x) . \tag{4.9}$$

Let $m_1, m_2, \ldots, m_p$ be some other functions of the state whose probability densities, generated by $\rho(x)$, are also concentrated around their respective mean values

$$\overline{m}_k = \mathrm{Tr}_x m_k(x)\rho(x), \quad k = 1, 2, \ldots, p. \tag{4.10}$$

The quantities $\overline{m}_k$ are thermodynamic variables. In the case of neural networks, $m_k(x)$ is the overlap between the state x and the prototype $\xi^{(k)}$. How the mean value $\overline{m}_k$ exactly depends on the set of prototype vectors will be clarified below. For the time being, let us simply assume that the Hamiltonian for Hebb's law can be expressed in terms of the overlaps and we shall thus write

$$H(x) = h(m_1(x), m_2(x), \ldots, m_p(x)). \tag{4.11}$$

If we modify prototype $\xi^{(k)}$ in such a way as to change $m_k(x)$ by a small amount $dm_k(x)$, then the energy associated with state x changes by a small amount

$$dH(x) = \frac{\partial h}{\partial m_k}(m_1(x), m_2(x), \ldots, m_p(x))dm_k(x).$$

This relation can be interpreted as if some external force would bring to the system an elementary quantity of work $\delta A(x) = dH(x)$. The mean value of the work resulting from a modification of the prototypes is thus

$$\begin{aligned} \delta A &= \mathrm{Tr}_x \delta A(x)\rho(x), \\ &= \mathrm{Tr}_x \left(\sum_{k=1}^{p} \frac{\partial h}{\partial m_k}(m_1(x), \ldots, m_p(x))dm_k(x) \right) \rho(x). \end{aligned} \tag{4.12}$$

Formula (4.12) leads in fact to the identification of the free energy F with the logarithm of the partition function Z, i.e.

$$-\beta F = \log Z. \tag{4.13}$$

This result is obtained by comparing the increments of both sides in (4.13) during a reversible process. Indeed, one has for the left hand side

$$d(-\beta F) = d(-F/kT) = -\frac{dF}{kT} + \frac{F}{kT^2}dT, \tag{4.14}$$

which yields, in view of (4.3) and (4.4),

$$d(-\beta F) = -\beta\delta A - U d\beta. \tag{4.15}$$

On the other hand, with expression (4.11) for the Hamiltonian, one finds for the right hand side of (4.13)

$$d(\log Z) = -\frac{1}{Z}\mathrm{Tr}_x\left[\left(\beta\sum_{k=1}^{p}\frac{\partial h}{\partial m_k}(m_1(x),\ldots,m_p(x))dm_k(x)\right)\right.$$
$$\left.\times e^{-\beta H(x)} + H(x)e^{-\beta H(x)}d\beta\right],$$
$$= -\mathrm{Tr}_x\left[\beta\rho(x)\sum_{k=1}^{p}\frac{\partial h}{\partial m_k}dm_k + \rho(x)H(x)d\beta\right]. \qquad (4.16)$$

This gives finally, using (4.9) and (4.12)

$$d(\log Z) = -\beta\delta A - U d\beta. \qquad (4.17)$$

Comparison of (4.15) with (4.17), gives the desired result (4.13), within some constant which is irrelevant in this context. To conclude, let us observe that we can legitimately consider that the free energy F depends only on β and on the mean values of the overlaps. Indeed, on the one hand, the first term in the right hand side of (4.16) can be written as the mean value of a quantity with respect to the Gibbs distribution and, on the other hand, the distributions of the overlaps are concentrated around their mean value. Therefore, we shall write from now on, $F(\overline{m}, \beta)$ where $\overline{m} = [\overline{m}_1, \overline{m}_2, \ldots, \overline{m}_p]^T$ is the mean overlap vector.

4.2 Mean field equations for finite p

Let us now see how the general equations of statistical mechanics recalled above can be applied to the analysis of recursive neural networks. In a first step, we shall compute the expression of the free energy per unit $f(\overline{m}, \beta) = F(\overline{m}, \beta)/n$, via the partition function Z and relation (4.13). This will lead to the *mean field equations* which describe the mean behaviour of the network with respect to the distribution (4.6) when the parameters of the network, and more particularly the synaptic weights, are provisionally considered to be fixed. In a second step, we should take the mean of these equations with respect to the parameter distribution, i.e. in practice, with respect to the statistical distribution of the prototypes. In fact, we shall see that there is no need to compute explicitly this second statistical mean, because it is automatically obtained by an appropriate choice of the macrovariables.

Networks operating in asynchronous updating mode are easier to analyze by this scheme because there exists a natural Hamiltonian : the energy function already introduced in Chapter 2. This will be the topic of Subsection 4.2.1. In contrast, application to the synchronous mode is less obvious because no natural Hamiltonian can be suggested, except however for the Little model, as we shall see in Subsection 4.2.2 [Little 74], [Peretto 84].

4.2.1 Mean field theory for asynchronous updating

We have seen in Chapter 2 (§ 2.1.2) that an energy function can be associated with a state vector and that, in asynchronous updating mode, the state of the network changes in such a way that the flipping of a unit x_i (from $+1$ to -1 or conversely) corresponds to an energy reduction. Starting from an initial state, the network evolves through a sequence of single unit modifications while the energy monotonically decreases until an equilibrium point is reached which corresponds to a local minimum of energy. This energy function suggests itself as a natural Hamiltonian for the asynchronous mode. For convenience, we shall assume in this chapter that the threshold vector is zero. We define thus the Hamiltonian by

$$H(x) = -\frac{1}{2} x^T W x \qquad (4.18)$$

where W is the synaptic matrix. As stated earlier, we shall restrict the analysis mainly to the zero diagonal Hebbian rule which, for practical reasons, is redefined here as

$$W = \frac{1}{n}(XX^T - pI), \qquad w_{ij} = \frac{1}{n}\sum_{h=1}^{p} \xi_i^{(k)} \xi_j^{(k)}, \qquad i \neq j \qquad (4.19)$$

where $X = [\xi^{(1)}, \xi^{(2)}, \ldots, \xi^{(p)}]$ is the matrix of the prototype vectors. The purpose of the normalization factor $1/n$ is to ensure that the free energy is an *extensive quantity*, i.e. proportional to the dimension n of the system, so that the free energy *per unit* is finite when n goes to infinity. The probability of observing an equilibrium state x is given by the Gibbs distribution (4.6) with $H(x)$ defined by (4.18). At a given temperature, a state vector x has higher probability of being observed if the energy associated with it is lower. However, the higher the temperature, the more the energy differences are smoothed out and the more the states tend to become equiprobable. Consequently, the flipping of a unit becomes possible, even though it corresponds to an energy increase. Conversely, at lower temperatures, the energy levels have a stronger influence on the probability of observing a given state. The recursive networks with deterministic dynamics according to (1.2) and investigated in the preceding chapters correspond to the limiting case $T = 0$.

For Hebb's law (4.19), the probability of a state becomes, in view of (4.6) and (4.18),

$$\rho(x) = Z^{-1} \exp\left[\frac{\beta}{2n} \sum_{k=1}^{p} \left(\sum_{i=1}^{n} x_i \xi_i^{(k)} \right)^2 - \frac{\beta p}{2} \right] \qquad (4.20)$$

where the term $\beta p/2$ in the argument of the exponential accounts for the zero diagonal in the synaptic matrix. Similarly, the partition function defined in (4.8) is given by

$$Z = \text{Tr}_x \exp \left[\frac{\beta}{2n} \sum_{k=1}^{p} \left(\sum_{i=1}^{n} x_i \xi_i^{(k)} \right)^2 - \frac{\beta p}{2} \right], \tag{4.21}$$

and this shows, in agreement with the assertion of the previous section, that the natural variables of the problem are in fact the overlaps with the prototypes, i.e.

$$m_k = \frac{1}{n} \sum_{i=1}^{n} x_i \xi_i^{(k)}, \quad m_k \in [-1,1], \quad (k = 1, 2, \dots, p). \tag{4.22}$$

This observation suggests that we should perform the change of variable from the state vector x to the overlap vector

$$m = \frac{1}{n} X^T x, \tag{4.23}$$

with

$$m = [m_1, m_2, \dots, m_p]^T. \tag{4.24}$$

Without going into the details, one can understand that, in order to compute the partition function Z in terms of the new variables, the trace operator should be replaced by a multiple integral over the p components of the vector m. This gives

$$Z = \exp \left[-\frac{\beta p}{2} \right] \int_{-\infty}^{+\infty} \exp \left[\frac{\beta n}{2} \| m \|^2 \right] J(m) \prod_{k=1}^{p} dm_k \tag{4.25}$$

where $J(m)$ stands for the equivalent of the Jacobian for the transformation (4.23). In the very simple case where there is only one prototype vector ($p = 1$), the expression of $J(m)$ can easily be computed [van Hemmen and Kühn 86]. For the more complicated situation considered here, it is preferable to avoid the explicit calculation of $J(m)$ and to derive directly the integral representation of Z in terms of m by some computational trick which relies on the *Laplace integration method*, recalled in Lemma 4.1 hereunder. This technique is also called *saddle point integration* or *steepest descent integration*.

Lemma 4.1 *Let $h(y)$ be a real continuous function which has an absolute minimum at y_0 and such that in this point $h''(y_0) > 0$. Assume moreover that $h(y)$ tends to $+\infty$ if $|y| \to \infty$ and that the integral $\int_{-\infty}^{+\infty} exp[-nh(y)]dy$ converges for sufficiently large n. Under these conditions, the following identity holds* [de Bruijn 58] :

$$\lim_{n \to \infty} \left(\frac{n}{2\pi} \right)^{1/2} \int_{-\infty}^{+\infty} e^{-nh(y)} dy = \lim_{n \to \infty} \frac{e^{-nh(y_0)}}{\sqrt{h''(y_0)}}. \tag{4.26}$$

Remarks • We shall use this result in a slightly more general setting where the function h, and thus the minimum y_0, depend on the parameter n. It is assumed in this case that the position and the value of the minimum tend to finite limits when $n \to \infty$.

• In the particular case where $h(y)$ is a second order polynomial in y with positive leading coefficient, the identity (4.26) holds even for finite values of n because it reduces to the property that the area under a Gaussian distribution is equal to unity. The extension of this identity to the multivariable case gives the following equality where C is a positive definite matrix of order p and where u and y are real p-vectors :

$$\exp\left[\frac{1}{2} u^T C^{-1} u \right] = (2\pi)^{-p/2} (\det C)^{1/2} \int_{-\infty}^{+\infty} \prod_{1}^{p} dy_k$$

$$\exp\left[-\frac{1}{2} y^T C y + y^T u \right]. \tag{4.27}$$

The latter equality, which is easily derived from the scalar case by means of the factorization $C = V^T V$, is often called the *Gaussian transformation* (see e.g. [Amit et al. 87a]). Its interest comes from the fact that it transforms the exponential of a quadratic form into an exponential of a linear form, which makes subsequent computation of the trace much easier, as we shall see below [van Hemmen and Kühn 86], [Stanley 71].

Let us now return to the calculation of the partition function. If one denotes by $g(x)$ the p-vector with components

$$g_k(x) = \sum_{i=1}^{n} x_i \xi_i^{(k)}, \quad (k = 1, 2, \ldots, p), \tag{4.28}$$

then expression (4.21) can be rewritten in the form

$$Z = \exp\left(-\frac{\beta p}{2} \right) \mathrm{Tr}_x \, \exp\left[\frac{\beta}{2n} \| g(x) \|^2 \right]. \tag{4.29}$$

On the other hand, applying identity (4.27) with $C = \beta n I_p$ and $u = \beta g(x)$, one obtains the equality

$$\exp\left[\frac{\beta}{2n} \| g(x) \|^2 \right] = \left(\frac{\beta n}{2\pi} \right)^{p/2} \int \prod_{1}^{p} dm_k$$

$$\exp\left[-\frac{\beta n}{2} \| m \|^2 + \beta m^T g(x) \right], \tag{4.30}$$

which yields for Z the expression

$$Z = \exp\left(-\frac{\beta p}{2}\right)\left(\frac{\beta n}{2\pi}\right)^{p/2}$$
$$\mathrm{Tr}_x \int \prod dm_k \exp\left[-\frac{\beta n}{2}\parallel m \parallel^2 + \beta m^T g(x)\right]. \tag{4.31}$$

It should be noticed that, in expressions (4.30) and (4.31), the m_k are so far
formal integration variables, but they can in fact be interpreted as the overlaps
(4.22) when $n \to \infty$. Indeed, in view of Lemma 4.1, the right hand sides of
these equations are dominated by the maximum of the integrand and this
maximum is attained for $m = n^{-1} g(x)$.

Exchanging the integration and trace operators in (4.31), one finds, in view
of (4.28),

$$Z = \exp\left(-\frac{\beta p}{2}\right)\left(\frac{\beta n}{2\pi}\right)^{p/2} \int \prod dm_k \exp\left[-\frac{\beta n}{2}\parallel m \parallel^2\right]$$
$$\mathrm{Tr}_x \exp\left[\beta \sum_{k=1}^{p} m_k \sum_{i=1}^{n} x_i \xi_i^{(k)}\right]. \tag{4.32}$$

On the other hand, the following sequence of equalities holds

$$\mathrm{Tr}_x \exp\left[\sum_{i=1}^{n} x_i v_i\right] = \mathrm{Tr}_x \prod_{i=1}^{n} \exp(x_i v_i) = \prod_{i=1}^{n}(e^{v_i} + e^{-v_i}),$$
$$= \prod_{i=1}^{n} 2 \cosh v_i, \tag{4.33}$$

and one obtains in this way the expression

$$Z = \exp\left(-\frac{\beta p}{2}\right)\left(\frac{\beta n}{2\pi}\right)^{p/2} \int \prod dm_k \exp\left[-\frac{\beta n}{2}\parallel m \parallel^2\right.$$
$$\left. + \sum_{i=1}^{n} \log 2 \cosh \beta \sum_{k=1}^{p} \xi_i^{(k)} m_k\right]. \tag{4.34}$$

Saddle point integration of Z leads, via formula (4.13), to the following expression for the free energy per unit

$$f(\overline{m},\beta) = \lim_{n\to\infty}\left[\frac{1}{2}\parallel \overline{m} \parallel^2 - \frac{1}{\beta n}\sum_{i=1}^{n} \log 2 \cosh \beta \sum_{k=1}^{p} \xi_i^{(k)} \overline{m}_k\right] \tag{4.35}$$

where $\overline{m} = [\overline{m}_1, \overline{m}_2, \ldots, \overline{m}_p]^T$ is the mean overlap vector. These mean values
of the overlaps at thermodynamic equilibrium are solutions of the saddle point
equations $\partial f/\partial \overline{m}_k = 0$. This yields

$$\overline{m}_k = \lim_{n \to \infty} \left[\frac{1}{n} \sum_{i=1}^{n} \xi_i^{(k)} \tanh \beta \sum_{\ell=1}^{p} \xi_i^{(\ell)} \overline{m}_\ell \right], \, (k = 1, 2, \ldots, p). \tag{4.36}$$

Among these saddle points, only the *minima* of f actually contribute to the integral (4.34). At these points the Hessian of f is positive definite, i.e.

$$A = \left[\frac{\partial^2 f}{\partial \overline{m}_k \partial \overline{m}_\ell} ; \quad \ell, k = 1, 2, \ldots, p \right] > 0. \tag{4.37}$$

This inequality will be called "stability condition" in the sequel.

As in Chapter 3, we should now compute the statistical mean of both sides in equations (4.35) and (4.36) with respect to the distribution of the prototype components $\xi_i^{(k)}$. In fact, it is not necessary to take this mean explicitly because $\overline{m}_k$, by its definition (4.22), as well as the right hand sides of (4.35) and (4.36) are written as sample means of quantities which depend on the $\xi_i^{(k)}$'s. Therefore, in view of the law of large numbers [Feller 66], these expressions converge to the statistical mean when $n \to \infty$. As short reference to this observation, expressions (4.35) and (4.36) are said to be *self-averaged* [Amit et al. 85a], [Provost and Vallee 83]. In the sequel we shall thus write

$$f(\overline{m}, \beta) = \frac{1}{2} \| \overline{m} \|^2 - \frac{1}{\beta} \ll \log 2 \cosh \beta \sum_{k=1}^{p} \xi_i^{(k)} \overline{m}_k \gg, \tag{4.38}$$

$$\overline{m}_k = \ll \xi_i^{(k)} \tanh \beta \sum_{\ell=1}^{p} \xi_i^{(\ell)} \overline{m}_\ell \gg \tag{4.39}$$

where the notation $\ll \cdot \gg$ represents the average with respect to the distribution of the prototype components $\xi_i^{(k)}$. In summary, equations (4.38) and (4.39) are obtained by a twofold averaging operation : the first one with respect to the Gibbs distribution (4.6) and represented by an overbar, followed by the second one with respect to the prototype distributions.

Remarks • The computation of the partition function, which lies at the basis of the mean field theory, can also be performed by other means than the method followed above. An alternative approach [Provost and Vallee 83], [Amit et al. 85a], uses a classical property of the Dirac function to replace expression (4.29) of the partition function by

$$Z = \exp \left(-\frac{\beta p}{2} \right) \text{Tr}_x \int \prod dm_k \exp \left[\frac{\beta n}{2} \| m \|^2 \right] \times$$
$$\times \delta(m - n^{-1} g(x)) \tag{4.40}$$

where the components of vector $g(x)$ are defined in (4.28). Next, the Dirac function is replaced by its inverse Laplace transform,

$$\delta(m) = (2\pi i)^{-p} \int_{-\infty}^{+\infty} \exp\left(-s^T m\right) \prod ds_k, \tag{4.41}$$

and this yields

$$Z = D \left(\frac{n\beta}{2\pi}\right)^p \mathrm{Tr}_x \int \prod dm_k \prod ds_\ell$$
$$\exp\left[\frac{\beta n}{2} \| m \|^2 + \beta s^T g(x) - \beta n s^T m\right] \tag{4.42}$$

where s denotes a p-vector of complex variables $s = [s_1, s_2, \ldots, s_p]^T$ and where D is a normalization constant. Next, the integral and trace operators are exchanged and, in view of definition (4.28) and identity (4.33), one obtains

$$Z = D \left(\frac{n\beta}{2\pi}\right)^p \int \prod dm_k \prod ds_\ell \exp\left[\frac{\beta n}{2} \| m \|^2 \right.$$
$$\left. -\beta n s^T m + \sum_{i=1}^n \log 2 \cosh \beta \sum_{k=1}^p \xi_i^{(k)} s_k\right]. \tag{4.43}$$

By Lemma 4.1, this integral is dominated by the value of the integrand at the saddle point when n tends to infinity, provided the integration contours are analytically deformed so that they pass through the saddle points. Equating to zero the derivatives of the exponent in (4.43) with respect to the integration variables m_k and s_ℓ, one finds

$$\overline{m}_k = \overline{s}_k, \tag{4.44}$$

$$(k = 1, 2, \ldots, p),$$

$$\overline{s}_k = \frac{1}{n} \sum_{i=1}^n \xi_i^{(k)} \tanh \beta \sum_{\ell=1}^p \xi_i^{(\ell)} \overline{s}_\ell, \tag{4.45}$$

and one recovers, as expected, the mean field equation (4.39) obtained above. On the other hand, if $\overline{s}_k$ is eliminated by means of (4.44), then the value of the integrand at the saddle point leads to expression (4.38) for the free energy per unit.

• Note that the requirement of a zero diagonal in the synaptic matrix leads to a factor $\exp(-\beta p/2)$ in expression (4.34) of the partition function. Since this factor does in fact not appear in (4.38) and (4.39), the conclusion is that the question of a zero or nonzero diagonal in the synaptic matrix does not affect the mean field equations for finite p.

• The thermodynamic extension of recursive networks has been mainly worked out in the framework of disordered systems physics because of the strong analogy with the spin glass model [Edwards and Anderson 75], [Collobert and Maruani 89], [Kirkpatrick and Sherrington 78], [Moore 84], [Stephen 83], [van

Hemmen 82]. Spin glasses are magnetic alloys formed, for instance, by dilute solutions of of manganese in copper or iron in gold. These impurities interact with each other by means of the conduction electrons and the couplings are either of the ferromagnetic ($w_{ij} > 0$) or antiferromagnetic type ($w_{ij} < 0$). The interest of these alloys comes from the fact that they exhibit a wide variety of stable or meta-stable states. The impurities are located at random sites of the lattice of the host metal and, from a magnetic point of view, they can be modeled as classical dipoles labelled by an index $i = 1, 2, \ldots, n$ and pointing in the direction x_i. These dipoles interact via the couplings w_{ij}. In the simplest approach, a spin interacts only with its nearest neighbours, while the equivalent of the recursive neural networks considered here, requires infinite range interactions where each spin is coupled to all others. In the Ising model [Moore 84], the Hamiltonian of such a spin glass is proportional to $\sum_i \sum_{j \neq i} w_{ij} x_i x_j$ and the system stabilizes in an equilibrium point which is a minimum of the free energy.

• In this subsection, we assumed that the neural network was in a heat bath. We also mentioned that the interaction with a heat bath was equivalent to adding a noise source to the system but the particular form of this interaction had not been specified. In the next subsection, we start from a given stochastic process and show that an energy function exists such that the corresponding Gibbs distribution is the equilibrium distribution of the process. This result establishes a precise link between the heat bath and the stochastic dynamics. Conversely, we will show that, given an energy function, it is always possible to find a corresponding stochastic process.

4.2.2   The Little model for synchronous updating

In Chapter 2 it was shown that, for synchronous operation mode, it was in general not possible to find an energy function which is monotonically decreasing along a state trajectory and it is precisely for this reason that cycles can appear. However, in the case of a synchronous process described by the Little model [Little 74] we shall show below, following Peretto's argument [Peretto 84], that a Hamiltonian does exist and that the equilibrium properties of the system are described by a Gibbs distribution of the form (4.6). With this distribution, one can then apply the mean field theory in the same way as in the preceding subsection [Amit et al. 85a].

Since the Hamiltonian is unknown for the time being, the starting point is not a Gibbs distribution as for asynchronous updating, but a stochastic evolution equation. In this approach, one assumes that the network in synchronous operation mode evolves according to a stationary first order Markov process [Peretto 84], [Glauber 63]. The probability $\Pr(x, t + 1)$ of finding the system in state x at time $t + 1$ is given by

$$\Pr(x, t+1) = \sum_y V(x|y) \Pr(y, t) \tag{4.46}$$

where $V(x|y)$ is the transition probability from state y to state x. Taking into account the normalization $\sum_x V(x|y) = 1$, one can rewrite (4.46) under the form

$$\begin{aligned}
\Pr(x, t+1) - \Pr(x, t) &= \sum_{y \neq x} V(x|y)\Pr(y, t) \\
&\quad - \sum_{y \neq x} V(y|x)\Pr(x, t).
\end{aligned} \tag{4.47}$$

This equation is the discrete time equivalent of a Boltzmann equation if, and only if, the transition probabilities satisfy the *detailed balance principle*

$$\frac{V(x|y)}{V(y|x)} = \frac{G(x)}{G(y)} . \tag{4.48}$$

The asymptotic behaviour of $\Pr(x, t)$ for $t \to \infty$ is elucidated in the lemma below where the following two definitions are used. A process is called *irreducible* if there are no sets of states S_1 and S_2 such that $V(x|y) = 0$ for all $x \in S_1$ and $y \in S_2$. A process is called *aperiodic* if $V(x|x) > 0$ for all x.

Lemma 4.2 *If a Markov process is irreducible and aperiodic and if the transition probabilities satisfy the detailed balance equation (4.48) then the occupation probability* $\Pr(x, t)$ *converges in time to the equilibrium distribution*

$$\lim_{t \to \infty} \Pr(x, t) = \frac{G(x)}{\sum_y G(y)} . \tag{4.49}$$

Proof Observe first that the expression $\sigma(x) = G(x)/\sum_y G(y)$ satisfies the equation

$$\sigma(x) = \sum_y V(x|y)\sigma(y) \tag{4.50}$$

and so is an equilibrium distribution. By standard Markov theory, the equilibrium distribution is unique because the process is irreducible and the occupation probability converges to $\sigma(x)$ since the process was also assumed to be aperiodic.   □

Remark • If we put

$$H(x) = -\frac{1}{\beta} \log G(x), \tag{4.51}$$

then the occupation probability at equilibrium is given by

$$\Pr(x, \infty) = \frac{1}{Z} e^{-\beta H(x)} \tag{4.52}$$

where Z is the partition function and this brings us back in the Gibbs distribution framework as used earlier for asynchronous updating with a Hamiltonian defined by (4.51).

With the Little model, the probability that a neuron i is in state x_i at time $t + 1$, given that the network was in state y at time t, is expressed by

$$\Pr(x_i|y) = \frac{\exp[\beta n^{-1} x_i h_i(y)]}{\exp[-\beta n^{-1} x_i h_i(y)] + \exp[\beta n^{-1} x_i h_i(y)]} \tag{4.53}$$

where $h_i(y) = \sum_{j \neq i} w_{ij} y_j$ is the synaptic potential at neuron i. In synchronous operation mode, the transition probability $V(x|y)$ is the product of n factors $\Pr(x_i|y)$ and this gives, in view of (4.53),

$$V(x|y) = \frac{\exp[\beta n^{-1} \sum_i x_i h_i(y)]}{\prod_{i=1}^{n} 2 \cosh[\beta n^{-1} h_i(y)]} . \tag{4.54}$$

These transition probabilities satisfy the detailed equilibrium equation (4.48). Indeed, since the synaptic matrix is symmetrical, one has

$$\frac{V(x|y)}{V(y|x)} = \frac{\prod_{i=1}^{n} 2 \cosh[\beta n^{-1} \sum_{j \neq i} w_{ij} x_j]}{\prod_{i=1}^{n} 2 \cosh[\beta n^{-1} \sum_{j \neq i} w_{ij} y_j]}, \tag{4.55}$$

which has the required form $G(x)/G(y)$ with

$$G(x) = \prod_{i=1}^{n} 2 \cosh[\beta n^{-1} \sum_{j \neq i} w_{ij} x_j]. \tag{4.56}$$

According to (4.51), the Hamiltonian of the equilibrium distribution is then given by

$$\begin{aligned} H(x) &= -\beta^{-1} \log G(x) \\ &= -\beta^{-1} \sum_{i=1}^{n} \log 2 \cosh(\beta n^{-1} \sum_{j \neq i} w_{ij} x_j). \end{aligned} \tag{4.57}$$

In order to establish the equations holding at thermodynamic equilibrium, we shall now apply mean field theory to the computation of the partition function. The result will be an integral expression in terms of the overlaps which is dominated by its saddle point value.

For Hebb's law with zero diagonal, the partition function (4.8) is given by

$$Z = \mathrm{Tr}_x \, \exp \left[\sum_{i=1}^{n} \log 2 \cosh \beta n^{-1} \sum_{k=1}^{p} \xi_i^{(k)} \sum_{j \neq i} \xi_j^{(k)} x_j \right].$$

(4.58)

In contrast with (4.29), the argument of the exponential can no longer be written as a vector norm and it is therefore no longer possible to use one of the identities (4.27) or (4.30) to introduce the overlaps in the expression of the partition function. Consequently, we shall rather resort to the alternative approach relying on a classical property of the Dirac function and which leads to the same results as was shown above. If we neglect the fact that $j \neq i$ in (4.58), then the partition function can be written in the form

$$Z = \mathrm{Tr}_x \int \prod dm_k \, \exp \left[\sum_{i=1}^{n} \log 2 \cosh \beta \sum_{k=1}^{p} \xi_i^{(k)} m_k \right]$$
$$\times \delta(m - n^{-1} g(x))$$

(4.59)

where the components of vector $g(x)$ are defined in (4.28). Replacing the Dirac function by its inverse Laplace transform (4.41), one obtains

$$Z = D \left(\frac{n\beta}{2\pi} \right)^p \mathrm{Tr}_x \int \prod dm_k \prod ds_\ell \, \exp \left[\beta s^T g(x) - \beta n \, s^T m \right.$$
$$\left. \sum_{i=1}^{n} \log 2 \cosh \beta \sum_{k=1}^{p} \xi_i^{(k)} m_k \right]$$

(4.60)

where D is a constant. Exchanging the trace and integral operators and taking identity (4.33) into account, one obtains

$$Z = D \left(\frac{n\beta}{2\pi} \right)^p \int \prod dm_k \prod ds_\ell \, \exp \left[\sum_{i=1}^{n} \log 2 \cosh \beta \sum_{k=1}^{p} \xi_i^{(k)} m_k \right.$$
$$\left. -\beta n \, s^T m + \sum_{i=1}^{n} \log 2 \cosh \beta \sum_{k=1}^{p} \xi_i^{(k)} s_k \right].$$

(4.61)

The integral is dominated by the value of the integrand at the saddle points and the latter satisfy the following equations

$$\bar{s}_k = \frac{1}{n} \sum_{i=1}^{n} \xi_i^{(k)} \tanh \beta \sum_{\ell=1}^{p} \xi_i^{(\ell)} \overline{m}_\ell,$$

(4.62)

$$\overline{m}_k = \frac{1}{n} \sum_{i=1}^{n} \xi_i^{(k)} \tanh \beta \sum_{\ell=1}^{p} \xi_i^{(\ell)} \bar{s}_\ell.$$

(4.63)

One can show that these equations imply $\bar{s}_k = \overline{m}_k$. Indeed, upon subtraction of these relations and multiplication by $\bar{s}_k - \overline{m}_k$, one finds that

$$\| \bar{s} - \overline{m} \|^2 = \frac{1}{n} \sum_{i=1}^{n} \left\{ \left[\sum_{\ell=1}^{p} \xi_i^{(\ell)} \bar{s}_\ell - \sum_{\ell=1}^{p} \xi_i^{(\ell)} \overline{m}_\ell \right] \right.$$

$$\times \left[\tanh \beta \sum_{\ell=1}^{p} \xi_i^{(\ell)} \overline{m}_\ell - \tanh \beta \sum_{\ell=1}^{p} \xi_i^{(\ell)} \overline{s}_\ell \right] \Bigg\} . \tag{4.64}$$

Since the hyperbolic tangent is an odd function, the product $(a - b)(\tanh b - \tanh a)$ is strictly negative if $a \neq b$. Consequently, if $\overline{s} \neq \overline{m}$, each term in the summation over i in the right hand side of (4.64) is negative or zero, whereas the left hand side is strictly positive. As a consequence, the equilibrium equations simplify to (4.39) and the free energy is given by

$$f(\overline{m}, \beta) = \| \overline{m} \|^2 - \frac{2}{\beta} \ll \log 2 \cosh \beta \sum_{k=1}^{p} \xi_i^{(k)} \overline{m}_k \gg . \tag{4.65}$$

The following conclusion can be drawn [Amit et al. 85a].

Theorem 4.3 *The thermodynamic extension of the synchronous operation mode according to the Little model leads exactly to the same mean field equations as for the asynchronous mode and the corresponding free energy is twice as large.*

Before we continue with the thermodynamic extension, it is useful to summarize the results obtained so far. It was assumed that, at equilibrium, the state vectors follow a Gibbs distribution (4.6) and, for the asynchronous mode, the Hamiltonian was automatically given by the energy function introduced in Chapter 2 (Section 2.1). Next, we have applied to this distribution the mean field theory and the equilibrium points have been obtained as minima of the free energy. This resulted in the mean field equations (4.38) and (4.39) with the additional information that, among the solutions of (4.38), only those which satisfy (4.37) are stable equilibrium points. We have also shown that, when the synchronous operation mode is modelled as a Markovian process, we obtain essentially the same mean field equations as in the asynchronous mode.

In the next section, we shall use the mean field equations to investigate in more details the properties of some particular solutions and to examine how the solutions are affected when the prototype distribution is biased or when the synaptic matrix is determined via the projection rule.

4.3 Solutions of the mean field equations for finite p

In the remaining part of this chapter we shall essentially restrict the analysis to the case where the prototype components $\xi_i^{(k)}$ are independent identically distributed random variables with equal probability of taking the values $+1$ and -1 :

$$\Pr\left(\xi_i^{(k)} = 1\right) = \Pr\left(\xi_i^{(k)} = -1\right) = 1/2,$$
$$\xi_i^{(k)} \text{ independent of } \xi_j^{(\ell)} \text{ if } k \neq \ell \text{ or } i \neq j. \tag{4.66}$$

Consequently, one has in particular,

$$\ll \xi_i^{(k)} \gg = 0, \qquad \ll \xi_i^{(k)}\, \xi_i^{(\ell)} \gg = \delta_{k\ell} \tag{4.67}$$

where $\delta_{k\ell}$ is the Kronecker delta and, in the mean, the prototypes are thus orthogonal. The case of biased distributions according to (3.56) will briefly be considered in Subsection 4.3.4. To simplify notation, the Boltzmann constant k will be incorporated in the temperature and, from now on, we shall thus write $\beta = 1/T$.

4.3.1 Mattis solutions

A Mattis solution [Mattis 76] is characterized by the fact that the mean state vector is macroscopically lined up with a particular prototype and orthogonal to the others. Thus, in terms of the mean overlap vector, we are looking for a solution of the mean field equations of the form

$$\overline{m} = [\overline{m}_1, 0, \ldots, 0]^T, \qquad \overline{m}_1 \neq 0. \tag{4.68}$$

This corresponds exactly to an associative memory behaviour of the network. The mean field equations (4.39) become for this case

$$\overline{m}_1 = \ll \xi_i^{(1)} \tanh \beta\, \xi_i^{(1)}\, \overline{m}_1 \gg, \tag{4.69}$$

$$0 = \ll \xi_i^{(k)} \tanh \beta\, \xi_i^{(1)}\, \overline{m}_1 \gg, \qquad k = 2, \ldots, p. \tag{4.70}$$

Since $\xi_i^{(1)}$ can take the values $+1$ or -1 and since the hyperbolic tangent is an odd function, one has

$$\tanh \beta\, \xi_i^{(1)}\, \overline{m}_1 = \xi_i^{(1)} \tanh \beta\, \overline{m}_1, \tag{4.71}$$

which shows, in view of (4.67), that equations (4.70) are automatically satisfied, whereas (4.69) now becomes

$$\overline{m}_1 = \tanh \beta\, \overline{m}_1. \tag{4.72}$$

From the graphical representation of the latter equation (see Figure 4.1), one can see that for $\beta < 1$, i.e. for $T > T_c = 1$, the only solution is $\overline{m}_1 = 0$. Two additional nonzero solutions, $\overline{m}_1' = -\overline{m}_1''$, exist as soon as $T < T_c = 1$. There are thus $2p$ Mattis solutions. When the temperature decreases and goes to zero, the absolute value of these two solutions tend to unity which means that the mean state vector coincides more and more closely with prototype $\xi^{(1)}$ or its negative.

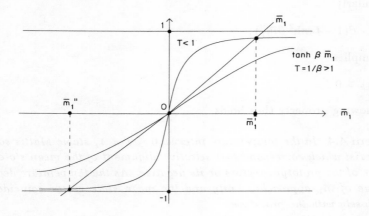

Figure 4.1 : Mattis solution for finite p.

As far as stability is concerned, one expects that the zero solution will be stable as long as $T > 1$ and that it becomes unstable when $T < 1$. Simultaneously, solutions $\overline{m}_1'$ and $\overline{m}_1''$ appear and are stable in the interval $0 \leq T < 1$. This result will now be established on a rigorous basis by applying stability condition (4.37). Taking into account expression (4.38) of the free energy, one has

$$\frac{\partial^2 f}{\partial \overline{m}_k \partial \overline{m}_\ell} = \delta_{k\ell} - \beta \ll \xi_i^{(k)} \xi_i^{(\ell)} \left[1 - \tanh^2 \beta \sum_{t=1}^{p} \xi_i^{(t)} \overline{m}_t \right] \gg, \qquad (4.73)$$

which, in view of (4.67), can be rewritten as

$$\frac{\partial^2 f}{\partial \overline{m}_k \partial \overline{m}_\ell} = \delta_{k\ell} - \beta \left[\delta_{k\ell} - \ll \xi_i^{(k)} \xi_i^{(\ell)} \tanh^2 \beta \sum_{t=1}^{p} \xi_i^{(t)} \overline{m}_t \gg \right]. \qquad (4.74)$$

For the Mattis solution (4.68), matrix A reduces to a diagonal whose elements A_{kk} are identical and equal to

$$A_{kk} = 1 - \beta \left(1 - \tanh^2 \beta \overline{m}_1 \right), \quad k = 1, 2, \ldots, p. \qquad (4.75)$$

Solution $\overline{m}_1 = 0$ is stable, i.e. $A > 0$, as long as $T = \beta^{-1} > 1$. Solutions $\overline{m}_1'$ and $\overline{m}_1''$ which appear when $T < 1$ are also stable. Indeed, at the crossing point $\overline{m}_1'$, the slope of the function $\tanh \beta \overline{m}_1$ is smaller than unity (see Figure 4.1). Thus,

$$1 > \beta (1 - \tanh^2 \beta \overline{m}_1') \qquad (4.76)$$

and similarly

$$1 > \beta(1 - \tanh^2 \beta \overline{m}_1''), \tag{4.77}$$

which implies

$$A_{kk} > 0. \tag{4.78}$$

The following property thus holds.

Theorem 4.4 *In the temperature interval $0 \leq T < 1$, stable Mattis solutions (4.68) exist which correspond to a selective alignment of the mean state vector with one of the prototype vectors or its negative. As the temperature decreases, the value of $\overline{m}_1$ approaches unity and the mean state vector coincides even more closely with the prototype.*

4.3.2   Mixture solutions and parasitic fixed points

The preceding chapters have shown that, in addition to the prototype vectors, a large number of parasitic fixed points exist in which the network can get trapped during the successive iterations. In particular, in Chapter 3 (Theorem 3.18) we have found that linear combinations of prototype vectors are preferential candidates for such parasitic fixed points. We shall see now that the thermodynamic extension provides additional evidence for this fact.

As an introduction to this problem, we start with a limited power series expansion of the mean field equation (4.39) near the origin. One finds that

$$\overline{m}_k = \ll \xi_i^{(k)} \left[\beta \sum_{\ell=1}^{p} \xi_i^{(\ell)} \overline{m}_\ell - \frac{1}{3} \beta^3 \left(\sum_{\ell=1}^{p} \xi_i^{(\ell)} \overline{m}_\ell \right)^3 \right] \gg, \tag{4.79}$$

whence, in view of (4.67),

$$\overline{m}_k = \beta \overline{m}_k - \beta^3 \overline{m}_k \| \overline{m} \|^2 + \frac{2}{3} \beta^3 \overline{m}_k^3. \tag{4.80}$$

The latter relation shows that, for each k, there exists a solution $\overline{m}_k = 0$, *independently* of the other components of the mean overlap vector $\overline{m}$. Moreover, dividing both sides of (4.80) by $\overline{m}_k$, one obtains

$$\frac{2}{3} \overline{m}_k^2 = T^2(T - 1) + \| \overline{m} \|^2 \tag{4.81}$$

which has two solutions for $\overline{m}_k$ with opposite signs, and which are again *independent* of the index k. The conclusion is that the mean field equations admit *symmetric mixture states* as solutions, of the form

$$\overline{m} = \mu_s [\underbrace{\pm 1, \pm 1, \ldots, \pm 1}_{s}, \underbrace{0, \ldots, 0}_{p-s}]^T \tag{4.82}$$

for which the mean state vector is a linear combination with equal weights of s prototypes. The total number of such solutions is equal to $\binom{p}{s} 2^s$ and thus grows exponentially with s. Equation (4.81) indicates moreover that this type of solution exists only if $T < T_c = 1$. We shall now examine the stability of these solutions and show that it depends essentially on the parity of s. To this end, we consider a typical representative of solutions (4.82), i.e.

$$\overline{m} = \mu_s [\underbrace{1, 1, \ldots, 1}_{s}, \underbrace{0, \ldots, 0}_{p-s}]^T . \tag{4.83}$$

Adding up the mean field equations (4.39) for the s nonzero components, one obtains

$$\mu_s = \frac{1}{s} \ll z_{i,s} \tanh \beta \mu_s z_{i,s} \gg \tag{4.84}$$

where

$$z_{i,s} = \sum_{\ell=1}^{s} \xi_i^{(\ell)} . \tag{4.85}$$

Equations (4.39), corresponding to the zero components of the vector (4.83), are of the form

$$0 = \ll \xi_i^{(k)} \tanh \beta \mu_s z_{i,s} \gg, \qquad k = s+1, \ldots, p, \tag{4.86}$$

and they are automatically satisfied since we have seen that a solution $\overline{m}_k = 0$ always exists, independently of the other components. An alternative way of verifying this consists in observing that, from definition (4.85), $\xi_i^{(k)}$ and $\tanh \beta \mu_s z_{i,s}$ are independent random variables and property (4.67) gives then the desired result.

Expression (4.74) for the elements of the stability matrix A becomes now

$$\frac{\partial^2 f}{\partial \overline{m}_k \partial \overline{m}_\ell} = \delta_{k\ell} - \beta \left[\delta_{k,\ell} - \ll \xi_i^{(k)} \xi_i^{(\ell)} \tanh^2 \beta \mu_s z_{i,s} \gg \right]. \tag{4.87}$$

The diagonal elements are identical and equal to

$$1 - \beta(1-q) \qquad \text{with} \quad q = \ll \tanh^2 \beta \mu_s z_{i,s} \gg, \tag{4.88}$$

whereas the off-diagonal elements are given by

$$\beta Q = \beta \ll \xi_i^{(k)} \xi_i^{(\ell)} \tanh^2 \beta \mu_s z_{i,s} \gg \tag{4.89}$$

if $k \leq s$ and $\ell \leq s$. All other elements of A are zero. Indeed, if k or ℓ is larger than s, the mean value in (4.89) can be factorized into a product of statistical means, one of which at least is zero in view of (4.67). Consequently, the stability matrix can be written

$$
A = \begin{bmatrix}
1 - \beta(1-q) & \beta Q & \cdots & \beta Q \\
\beta Q & 1 - \beta(1-q) & \beta Q & \beta Q \\
\vdots & & \ddots & \\
\beta Q & \cdots & \beta Q & 1 - \beta(1-q)
\end{bmatrix}
$$

$$
+ \; [1 - \beta(1-q)] I_{p-s} \tag{4.90}
$$

and one easily verifies that A has three types of eigenvalues :

$$
\lambda_1 = 1 - \beta(1-q) + \beta(s-1)Q, \qquad \text{simple eigenvalue}, \tag{4.91}
$$

$$
\lambda_2 = 1 - \beta(1-q), \qquad \text{of multiplicity } (p-s), \tag{4.92}
$$

$$
\lambda_3 = 1 - \beta(1-q) - \beta Q, \qquad \text{of multiplicity } (s-1). \tag{4.93}
$$

In reference [Amit et al. 85a] it is shown that $Q > 0$ when $T < 1$ and the sign of the smallest eigenvalue, i.e. λ_3, is thus critical for stability. In order to analyze the behaviour of the solutions near $T = 1$, expression (4.84) is expanded in power series of μ_s yielding

$$
\mu_s \simeq \beta \mu_s - \frac{\beta^3 \mu_s^3}{3s} \ll z_{i,s}^4 \gg . \tag{4.94}
$$

Using the fact that $\ll z_{i,s}^4 \gg = s(3s-2)$ and setting $T = 1 - t$, one finds

$$
\mu_s^2 \simeq \frac{3t}{3s-2}. \tag{4.95}
$$

If we also expand expressions (4.88) and (4.89) of q and Q in power series of t, we obtain, in view of (4.95) and of the fact that $\ll z_{i,s}^2 \gg = s$,

$$
q \simeq \frac{3st}{3s-2} \qquad \text{and} \qquad Q \simeq \frac{2q}{s}. \tag{4.96}
$$

Introducing these values in (4.93), we find

$$
\lambda_3 \simeq -t + q - Q \simeq \frac{-4t}{3s-2} < 0, \tag{4.97}
$$

and this shows that the symmetric mixture states are unstable in the neighbourhood of $T = 1$.

Near $T = 0$, one should distinguish between odd and even values of s. Indeed, if s is odd, $z_{i,s}$ is never zero whereas $z_{i,s}$ can effectively become zero in the opposite case. For even s and $z_{i,s} \neq 0$, one observes that $\tanh^2 \beta \mu_s z_{i,s} \to 1$ when $\beta = T^{-1} \to \infty$. However, if $z_{i,s} = 0$, then $\tanh^2 \beta \mu_s z_{i,s} = 0$. Hence, $q = 1 - \Pr(z_{i,s} = 0)$ and thus $1 - q > 0$, with the consequence that λ_2 becomes negative when $\beta \to \infty$ and symmetric mixture states with even s are thus unstable. If s is odd, then $z_{i,s}$ is always nonzero and $q \to 1$ while $Q \to 0$ when $T \to 0$. Consequently, the three eigenvalues tend to unity and the mixture states with odd s are stable. It is the crossover of λ_3 with zero which gives, for each value of s, the temperature below which the mixture states become stable. By way of illustration, for $s = 3$, this temperature is $T = 0.461$ and, more generally, the temperature threshold decreases with s approximately as $T = 1/\sqrt{s}$ when s becomes large. Hence, only the odd-s symmetric mixture states with $s < T^{-2}$ are stable. The following conclusion thus holds [Amit et al. 85a].

Theorem 4.5 *Symmetric mixture states (4.83) of even order s are always unstable. Those of odd order are stable below a temperature threshold which decreases approximately as $1/\sqrt{s}$.*

Remarks • In the temperature interval $0.461 < T < 1$, there are no parasitic fixed points generated by symmetric mixture states. One concludes therefore that addition of a certain amount of thermal noise improves the associative memory performance because it reduces the risk of the network becoming trapped in a specific type of parasitic fixed point. In practice, an annealing process is applied to the network by which the temperature is progressively reduced to zero [van Laarhoven and Aarts 87] .

• Asymmetric mixture states of the form

$$\overline{m} = [\alpha, \alpha, \ldots, \alpha, \beta, \ldots, \beta, 0, \ldots, 0]^T \tag{4.98}$$

also exist and they too contribute to generating parasitic fixed points. Their properties are discussed in [Amit et al. 85a].

4.3.3 Existence of cycles in the Little model

We have seen in Subsection 4.2.2 that Little's model is described by the same mean field equations as for asynchronous updating. This may seem contradictory because, for symmetric synaptic matrices with zero diagonal, cycles can exist in synchronous mode (§ 2.1.3) but not for asynchronous operation.

The answer is that cycles can effectively occur for the Little model, that they cannot be observed at the level of the overlaps $\overline{m}_k$ but rather in the individual components of the state vector [Amit 87].

Using formula (4.19) of Hebb's law, equation (1.23) of a fixed point can be expressed as

$$x_i = \text{Sgn}\left[\frac{1}{n}\sum_{k=1}^{p}\xi_i^{(k)}\sum_{j=1}^{n}\xi_j^{(k)}x_j - \frac{p}{n}x_i\right], \qquad i = 1, 2, \ldots, n. \tag{4.99}$$

Definition (4.22) of the overlaps allows the x_i to be rewritten in the form

$$x_i = \text{Sgn}\left[\sum_{k=1}^{p}\xi_i^{(k)}m_k - \frac{p}{n}x_i\right], \qquad i = 1, 2, \ldots, n, \tag{4.100}$$

leading to the conclusion

$$m_\ell = \frac{1}{n}\sum_{i=1}^{n}\xi_i^{(\ell)}\text{Sgn}\left[\sum_{k=1}^{p}\xi_i^{(k)}m_k - \frac{p}{n}x_i\right]. \tag{4.101}$$

If $\sum_{k=1}^{p}\xi_i^{(k)}m_k \neq 0$ for all i, one can neglect the term $p\,x_i/n$ when n becomes large since p is assumed to stay finite. In particular, the Mattis solution (4.68) satisfies this hypothesis since in that case $\sum_{k=1}^{p}\xi_i^{(k)}m_k$ simplifies to $m_1\xi_i^{(1)}$. Equations (4.101) are then identical to the mean field equations (4.39) with $T = 0$.

However, if $\sum_{k=1}^{p}\xi_i^{(k)}m_k = 0$ for some i, then component x_i will flip at each iteration of the dynamic equations. This can, among others, occur in the case of symmetric mixture solutions (4.83) of even order s. In such a case,

$$\sum_{k=1}^{p}\xi_i^{(k)}m_k = \mu_s\sum_{k=1}^{s}\xi_i^{(k)} \tag{4.102}$$

and the sum in the right hand side can indeed become zero. More specifically, if $s = 2$, for instance, this will happen for all components i where prototypes $\xi^{(1)}$ and $\xi^{(2)}$ have opposite signs. In the synchronous updating mode, the vector m is the same for each of the n equations (4.100) and certain components will thus flip. However, as we shall see below, these components do not contribute to the value of the overlap vector, with the consequence that $m(t+1) = m(t)$ and these components will thus flip back to their original value at the next iteration. Therefore, symmetric mixture solutions of even order can give rise to cycles of length 2 which can be observed at the level of the individual components but not at the level of the overlap values.

It remains thus to be shown that the components which flip back and forth do not contribute to the overlap values. For the first s prototypes, this amounts to proving that

$$\frac{1}{n} \sum_i {}' \xi_i^{(\ell)} x_i = \mu_s, \quad 1 \le \ell \le s, \tag{4.103}$$

where $\sum'$ denotes a summation restricted to the elements x_i which do not flip. Adding up the s equations (4.103) one has thus to show that

$$\frac{1}{sn} \sum_{\ell=1}^{s} \sum_i {}' \xi_i^{(\ell)} x_i = \mu_s. \tag{4.104}$$

Using expressions (4.100), (4.102) and (4.85) successively, one can verify that the components x_i which do not flip are given by

$$x_i = \text{Sgn}(\mu_s z_{i,s}). \tag{4.105}$$

Substituting the latter expression for x_i, the left hand side of (4.104) becomes for large n

$$\frac{1}{s} \ll z_{i,s} \, \text{Sgn}(\mu_s z_{i,s}) \gg, \tag{4.106}$$

which is, indeed, equal to μ_s, in view of expression (4.84) when $T = 0$. Moreover, for $k > s$, the contribution to m_k should be zero for all components, irrespective of whether they flip or not. For the components which do not flip, one has, in view of (4.105),

$$\frac{1}{n} \sum_i {}' \xi_i^{(k)} x_i = \ll \xi_i^{(k)} \text{Sgn}(\mu_s z_{i,s}) \gg, \quad \text{for} \quad k > s \tag{4.107}$$

and the mean value of the right hand side is zero since $\xi_i^{(k)}$ is independent of $z_{i,s}$. As for the components x_i which do flip, they depend at most on the $\xi_i^{(\ell)}$ ($\ell \le s$) because, for these components, the right hand side of (4.102) should vanish. Therefore, they are independent of the $\xi_i^{(k)}$ for $k > s$. Consequently, if $\sum_i''$ denotes the sum over the components which do flip, one has

$$\frac{1}{n} \sum_i {}'' \xi_i^{(k)} x_i = \ll \xi_i^{(k)} x_i \gg = 0, \quad \text{for} \quad k > s. \tag{4.108}$$

4.3.4   Biased prototypes

Let us now examine what kind of information can be derived from the mean field equations in the case of biased prototypes, characterized by distribution (3.56), and which have already been considered in Chapter 3 (§ 3.3.1) in the framework of the statistical approach.

If we stick to the formulation (4.19) of Hebb's law, one immediately observes that Mattis solutions (4.68) are no longer possible. Indeed, in order to satisfy the mean field equations (4.70) corresponding to the zero components in $\overline{m}$, one should have $\ll \xi_i^{(k)} \xi_i^{(1)} \gg = 0$, and this is not compatible with distribution (3.56) because it imposes

$$\ll \xi_i^{(k)} \xi_i^{(1)} \gg = \ll \xi_i^{(k)} \gg \cdot \ll \xi_i^{(1)} \gg = a^2. \tag{4.109}$$

This brings us back to the drastic capacity reduction already mentioned in Subsection 3.3.1, although the result manifests itself here somewhat differently. In order to avoid this problem, we should adopt the modified Hebbian rule (3.63) with the normalization factor $1/n$ instead of $1/p$. In this case, the mean field equations (4.39) and expression (4.38) for the free energy become [Amit et al. 87a],

$$\overline{m}_k = \ll (\xi_i^{(k)} - a) \tanh \beta \sum_{\ell=1}^{p} (\xi_i^{(\ell)} - a) \overline{m}_\ell \gg, \tag{4.110}$$

$$f(\overline{m}, \beta) = \frac{1}{2} \parallel \overline{m} \parallel^2 - \frac{1}{\beta} \ll \log 2 \cosh \beta \sum_{\ell=1}^{p} (\xi_i^{(\ell)} - a) \overline{m}_\ell \gg, \tag{4.111}$$

provided we take as new definition of the mean overlaps

$$\overline{m}_k = \frac{1}{n} \sum_{j=1}^{n} (\xi_j^{(k)} - a) \overline{x}_j. \tag{4.112}$$

It is easily verified that a Mattis solution of the form (4.68) becomes possible because the mean field equations (4.110) corresponding to the zero components of $\overline{m}$ are now automatically satisfied, since

$$\ll (\xi_i^{(k)} - a)(\xi_i^{(\ell)} - a) \gg = (1 - a^2) \, \delta_{k\ell}. \tag{4.113}$$

On the other hand, $\overline{m}_1$ is solution of equation

$$\overline{m}_1 = \ll (\xi_i^{(1)} - a) \tanh \beta (\xi_i^{(1)} - a) \overline{m}_1 \gg, \tag{4.114}$$

which can also be written as

$$\overline{m}_1 = \frac{1}{2}(1 - a^2)[\tanh \beta(1 - a)\overline{m}_1 + \tanh \beta(1 + a)\overline{m}_1]. \tag{4.115}$$

Here too, a nonzero solution exists only below some threshold temperature, the value of which decreases for increasing values of the bias a. Indeed, a power series expansion of the right hand side of (4.115) near $\overline{m}_1 = 0$ and up to terms of order three, gives

$$\overline{m}_1^2 \simeq \frac{3T^2}{1 + 3a^2} \frac{1 - a^2 - T}{1 - a^2} \tag{4.116}$$

and this equation has a solution only if $T < T_c = 1 - a^2$. Near $T_c(a)$, the $2p$ Mattis solutions are approximately given by

$$\overline{m}_1^2 \simeq \frac{3T^2(T_c - T)}{T_c(1 + 3a^2)}.$$
(4.117)

When the temperature goes to zero ($\beta \to \infty$), the absolute value of the hyperbolic tangent tends to unity and equation (4.115) yields then

$$\overline{m}_1 = \pm(1 - a^2).$$
(4.118)

Contrary to what this expression suggests, the mean state vector coincides then exactly with prototype $\xi^{(1)}$ (or its negative) even when $a \neq 0$. Indeed, in view of (3.63) and (4.112), the fixed point equations (1.23) become now

$$\overline{x}_i = \text{Sgn}(\xi_i^{(1)} - a)\overline{m}_1$$
(4.119)

whence, for $n \to \infty$,

$$
\begin{aligned}
\frac{1}{n} \sum_{i=1}^{n} \overline{x}_i &= \ll \text{Sgn}(\xi_i^{(1)} - a)\,\overline{m}_1 \gg, \\
&= \frac{1}{2}(1 + a)\,\text{Sgn}(1 - a)\overline{m}_1 - \frac{1}{2}(1 - a)\,\text{Sgn}(1 + a)\overline{m}_1, \\
&= a\,\text{Sgn}\,\overline{m}_1.
\end{aligned}
$$
(4.120)

This last expression, combined with (4.118) and definition (4.112) leads to

$$\frac{1}{n} \sum_{j=1}^{n} \xi_j^{(1)}\,\overline{x}_j = \pm 1.$$
(4.121)

Since $\overline{x}$ and $\xi^{(1)}$ are elements of $\{-1, 1\}^n$, this implies necessarily that $\overline{x} = \pm\xi^{(1)}$.

Taking into account expression (4.111) of the free energy, one can write an element (k, ℓ) of the stability matrix A for a Mattis solution (4.68) as

$$
\frac{\partial^2 f}{\partial \overline{m}_k \partial \overline{m}_\ell} = \delta_{k\ell} - \beta \ll (\xi_i^{(k)} - a)(\xi_i^{(\ell)} - a)
$$
$$
[1 - \tanh^2 \beta(\xi_i^{(1)} - a)\overline{m}_1] \gg
$$
(4.122)

and it is easily seen that this matrix is diagonal because, for $k \neq \ell$, one has, in view of (3.57),

$$\ll (\xi_i^{(k)} - a)(\xi_i^{(\ell)} - a) \gg = \ll \xi_i^{(k)} - a \gg \ll \xi_i^{(\ell)} - a \gg = 0.$$
(4.123)

For the solution $\overline{m}_1 = 0$, all diagonal elements are identical and one can verify that their common value is equal to $1 - \beta(1 - a^2)$ by using the identity $\ll (\xi_i^{(k)} - a)^2 \gg = 1 - a^2$. This type of solution is thus stable as long as $T > T_c = 1 - a^2$. Below this critical temperature value, solution (4.117) becomes stable. Indeed, expansion of the hyperbolic tangent near the origin shows that element $(1,1)$ of matrix A is given by

$$A_{1,1} = 1 - \beta(1 - a^2) + \beta^3\, \overline{m}_1^2 \ll (\xi_i^{(1)} - a)^4 \gg . \qquad (4.124)$$

Replacing $\ll (\xi_i^{(1)} - a)^4 \gg$ by its value $(1 - a^2)(1 + 3a^2)$ and $\overline{m}_1^2$ by expression (4.117), one obtains

$$A_{1,1} = 2\,\frac{T_c - T}{T} > 0. \qquad (4.125)$$

As for the other diagonal elements $A_{k,k}$ ($k \geq 2$), one can see, using similar arguments, that they are also identical and equal to

$$A_{k,k} = 2\,\frac{T_c - T}{T}\,\frac{1 - 3a^2}{1 + 3a^2}, \;\; (k \geq 2). \qquad (4.126)$$

This shows that solution (4.117) is stable as long as $a^2 < 1/3$ (see reference [Amit et al. 87a]).

In the same framework one can also analyze symmetric mixture solutions of the form (4.83). In contrast to the unbiased case, solutions of even order s are not necessarily unstable which means that the number of parasitic fixed points generated by this type of solutions is now twice as large. A remedy to this problem can be provided by combining the modified Hebb rule (3.63) with a constraint on the dynamic equations. It consists in forcing the state vectors to have a mean value equal to the bias a, by imposing

$$\frac{1}{n}\sum_{i=1}^{n} x_i = a. \qquad (4.127)$$

One can show that, under these conditions, combinations of two or three prototypes are no longer solutions of the mean field equations. The same conclusion holds for the negative of the prototypes, for the obvious reason that they do not satisfy (4.127) (see reference [Amit et al. 87a]).

4.3.5 The projection rule

In this subsection, we shall rely on the results of reference [Kanter and Sompolinsky 87] in order to establish the mean field equations for the projection rule defined in Chapter 1 (§ 1.2.3). For convenience, we shall not impose a zero diagonal, since we have seen in Subsection 4.2.1 that, in any case, this does not affect the final equations. The very principle of the projection rule suggests that we should decompose the mean state vector $\bar{x}$ into its projections on the subspace $\mathcal{X}$ spanned by the prototype vectors and the orthogonal complement η. We shall thus write the mean vector with respect to the Gibbs distribution (4.6) in the form

$$\bar{x} = \sum_{k=1}^{p} \bar{b}_k \, \xi^{(k)} + \bar{\eta} = X \bar{b} + \bar{\eta} \tag{4.128}$$

where the vector $\bar{b} = [\bar{b}_1, \bar{b}_2, \ldots, \bar{b}_p]^T$ of the mean components is given by

$$\bar{b} = (X^T X)^{-1} X^T \bar{x}. \tag{4.129}$$

Let us now follow the approach of Subsection 4.2.1. With the Hamiltonian (4.18) and the synaptic matrix (1.35), the partition function can be expressed as

$$Z = \text{Tr}_x \, \exp[\frac{\beta}{2} x^T X C^{-1} X^T x] \tag{4.130}$$

where $C = X^T X$. Using identity (4.27) with $u = \sqrt{\beta} X^T x$ and $y = \sqrt{\beta n} v$, we can rewrite the partition function in the form

$$Z = \text{Tr}_x \left(\frac{\beta n}{2\pi}\right)^{p/2} (\det C)^{1/2} \int \prod dv_k \, \exp$$
$$\left[-\frac{1}{2} \beta n v^T C v + \sqrt{n} \beta v^T X^T x\right]. \tag{4.131}$$

The components v_k of vector v are integration variables in expression (4.131) just as in Subsection 4.2.1. To within a constant factor, these components can however be interpreted as the components of the state vector with respect to the prototypes. Indeed, in view of Lemma 4.1, the right hand side of (4.131) is dominated by the maximum of the integrand when $n \to \infty$ and this maximum is given by

$$v = n^{-1/2} b = n^{-1/2} (X^T X)^{-1} X^T x. \tag{4.132}$$

Exchanging the integration and trace operators and using identity (4.33), one obtains

$$Z = \left(\frac{\beta n}{2\pi}\right)^{p/2} (\det C)^{1/2} \int \prod dv_k \, \exp$$
$$\left[-\frac{1}{2} \beta n v^T C v + \sum_{i=1}^{n} \log 2 \cosh \beta \sqrt{n} \sum_{k=1}^{p} \xi_i^{(k)} v_k\right]. \tag{4.133}$$

By means of a saddle point integration, one finds that the free energy is given by

$$f(\overline{v},\beta) = \frac{1}{2}\,\overline{v}^T\,C\,\overline{v} - \frac{1}{\beta n}\sum_{i=1}^{n}\log 2\cosh\beta\sqrt{n}\sum_{\ell=1}^{p}\xi_i^{(\ell)}\,\overline{v}_\ell. \tag{4.134}$$

In view of (4.132) and the fact that $C = X^T X$, this expression can be rewritten as

$$f(\overline{b},\beta) = \frac{1}{2n}\,\overline{b}^T(X^T X)\overline{b} - \frac{1}{\beta n}\sum_{i=1}^{n}\log 2\cosh\beta\sum_{\ell=1}^{p}\xi_i^{(\ell)}\overline{b}_\ell \tag{4.135}$$

and, when $n \to \infty$, one obtains

$$f(\overline{b},\beta) = \frac{1}{2}\parallel\overline{b}\parallel^2 - \frac{1}{\beta} \ll \log 2\cosh\beta\sum_{\ell=1}^{p}\xi_i^{(\ell)}\overline{b}_\ell \gg. \tag{4.136}$$

It is clear now that this expression has exactly the same form as (4.38) and the following property thus holds.

Theorem 4.6 *The mean field equations for Hebb's law and the projection rule are identical, provided that the mean state vector is represented by its overlaps $\overline{m}_k$ in the first case and by the components $\overline{b}_k$ along the prototypes in the second case. In particular, both construction rules for the synaptic matrix lead to the same results concerning the existence and stability of Mattis solutions and mixture states.*

4.4 The mean field equations for $p \sim \alpha n$

The analysis performed in Subsections 4.2.1 and 4.2.2 relied on the assumption that the number of prototypes p was finite. In order to investigate the behaviour of the networks near saturation, a new derivation of the relevant equations is in principle required. However, this leads to rather lengthy developments; for a detailed account we refer to references [Amit et al. 87b] and [Amit et al. 87a]. Here, we shall simply give an outline of the main ideas and write down the final form of the mean field equations. The analysis is limited to asynchronous updating.

4.4.1 General case

When the number of stored prototypes tends to infinity, the possibility exists that the overlap of the state vector with each prototype tends to zero. This could in particular occur for orthogonal prototypes since in this case one can show that $\parallel m \parallel\leq 1$. In order to exclude this uninteresting type of solution from the outset, we shall assume that the state vector has macroscopic overlaps with a *finite* number ν of prototypes which, for this reason, are called *main prototypes*; the correlation with the remaining $p - \nu$ *secondary prototypes* will be represented by a noise source. We define thus the ν-vector

$$\overline{m} = [\overline{m}_1, \overline{m}_2, \ldots, \overline{m}_\nu]^T \tag{4.137}$$

whose components are the mean overlaps

$$\overline{m}_k = \frac{1}{n} \sum_{i=1}^{n} \xi_i^{(k)} \, \overline{x}_i, \qquad k = 1, 2, \ldots, \nu, \tag{4.138}$$

with the ν main prototypes. In order to clarify the steps leading to the expression of the free energy, let us start from formula (4.32) of the partition function where we now put $p = \alpha n$. In the sum $\sum_{i=1}^{n} x_i \sum_{k=1}^{\alpha n} m_k \, \xi_i^{(k)}$ which appears as argument of the exponential, we separate the terms related to the main prototypes from the others and rewrite this sum as

$$\sum_{i=1}^{n} x_i \left(\sum_{\ell=1}^{\nu} \xi_i^{(\ell)} m_\ell + \sum_{\ell=\nu+1}^{\alpha n} \xi_i^{(\ell)} m_\ell \right). \tag{4.139}$$

For $n \to \infty$, the sum over the secondary prototypes is composed of an infinite number of independent random variables $\xi_i^{(\ell)} m_\ell$ having zero mean and variance m_ℓ^2, as a consequence of (4.67). In view of the central limit theorem [Cramér 57], this sum tends to a zero mean Gaussian variable and its variance, averaged over the Gibbs distribution (4.6), is given by

$$\alpha \, r = \sum_{\ell=\nu+1}^{\alpha n} \overline{m}_\ell^2. \tag{4.140}$$

To compute the partition function, the *replica method* takes as starting point the identity

$$\log Z = \lim_{\tau \to \infty} \frac{Z^\tau - 1}{\tau} \tag{4.141}$$

and calculates Z^τ as the product of τ partition functions corresponding to τ distinct realizations or *replica* of the system under consideration. The Edward-Anderson *order parameter*

$$q_{\rho,\sigma} = \frac{1}{n} \sum_{i=1}^{n} x_i^{(\rho)} x_i^{(\sigma)} \tag{4.142}$$

is introduced, where ρ and σ are indices referring to different realizations [Edwards and Anderson 75]. In the more restricted framework of the *symmetric replica theory*, one assumes that, at thermodynamic equilibrium, these parameters all take a common value q. Under these conditions, one can show that the free energy is given by

$$
\begin{aligned}
f \; = \; & \frac{1}{2}\alpha + \frac{1}{2}\sum_{k=1}^{\nu}\overline{m}_k^2 + \frac{\alpha}{2\beta}\left[\log(1-\beta+\beta q) - \frac{\beta q}{1-\beta+\beta q}\right] \\
& + \; \frac{\alpha\beta r}{2}(1-q) - \frac{1}{\beta\sqrt{2\pi}}\int dz\, e^{-z^2/2} \\
& \times \; \ll \log 2\cosh\beta\left[\sqrt{\alpha r}\,z + \sum_{k=1}^{\nu}\xi_i^{(k)}\overline{m}_k\right] \gg
\end{aligned}
\tag{4.143}
$$

where z is a Gaussian variable with zero mean and unit variance [Amit et al. 87b]. The mean field equations are obtained by equating to zero the partial derivatives of f with respect to $\overline{m}_k$, q and r. This gives

$$
\overline{m}_k = \ll \xi_i^{(k)}\tanh\beta\left[\sqrt{\alpha r}\,z + \sum_{\ell=1}^{\nu}\xi_i^{(\ell)}\overline{m}_\ell\right]\gg,
\tag{4.144}
$$

$$
r = \frac{q}{(1-\beta+\beta q)^2},
\tag{4.145}
$$

$$
q = \ll \tanh^2\beta\left[\sqrt{\alpha r}\,z + \sum_{\ell=1}^{\nu}\xi_i^{(\ell)}\overline{m}_\ell\right]\gg,
\tag{4.146}
$$

where the notation $\ll \cdot \gg$ now stands for a combined mean with respect to the distribution of the $\xi_i^{(k)}$ $(k=1,2,\ldots,\nu)$ and with respect to the noise z. These equations have two types of stable solutions :

• A solution $\overline{m} = 0$, $r \neq 0, q \neq 0$ which has no macroscopic overlap with any of the main prototypes and which therefore does not correspond to an associative memory behaviour of the network.

• Solutions $\overline{m} \neq 0$ which, as we shall see, exist only if α is sufficiently small (typically $\alpha < \alpha_c \simeq 0.14$ for $T = 0$) and which are useful for pattern retrieval. Among these solutions, the most important ones are of the type

$$
\overline{m} = [\overline{m}_1, 0, \ldots, 0]^T
\tag{4.147}
$$

where the mean state vector is essentially lined up with a single prototype.

Let us now examine in somewhat more detail the properties of solutions (4.147) when T tends to zero and, to this end, let us take the statistical mean of the right hand side in (4.144) with respect to the Gaussian noise z. One finds that

$$\frac{1}{\sqrt{2\pi}} \int_{-\infty}^{+\infty} e^{-z^2/2} \tanh \beta(\sqrt{\alpha r}\, z + x)dz \ \text{ where } x = \xi_i^{(1)} \overline{m}_1. \tag{4.148}$$

When $|z|$ is sufficiently large, the hyperbolic tangent has the same sign as z and, since the contribution of an odd integrand is zero, the integral (4.148) becomes, for $T = \beta^{-1}$ tending to zero,

$$\sqrt{\frac{2}{\pi}} \int_0^{x/\sqrt{\alpha r}} e^{-z^2/2}\, dz = 2\,\mathrm{erf}\left(\frac{x}{\sqrt{\alpha r}}\right). \tag{4.149}$$

Equation (4.144) simplifies to

$$\overline{m}_1 = 2 \ll \xi_i^{(1)}\,\mathrm{erf}\left(\frac{\xi_i^{(1)}\overline{m}_1}{\sqrt{\alpha r}}\right) \gg \tag{4.150}$$

where the mean $\ll \cdot \gg$ is now over the distribution of the $\xi_i^{(1)}$ only. However, since erf is an odd function, the solution for $T \to 0$ can be written as

$$\overline{m}_1 = 2\,\mathrm{erf}\left(\frac{\overline{m}_1}{\sqrt{\alpha r}}\right) = \sqrt{\frac{2}{\pi}} \int_0^{\overline{m}_1/\sqrt{\alpha r}} e^{-z^2/2}\, dz \tag{4.151}$$

where r remains to be computed from equations (4.145) and (4.146). When $\beta \to \infty$, one can see that $q \to 1$, while

$$r = \frac{1}{(1-G)^2} \tag{4.152}$$

with

$$G = \beta(1 - q) = \beta \ll \cosh^{-2} \beta\left[\sqrt{\alpha r}\, z + x\right] \gg . \tag{4.153}$$

In the latter expression, the mean with respect to the noise variable z, can be written more explicitly as the integral

$$\frac{1}{\sqrt{2\pi}} \int_{-\infty}^{+\infty} \exp\left\{ -\frac{z^2}{2} - \log \cosh^2 \beta\left[\sqrt{\alpha r}\, z + x\right] \right\} dz . \tag{4.154}$$

Since $\beta \to \infty$, it suffices to expand the argument of the exponential near $z = -x/\sqrt{\alpha r}$ and this yields

$$\frac{1}{\sqrt{2\pi}} \int_{-\infty}^{+\infty} \exp\left[-\frac{z^2}{2} - \beta^2(\sqrt{\alpha r}\, z + x)^2 \right] dz . \tag{4.155}$$

Applying finally Lemma 4.1, one obtains

$$G = \frac{1}{\sqrt{2\alpha r}} \exp\left(-\frac{\overline{m}_1^2}{2\alpha r}\right). \tag{4.156}$$

The three equations (4.151), (4.152) and (4.156) can be combined into a single
equation in terms of the variable $y = \overline{m}_1/\sqrt{\alpha r}$, i.e.

$$y = \frac{2\sqrt{2}\,\text{erf}(y)}{\sqrt{2\alpha} + \exp\left(-y^2/2\right)}.$$ (4.157)

Remark • Except for the factor $\sqrt{r}$ in the upper integration limit, equation
(4.151) is identical to formula (3.29) obtained by Kinzel. The thermodynamic
extension offers thus the advantage that it takes into account the noise due to
the correlation of the state vector with the secondary prototypes. It is also
interesting to compare equations (4.151) and (4.72). Since the erf and tanh
functions have similar shapes, one concludes that the mean field equations
for $p = \alpha n$ and $T = 0$ are qualitatively equivalent to those for finite p and
$T \sim \sqrt{\alpha r}$. In other words, one can consider that the correlation between the
state vector and the secondary prototypes (represented by αr) has the same
effect as thermal noise and leads thus to residual errors ($\overline{m}_1 \neq 1$) even when
$T = 0$.

Equation (4.157) always has a solution $y = \overline{m}_1 = 0$, which is uninteresting
from the point of view of associative memories; it is the only possible solution
if α is too large. However, when $\alpha < \alpha_c \simeq 0.14$, two nonzero solutions appear,
having opposite signs and absolute values close to unity which means that the
state vector coincides almost exactly with prototype $\xi^{(1)}$. Indeed, even for
$\alpha = 0.14$, the value of $|\overline{m}_1|$ is about 0.96, which, in view of (3.28), corresponds
to a residual error rate $d/n \simeq 2\%$ where d is the Hamming distance between the
two vectors. Just as for the case of finite p, there are thus $2p = 2\alpha n$ solutions
of the type (4.147). When $\alpha \to 0$, the value of $|\overline{m}_1|$ tends exponentially fast
to unity. Indeed, in this case, expression (4.156) shows that $G \to 0$ and hence
that $r \to 1$. Moreover, from (4.151) one deduces that

$$1 - \overline{m}_1 = \sqrt{\frac{2}{\pi}} \int_{\overline{m}_1/\sqrt{\alpha}}^{\infty} e^{-z^2/2}\, dz.$$ (4.158)

Applying then the asymptotic formula (3.49), where the function Q is given
by (3.46), one finds that

$$1 - \overline{m}_1 \simeq \sqrt{\frac{2\alpha}{\pi}}\, e^{-1/2\alpha}.$$ (4.159)

These $2p$ solutions thus converge monotonically towards the $2p$ Mattis solutions
examined in Subsection 4.3.1. It should also be observed that these results are
in good qualitative agreement with those obtained by the statistical approach of
Subsection 3.2.2. Indeed, if one assumes that the overlaps with the prototypes

$\xi^{(\nu+1)} \ldots \xi^{(\alpha n)}$ are all identical and equal to $1/\sqrt{n}$, then the variance r is equal to unity, in view of (4.140) and equation (4.151) is then identical to (3.29) obtained in reference [Kinzel 85].

Taking into account relation (3.28) and the approximate value (4.159), one observes that the residual error rate is given by

$$\frac{d}{n} \simeq \sqrt{\frac{\alpha}{2\pi}}\, e^{-1/2\alpha}. \tag{4.160}$$

This residual error rate can be made arbitrarily small, provided that α is sufficiently small, but still different from zero. In other words, we recover here, in the framework of the thermodynamic extension, the same qualitative conclusion as in Subsection 3.3.3, namely, that the number of stored prototypes p can grow linearly with n, provided that some residual error rate is tolerated. However, there is a quantitative disagreement between (4.160) and Newman's result [Newman 88], because (4.160) indicates that the radius of the energy barrier decreases faster than the relation $\rho \sim e^{-1/2\alpha}$ indicated in the second remark following Theorem 3.15. This leads to the property below.

Theorem 4.7 *When the number of prototypes increases proportionally to the number of neurons, as $p \sim \alpha n$, then the network will behave as an associative memory only if $\alpha < \alpha_c \simeq 0.14$. The residual error rate after convergence is of the order of $\sqrt{\alpha}\, e^{-1/2\alpha}$.*

Remarks • The replica method introduced by Kirkpatrick and Sherrington [Kirkpatrick and Sherrington 78] has been applied by several authors to the investigation of recursive networks. A critical point of this theory is to justify that the expressions of Z^τ obtained for integer τ can be analytically continued to noninteger values when $\tau \to 0$ [Kirkpatrick and Sherrington 78], [Stephen 83], [Derrida 81], [Thouless et al. 77]. Moreover, the theory of *symmetric replica* assumes that the minimum of the free energy is reached for identical values of the order parameters $q_{\rho,\sigma}$ for the different replica. It is known that, for $T = 0$ this hypothesis leads to (weakly) negative values of the entropy when the state vector coincides with a prototype [Mézard et al. 86], [Thouless et al. 77]. In order to remove the limitations resulting from this hypothesis, a scheme for *replica symmetry breaking* has been proposed [Parisi 80] with the effect that the value 0.14 of α_c is corrected into 0.145, which is indeed closer to the experimental observations. [Crisanti et al. 86].

• If it is required that the *absolute* number d of residual errors should go to zero when $n \to \infty$, then relation (4.160) imposes that $\alpha = p/n < 1/2\log n$. This is exactly the limitation $p < n/2\log n$ established in Theorem 3.9.

For $T \neq 0$, solutions of the type (4.147) with $\overline{m}_1 \neq 0$ still exist provided α is smaller than some critical value $\alpha_c(T)$. This threshold value decreases when the temperature increases to unity, as shown in Figure 4.2.

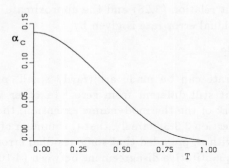

Figure 4.2 : Critical memory occupation α_c as a function of temperature T. (Reprinted by permission of Academic Press Inc. ©1987)

For $T > 1$, only the solution $\overline{m}_1 = 0$ exists, just as for finite values of p.

4.4.2   Some particular cases

We shall now briefly point out some results concerning mixture solutions, biased prototypes, the projection rule and nonlinear synaptic weights in networks near saturation $(p \sim \alpha n)$.

Just as for finite p, symmetric mixture solutions exist here too. These are characterized by a ν-vector (4.137) of the form

$$\overline{m} = \mu_s [\underbrace{\pm 1,\ \pm 1, \ldots, \pm 1}_{s}, \underbrace{0, \ldots, 0}_{\nu - s}]^T. \tag{4.161}$$

For $T = 0$, only mixed solutions of odd order s are stable, while those of even order are unstable, as was the case for finite p. The mixed solutions exist only if $\alpha < \alpha_s$ and the value of α_s decreases as $1/s$ when s becomes large.

For prototypes biased according to distribution (3.56), the mean field equations (4.144)–(4.146) keep the same general form. With the modified Hebbian rule (3.63), these equations can be written as (see reference [Amit et al. 87a]) :

$$\overline{m}_k = \ll (\xi_i^{(k)} - a)\ \tanh \beta \left[\sqrt{\alpha r}\, z + \sum_{\ell=1}^{\nu} (\xi_i^{(\ell)} - a)\, \overline{m}_\ell \right] \gg, \tag{4.162}$$

$$r = \frac{q(1 - a^2)^2}{[1 - \beta(1 - a^2)(1 - q)]^2}, \tag{4.163}$$

$$q = \ll \tanh^2 \beta \left[\sqrt{\alpha r}\, z + \sum_{\ell=1}^{\nu} (\xi_i^{(\ell)} - a)\, \overline{m}_\ell \right] \gg .$$ (4.164)

The main effect of the bias a is that it lowers the critical value α_c below which solutions of the type (4.147) exist with $\overline{m}_1 \neq 0$. The dependence of α_c on a is approximately given by

$$\alpha_c(a) \sim \alpha_c (1 - |a|)^2.$$ (4.165)

This result is consistent with the bound (3.67) obtained for finite p via the statistical approach. Here too, modification (3.63) of the Hebbian rule is not sufficient to remove completely the detrimental effect of the bias. A more satisfactory solution consists in combining (3.63) with constraint (4.127). The main result is that the value $\alpha_c(a)$ below which prototypes can be stored is now considerably larger than the value given by (4.165) and even larger than $\alpha_c(0) = 0.14$ for almost all values of a as seen in Figure 4.3 [Amit et al. 87a].

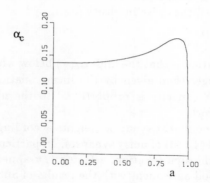

Figure 4.3 : Critical memory occupation rate α_c as a function of bias a. (Reprinted by permission of American Physical Society ©1987)

Investigation of the projection rule in the case $p \sim \alpha n$ [Kanter and Sompolinsky 87] does not bring new results, except that the number of stored prototypes can be equal to the dimension n of the network, i.e. $\alpha_c = 1$, provided the temperature is low enough, although not necessarily zero. This conclusion is not really surprising since it was shown in Subsection 1.2.3 that the projection rule guarantees by construction that the prototypes are fixed points, at least for $T = 0$ and as long as $p \leq n$.

Sompolinsky examines the case where some zero mean Gaussian noise ζ_{ij} is superimposed on the synaptic weights computed by Hebb's law [Sompolinsky 86], [Sompolinsky 87]. This gives the expression

$$w_{ij} = \frac{J}{n} \sum_{k=1}^{p} \xi_i^{(k)} \xi_j^{(k)} + \zeta_{ij}. \tag{4.166}$$

The relative noise intensity is measured by the parameter

$$\Delta = \zeta/J, \tag{4.167}$$

where ζ is the variance of the noise, and it is assumed that the noise is not correlated with the prototypes. It is shown in reference [Sompolinsky 86] that networks with nonlinear synapses as well as partially connected networks (so-called *diluted networks*), can be reduced to the model (4.166). In particular, for diluted networks, the synaptic weights are written as

$$w_{ij} = \frac{c_{ij}}{n\gamma} \sum_{k=1}^{p} \xi_i^{(k)} \xi_j^{(k)} \tag{4.168}$$

where $c_{ij} = c_{ji}$ is a random variable taking the values $+1$ and 0 with probability γ and $(1 - \gamma)$ respectively. One can show that this situation can be reduced to the model (4.166) with the noise intensity given by

$$\Delta = [\alpha(1 - \gamma)/\gamma]^{1/2}. \tag{4.169}$$

A result of this investigation is that the limit $\alpha_c(\gamma)$ below which prototypes can be stored is slightly larger than given by the linear relation $\alpha_c(\gamma) = \gamma \, \alpha_c(1)$ which assumes that the capacity is proportional to the number of synaptic connections in the network.

Similarly, the case of nonlinear synaptic weights according to (3.89) can also be reduced to the model (4.166) of noisy synapses. In particular, for the clipped Hebb rule, where f is the sign function, a factor $1/\pi$ appears in the capacity estimates which is in good agreement with the results of Subsection 3.3.2. The problem of nonlinear synaptic weights has also been examined by van Hemmen and, more particularly, the problem of removing the large number of parasitic fixed points generated in this case [van Hemmen 87].

Chapter 5

Higher order networks

The different approaches developed in the preceding chapters have shown that the network storage capacity is limited in that it grows at most linearly with the dimension of the network, whereas the total number of state vectors increases exponentially as 2^n. One way of increasing the capacity is to exploit, not only the information provided by the individual elements of the state vector, as we have done so far, but also the correlations between these elements. According to this idea, the synaptic potential is then defined as a linear combination of the components x_j and the products $x_j x_k$ between the components of the state vector. This leads then to the following form for the dynamic equations :

$$x_i(t+1) = \text{Sgn}\left[\sum_j w_{ij}\, x_j(t) + \sum_j \sum_{k>j} w_{ijk}\, x_j(t)x_k(t) - \theta_i\right]. \qquad (5.1)$$

The threshold function on the right hand side shows that the discrimination between two state vectors is now performed in a feature space of dimension $n + n(n-1)/2$ instead of n and this should, in principle, lead to a better separability and thus to a corresponding increase in capacity. Obviously, one can pursue this line and include in the synaptic potential also higher order interactions represented by triplets $x_j x_k x_\ell$, quadruplets, etc.

This way of introducing higher order networks, i.e. directly at the level of the dynamic equations, has the advantage of being conceptually straightforward. Its main drawback, however, is that some important properties derived in the preceding chapters do not carry over. Therefore, this approach will be temporarily shelved but will be briefly resumed in Section 5.2. In contrast, the extension proposed by Baldi is potentially more powerful, precisely because it preserves some of the important tools which are necessary to examine among other things the existence of cycles in higher order networks [Baldi 88b]. Baldi's approach, which takes the energy function as starting point, will be developed in the next section.

133

5.1   Extension via the energy function

5.1.1   Main properties

For convenience, the dynamic equations (1.2) and the energy function (2.14) are repeated below in the particular case of a zero diagonal synaptic matrix :

$$x_i(t+1) = \text{Sgn}\left[\sum_{j \neq i} w_{ij}\, x_j(t) - \theta_i\right], \qquad i = 1, 2, \ldots, n, \tag{5.2}$$

$$E(x) = -\sum_{i=1}^{n} \sum_{j>i} w_{ij}\, x_i\, x_j + \sum_{i=1}^{n} \theta_i\, x_i + \theta_0. \tag{5.3}$$

One observes that the dynamic equations (5.2) can be rewritten in terms of the energy in the form

$$x_i(t+1) = \text{Sgn}\left[-\partial E / \partial x_i\right], \qquad i = 1, 2, \ldots, n, \tag{5.4}$$

with the convention, analogous to (1.3), that $x_i(t+1) = x_i(t)$ if $\partial E / \partial x_i = 0$.

The extension of the asynchronous mode to higher order networks consists now in taking for the energy function an algebraic form of degree $d > 2$ and in keeping the dynamic equations as given by (5.4). To describe this extension more formally, we consider the set $\mathcal{N} = \{1, 2, \ldots, n\}$ and we denote by $\mathcal{N}_i$ the subset $\mathcal{N} \setminus \{i\}$ obtained by deleting element i. Let J and J_i be subsets respectively of $\mathcal{N}$ and $\mathcal{N}_i$. For any state vector $x \in \{-1, 1\}^n$, one defines the *monomial* x_J by

$$x_J = \prod_{k \in J} x_k \tag{5.5}$$

and $|J|$ is called the *degree of the monomial*. A *multilinear form of degree d* in the n components of a vector x, is a polynomial expression of the type

$$P_{\mathcal{N}}^d(x) = \sum_{J} w_J\, x_J, \qquad w_J \in \mathbf{R}, \tag{5.6}$$

where the sum extends over certain well defined subsets J of $\mathcal{N}$ such that $|J| \leq d$.

A *homogeneous multilinear form of degree d* is defined as

$$\overline{P}_{\mathcal{N}}^d(x) = \sum_{J \in \overline{\mathcal{D}}} w_J\, x_J, \qquad \overline{\mathcal{D}} = \{J \subset \mathcal{N} : |J| = d\}, \tag{5.7}$$

and a *complete multilinear form of degree d* by

$$\hat{P}_{\mathcal{N}}^d(x) = \sum_{J \in \hat{\mathcal{D}}} w_J\, x_J, \qquad \hat{\mathcal{D}} = \{J \subset \mathcal{N} : |J| \leq d\}. \tag{5.8}$$

For homogeneous and complete multilinear forms of degree d in n variables, the number of degrees of freedom is given by

$$r(n,d) = \binom{n}{d} \text{ for } \overline{\mathcal{D}}, \text{ and } r(n,d) = \sum_{i=0}^{d} \binom{n}{i} \text{ for } \hat{\mathcal{D}}, \tag{5.9}$$

respectively. On the other hand, for an arbitrary multilinear form of degree d, the following decomposition holds,

$$P_{\mathcal{N}}^{d}(x) = x_i P_{\mathcal{N}_i}^{d-1}(x) + P_{\mathcal{N}_i}^{d}(x), \tag{5.10}$$

where the forms on the right hand side are homogeneous or complete together with the form on the left hand side. If we put

$$E = -P_{\mathcal{N}}^{d}(x), \tag{5.11}$$

then the dynamic equation (5.4) can be written as

$$x_i(t+1) = \text{Sgn}\left[P_{\mathcal{N}_i}^{d-1}(x(t))\right], \tag{5.12}$$

where $P_{\mathcal{N}_i}^{d-1}$ has $r(n-1, d-1)$ degrees of freedom.

Example A homogeneous form of degree $d = 3$ in $n = 4$ variables (x_1, x_2, x_3, x_4) has $\binom{4}{3} = 4$ degrees of freedom and is written explicitly as

$$\overline{P}_{\mathcal{N}}^{3}(x) = x_1[w_{123}\, x_2\, x_3 + w_{124}\, x_2\, x_4 + w_{134}\, x_3\, x_4] + [w_{234}\, x_2\, x_3\, x_4],$$

where the first expression between brackets is the homogeneous form $\overline{P}_{\mathcal{N}_1}^{2}$ and the second expression is the homogeneous form $\overline{P}_{\mathcal{N}_1}^{3}$. In particular, the dynamic equation (5.12) for asynchronous updating of element x_1 becomes

$$x_1(t+1) = \text{Sgn}[w_{123}\, x_2 x_3 + w_{124}\, x_2 x_4 + w_{134}\, x_3 x_4],$$

where the values of the elements x_2, x_3, x_4 are taken at time t.

Remarks • In view of expression (5.12) of the dynamic equations, it is clear that higher order networks can be considered as threshold functions in a space of dimension $r(n-1, d-1)$. As we shall see in the next section, it is precisely this higher dimensionality which accounts for a corresponding increase in capacity, but at the cost of a larger number of synaptic weights.

• Since the elements of the state vector take on the values $+1$ or -1, only the powers 0 and 1 of the variables have to be considered and there is thus no loss of generality in restricting the energy to multilinear forms.

Since the energy is a multilinear form, a modification of the i-th component of the state vector produces an energy variation given by

$$\Delta E = [x_i(t+1) - x_i(t)] \frac{\partial E}{\partial x_i}. \tag{5.13}$$

Consequently, the dynamic equation (5.4) is equivalent to the updating rule

$$x_i(t+1) = -x_i(t) \quad \text{if and only if} \quad \Delta E < 0 \tag{5.14}$$

and the following property thus holds [Baldi 88b].

Theorem 5.1 *Higher order networks, for which the dynamic equations are expressed in terms of an energy function according to (5.4) and (5.11), are devoid of cycles under asynchronous updating. The fixed points are local minima of the energy.*

Remarks • This result is simply the transposition of Theorem 2.1 to higher order networks. In contrast, for synchronous updating, there is no similar version of Theorem 2.4 and, as a consequence, cycles cannot be excluded, even if the dynamic equations are expressed in terms of an energy function as in (5.4). However, we shall see in the next subsection that, for a particular extension of Hebb's law, cycles are excluded even for the synchronous operating mode.

• It can be seen that the particular form (5.14) of the asynchronous updating rule induces a partial ordering on the vertices of the hypercube C^n. Indeed, consider the edge connecting a vertex x to one of its neighbours $y \in N_1(x)$. If this edge is oriented in the sense $x \to y$, when $E(x) > E(y)$, then it is easily seen that this yields an *acyclic orientation* of the hypercube [Baldi 88a], [Baldi 88b]. This acyclic orientation can be interpreted as an energy landscape where the local minima are fixed points of the network. The *indegree* and *outdegree* of a vertex are respectively defined as the number of edges pointing towards the vertex or leaving it. With this terminology, a fixed point is characterized by a zero outdegree and an indegree equal to n. So far, it has been implicitly assumed that the coefficients w_J of the multilinear forms have been adjusted in such a way that the energy never takes on the same value at two vertices at unit Hamming distance. It is not difficult to see that this is always possible, even if the coefficients are constrained to be rational or integer numbers.

For homogeneous forms, the obvious identity $\overline{P}_N^d(-x) = (-1)^d \, \overline{P}_N^d(x)$, leads to the following property [Baldi 88a].

Theorem 5.2 *Consider a network for which the energy is a homogeneous form of degree d and let x be a fixed point. If d is even, $-x$ is also a fixed point, but if d is odd, $-x$ is a relative maximum of the energy. This property extends in an obvious way to energy functions which are even or odd multilinear forms.*

5.1.2 Generalization of Hebb's rule to higher orders

In Chapter 1 (§ 1.2.2), we have seen that Hebb's law determines the synaptic weights as $w_{ij} = p^{-1} \sum_{k=1}^{p} \xi_i^{(k)} \xi_j^{(k)}$. In the extension of the Hebbian rule proposed by Baldi, the coefficients w_J in the multilinear form (5.6) are defined as

$$w_J = \sum_{k=1}^{p} \xi_J^{(k)}, \tag{5.15}$$

(see reference [Baldi 88a]). For example, the coefficient of monomial $x_1 x_3 x_4$ is $w_{134} = \sum_{k=1}^{p} \xi_1^{(k)} \xi_3^{(k)} \xi_4^{(k)}$. This extension is however not the only possible one. Lee and his coauthors propose the following expression for the energy function,

$$E(x) = - \sum_{k=1}^{p} (x^T \xi^{(k)})^d, \tag{5.16}$$

and it can be verified that it reduces to a sum of homogeneous multilinear forms of the same parity as d by taking into account that x and ξ are elements of $\{-1, 1\}^n$ [Lee et al. 86]. In this case, coefficient w_J of monomial x_J is of the form

$$w_J = \alpha(|J|) \sum_{k=1}^{p} \xi_J^{(k)}, \tag{5.17}$$

where $\alpha(|J|)$ is a natural number which depends on the degree $|J|$ of the monomial. Comparison of the expressions (5.15) and (5.17) shows that the energy function (5.16) is an alternative extension of Hebb's law to higher order networks.

We have seen in Subsection 1.2.2, that the Hebbian rule guarantees exact retrieval of the prototype vectors when they are mutually orthogonal. This property also holds true for higher order networks and, for the generalized Hebb rule (5.15), a proof can be found in [Baldi 88a]. For the extension (5.16), the argument is even simpler. Indeed, starting from the expression (5.16) of the energy, one has

$$\frac{\partial E}{\partial x_i} = -d \sum_{k=1}^{p} \left(x^T \xi^{(k)} \right)^{d-1} \xi_i^{(k)}. \tag{5.18}$$

In particular, when $x(t) = \xi^{(1)}$, this yields

$$\frac{\partial E}{\partial x_i} = -d n^{d-1} \xi_i^{(1)}, \tag{5.19}$$

and the dynamic equation (5.4) gives then $x_i(t+1) = \xi_i^{(1)}$.

The extension of Hebb's law, by specification of the energy function (5.16), has the advantage that it guarantees the absence of cycles, even for synchronous updating, at least for even values of the degree d. This property is stated in the following theorem [Lee et al. 86].

Theorem 5.3 *Higher order networks in synchronous mode, with expression (5.16) as energy function and (5.4) as dynamic equation, are free of cycles for even values of the degree d.*

Proof The energy variation

$$\Delta E = E(x(t) + \delta x) - E(x(t)), \tag{5.20}$$

with $\delta x = x(t+1) - x(t)$, can be expressed as

$$\Delta E = \sum_{i=1}^{n} [x_i(t+1) - x_i(t)] \frac{\partial E}{\partial x_i} + R, \tag{5.21}$$

where, in view of (5.16), R is given by

$$R = -\sum_{k=1}^{p} \sum_{j=2}^{d} \binom{d}{j} (x(t)^T \xi^{(k)})^{d-j} (\delta x^T \xi^{(k)})^j. \tag{5.22}$$

For each component in which the state vectors $x(t+1)$ and $x(t)$ disagree, the first term in (5.21) gives a negative contribution, equal to $-2|\partial E/\partial x_i|$. As for the R term, it is shown hereafter that it is also negative, with the consequence that the energy is monotonically decreasing along a trajectory and that cycles therefore cannot exist. In order to show that R is indeed negative, one observes that it can be rewritten as

$$R = -\sum_{k=1}^{p} \left(x(t)^T \xi^{(k)} \right)^d \sum_{j=2}^{d} \binom{d}{j} z^j, \tag{5.23}$$

with

$$z = \left[\delta x^T \xi^{(k)} \right]^j / \left[x(t)^T \xi^{(k)} \right]^j. \tag{5.24}$$

Because of the fact that d is even, it suffices thus to show that the function

$$f_q(z) = \sum_{j=2}^{2q} \binom{2q}{j} z^j = (1+z)^{2q} - (1+2qz), \tag{5.25}$$

is always positive which is true since $(1+z)^{2q}$ is convex in z and tangential to the straight line

$$y = 1 + 2qz \qquad (5.26)$$

at $z = 0$. □

Remarks • The property stated in Theorem 5.3 can be seen as a natural extension of Theorem 2.4 because, for even values of d, expression (5.16) is indeed negative definite. On the other hand, in the particular case $d = 2$, it can be written as

$$E = -x^T \left(\sum_{k=1}^{p} \xi^{(k)} \xi^{(k)T} \right) x = -x^T X X^T x, \qquad (5.27)$$

which is identical to expression (2.7) of the energy for the usual Hebbian law (1.25) and for zero threshold function.

• For odd values of d, it is in general no longer possible to show that the energy is monotonically decreasing and cycles may thus show up in synchronous updating mode for the generalized Hebb rule (5.16).

5.2 Extension via the dynamic equations

The learning techniques considered in Chapter 6 as well as the pseudo-inverse rule for higher order networks (see references [Personnaz et al. 87a], [Guyon et al. 88a]) deviate radically from the approach developed in the preceding section in that the extension is not performed on the energy function but directly on the dynamic equations. In the latter case, the argument of the sign function in (5.4) is not necessarily the partial derivative of a scalar function of the state vector. Consequently, it is in general no longer possible to find an energy function which is monotonically decreasing along a trajectory of the network. Therefore, cycles may appear, even for asynchronous updating.

One defines a vector of monomials

$$g = [x_J, x_K, \ldots]^T, \qquad J, K \in \overline{\mathcal{D}} \text{ or } \hat{\mathcal{D}}, \qquad (5.28)$$

where, in principle, g contains all elements of the sets $\overline{\mathcal{D}}$ or $\hat{\mathcal{D}}$ defined in (5.7) and (5.8). For example, in the case $n = 3$, $d = 2$, the vector g is explicitly given by

$$g = [x_1 x_2, \ x_1 x_3, \ x_2 x_3]^T, \qquad (5.29)$$

$$g = [1, \ x_1, \ x_2, \ x_3, \ x_1 x_2, \ x_1 x_3, \ x_2 x_3]^T, \qquad (5.30)$$

according to whether the set considered is $\overline{\mathcal{D}}$ or $\hat{\mathcal{D}}$. The dimension of vector g is $r(n, d)$ as defined in (5.9). In practice, the pseudo-inverse rule (see § 1.2.3) for higher order networks applies mainly for synchronous updating and the dynamic equations are then

$$x(t+1) = \text{Sgn}\,[W\,g(t)], \tag{5.31}$$

where the synaptic matrix W has dimension $n \times r(n,d)$. In order to impose the prototypes $\xi^{(1)}, \xi^{(2)}, \dots, \xi^{(p)}$ as fixed points, one computes W as solution of the equation

$$W\,\Gamma = X, \tag{5.32}$$

where X is the matrix (1.21) of the prototype vectors and where Γ is the matrix

$$\Gamma = [\gamma^{(1)}, \gamma^{(2)}, \dots, \gamma^{(p)}]. \tag{5.33}$$

Here the definition of $\gamma^{(k)}$ is similar to that given in (5.28) for vector g but with $\xi^{(k)}$ instead of x. More precisely, one has

$$\gamma^{(k)} = [\xi_J^{(k)}, \xi_K^{(k)}, \dots]^T, \qquad J, K \in \overline{\mathcal{D}} \text{ or } \hat{\mathcal{D}}. \tag{5.34}$$

In particular, the row dimension of Γ is $r(n,d)$. If Γ has full column rank, a solution of (5.32) is given by

$$W = X(\Gamma^T\Gamma)^{-1}\,\Gamma^T. \tag{5.35}$$

With the pseudo-inverse rule defined in Subsection 1.2.3, the number of prototypes which could be stored was limited to $p \leq n$. Here, we see that for higher order networks the limit lies in principle much higher, since it is now given by $p \leq r(n,d)$ [Baldi and Venkatesh 87].

5.3   Absolute capacity limits - total number of fixed points

So far, we have seen how to perform the extension of recursive networks to higher order interactions, either via the energy function, with the advantage that cycles can be excluded for certain updating modes, or directly via the dynamic equations. Let us now examine how the absolute capacity limitations can be generalized. Reference [Baldi 88b] gives the following extension of Theorem 2.12.

Theorem 5.4 *If, for any set of p vectors in $\{-1, 1\}^n$, there exists a multilinear form of degree d for the energy function, such that these p vectors become fixed points of the system (i.e. local minima of the energy), then an upper bound for the capacity is given by*

$$p \leq r(n-1, d-1), \tag{5.36}$$

where $r(n,d)$ is defined in (5.9) for homogeneous and complete multilinear forms. Moreover, if each set of p vectors is nondegenerate, then a lower bound on the capacity is

$$p \geq \frac{r(n,d)}{n+1}. \tag{5.37}$$

Proof Let $\xi^{(1)}, \xi^{(2)}, \ldots, \xi^{(p)}$ be a set of p binary vectors. By assumption, there exists a multilinear form $P_{\mathcal{N}}^d$ such that, according to the dynamic equation (5.12),

$$\xi_i^{(k)} = \text{Sgn}\,[P_{\mathcal{N}_i}^{d-1}(\xi^{(k)})], \quad i = 1, 2, \ldots, n, \quad k = 1, 2, \ldots, p. \tag{5.38}$$

We have seen in Section 1.1, that the right hand side can be considered as a threshold function defined in p points but where the number of variables is now $r(n-1, d-1)$. Thus, for the example given in Subsection 5.1.1, of a homogeneous form of degree $d = 3$ in $n = 4$ variables, the equations (5.38) for $i = 1$ become here

$$\text{Sgn}\left\{ [w_{123}\ w_{124}\ w_{134}] \begin{bmatrix} \xi_2^{(1)}\xi_3^{(1)} & \cdots & \xi_2^{(p)}\xi_3^{(p)} \\ \xi_2^{(1)}\xi_4^{(1)} & \cdots & \xi_2^{(p)}\xi_4^{(p)} \\ \xi_3^{(1)}\xi_4^{(1)} & \cdots & \xi_3^{(p)}\xi_4^{(p)} \end{bmatrix} \right\}$$

$$= \left[\xi_1^{(1)} \quad \cdots \quad \xi_1^{(p)} \right]. \tag{5.39}$$

By hypothesis, there exists, for each of the 2^p possible right hand sides, a corresponding vector of coefficients $[w_{123}\ w_{124}\ w_{134}]^T$ which satisfies (5.39). More generally, the assumptions imply that the number $B_{r(n-1,d-1)}^p$ of threshold functions in $r(n-1, d-1)$ variables and specified in p points is at least equal to 2^p. By analogy with the proof of Theorem 2.12, one obtains then inequality (5.36).

In order for $\xi^{(k)}$ to be a fixed point of the network, it suffices to find for the energy a multilinear form $P_{\mathcal{N}}^d$, such that it takes some arbitrary value a in $\xi^{(k)}$ and some higher value $b > a$ in each of the n neighbours of $\xi^{(k)}$ (i.e. the n vertices located at unit Hamming distance from $\xi^{(k)}$). This gives for the p prototypes $\xi^{(k)}$ a system of $p(n+1)$ equations in the $r(n, d)$ unknown coefficients of $P_{\mathcal{N}}^d$. The set of vectors $\xi^{(1)}, \xi^{(2)}, \ldots, \xi^{(p)}$ is said to be nondegenerate if this system of equations is soluble when the number of equations is smaller or equal to the number of unknowns, i.e. if $p(n+1) \leq r(n, d)$. The minimum value for p satisfying this inequality leads to the lower bound (5.37). Taking into account the expressions (5.9) of $r(n, d)$, it is clear that the capacity limits obtained for higher order networks can be considerably larger than in the classical situation $d = 2$ considered in Theorems 2.12 and 2.13. $\qquad\square$

Remark • At first glance, one may think that the argument used above not only imposes fixed points at some prescribed locations, but also imposes a basin of attraction of unit radius around each of these points. In general this is not so because, if y is a vector at unit Hamming distance from $\xi^{(k)}$, one has by construction $E(y) > E(\xi^{(k)})$ but y itself can have a neighbour $z \neq \xi^{(k)}$ and such that $E(z) < E(y)$. The oriented graph in the neighbourhood of $\xi^{(k)}$ and illustrating this situation, is shown in Figure 5.1. However this technique

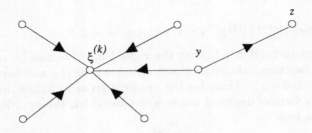

Figure 5.1 : Example of an oriented graph around a fixed point.

can easily be extended to the storage of cycles [Baldi 88b]. First, it should be recalled that the forms $P_{\mathcal{N}_i}^{d-1}(x)$ in the right hand side of equation (5.12) are in fact the partial derivatives of the same multilinear form $P_{\mathcal{N}}^{d}(x)$. In order to generate some predetermined cycle by an asynchronous network, it will be sufficient to take multilinear forms $P_{\mathcal{N}_i}^{d-1}$ which are completely independent from each other. For each element x_i, one has then $r(n-1, d-1)$ degrees of freedom and, for each edge orientation in C^n parallel to component i, one obtains an inequality in these $r(n-1, d-1)$ coefficients. In order to store a cycle of length m, one has to impose the orientation of the m edges of the cycle and of the $m(n-1)$ edges adjacent to the cycle, as illustrated in Figure 5.2.

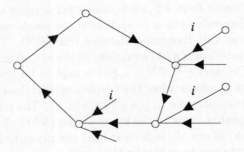

Figure. 5.2 : Oriented graph of a cycle.

Along each direction i, there are thus at most m constraints and the problem can in principle be solved if $m < r(n-1, d-1)$.

Just as in Chapter 3, one can also apply here the Cover argument [Cover 65] to show that, asymptotically, the capacity can reach the value $2r(n-1, d-1)$. The nondegeneracy hypothesis which has to be satisfied here is that, for all i $(i = 1, 2, \ldots, n)$, the multilinear form $P_{\mathcal{N}_i}^{d-1}(x)$ can assume arbitrary prescribed values in any subset of at most $r(n-1, d-1)$ points taken in the set $\{\xi^{(1)}, \xi^{(2)}, \ldots, \xi^{(p)}\}$. The proof is similar to that given for Theorem 3.1 where n should be replaced by $r(n-1, d-1)$ since this is the dimension of the space on which the threshold functions at the right hand side of (5.12) are defined. Consequently, the following generalization of Theorem 3.1 is obtained.

Theorem 5.5 *In the nondegenerate case defined above, the capacity can reach the value $p = 2r(n-1, d-1)$, in the sense that, for all $\epsilon > 0$, the probability that a fraction $(1 - \epsilon)$ of the $2r(n-1, d-1)$ vectors can be imposed as fixed points, tends to unity, when the dimension of the network tends to infinity.*

Remark • In Section 2.1, we have already pointed out that recursive networks may provide an efficient computational tool for the solution of optimization problems with combinatorial complexity. The condition was that the cost function should have the form of an energy function associated with the network. This field of application is now considerably extended by the introduction of higher order networks in that the cost function is no longer restricted to be quadratic but can, in principle, be of arbitrary degree. Reference [Baldi 88b] gives an example of an optimization problem arising in coding theory, where the cost function is of degree four.

The analysis below [Baldi and Venkatesh 87] gives an estimate of the total number of fixed points in a higher order recursive network and generalizes in this way the result of Theorem 3.19.

Theorem 5.6 *Assume that the energy function is a homogeneous multilinear form and that its coefficients w_J are independent Gaussian random variables with zero mean and unit variance. An asymptotic estimate of the number of fixed points is given by*

$$F \simeq k_d \, 2^{c_d n}, \tag{5.40}$$

where the constants k_d and c_d depend only on the degree d of the energy function.

Proof Since the proof closely follows that of Theorem 3.19, it will be sufficient to point out how the different expressions should be adapted. Taking into account (5.12), the synaptic potential h_i for the state vector $x = [1, 1, \ldots, 1]^T$ is given by

$$h_i = \overline{P}_{\mathcal{N}_i}^{d-1}(x) = \sum_{|J_i|=d-1} w_{i,J_i} \tag{5.41}$$

and, when $n \to \infty$, its distribution tends towards a zero mean Gaussian distribution. The variance is equal to $\binom{n-1}{d-1}$, which is the number of terms in the right hand side of (5.41). On the other hand, the potentials h_i and h_j are correlated and the mean value of the product

$$h_i h_j = \sum_{J_i} \sum_{J_j} w_{i,J_i} w_{j,J_j}, \tag{5.42}$$

is equal to

$$\mathcal{E}(h_i h_j) = \binom{n-2}{d-2}. \tag{5.43}$$

Indeed, there are $\binom{n-2}{d-2}$ subsets of size d in $\mathcal{N}$ which contain both elements i and j. One defines again equivalent Gaussian variables z_i, similar to those of equation (3.118), with $\alpha = \binom{n-2}{d-1}^{1/2}$ and $\beta = \binom{n-2}{d-2}^{1/2}$, since $\mathcal{E}(z_i^2) = \alpha^2 + \beta^2 = \binom{n-1}{d-1}$ and $\mathcal{E}(z_i z_j) = \beta^2$. The number of fixed points is given by expression (3.119) which, by the change of variable $u = -\alpha^{-1}\beta t$, can be written as

$$F = \left(\frac{n-d}{2\pi(d-1)}\right)^{1/2} \int_{-\infty}^{\infty} \left\{2 Q(u) \exp\left[-u^2/2(d-1)\right]\right\}^n$$
$$\exp\left[u^2 d/2(d-1)\right] du, \tag{5.44}$$

where the function Q is defined in (3.46). Since we want to compute the right hand side of this expression by a saddle point integration, we put, just as in Theorem 3.19,

$$\exp[h(u)] = 2 Q(u) \exp[-u^2/2(d-1)],$$
$$\gamma(u) = \exp[u^2 d/2(d-1)]. \tag{5.45}$$

In view of Lemma 4.1, one obtains then the asymptotic expression

$$F \simeq \frac{\gamma(u_0)}{(d-1)^{1/2}\sqrt{-h''(u_0)}} \exp[nh(u_0)], \tag{5.46}$$

where u_0 is the maximum of $h(u)$, i.e. the solution of the equation

$$(d-1) e^{-\frac{u^2}{2}} + (2\pi)^{1/2} u\, Q(u) = 0. \tag{5.47}$$

This gives the estimate (5.40) where k_d et c_d are well defined constants. In fact, coefficient c_d in the exponent varies from 0.2874 for $d = 2$ to 0.9916 for $d = 1000$, which means that for large values of the degree d, almost all vectors are fixed points. Gross and Mézard have obtained a similar result for the total number of fixed points in the framework of a mean field theory applied to a thermodynamic extension of higher order networks [Gross and Mézard 84]. □

5.4 Direct attraction

The purpose of this section is to examine how Theorem 3.10, which constitutes one of the main results of Subsection 3.3.2, can be extended to higher order networks. To start with, we shall assume that the energy function is a homogeneous form (5.7) of degree d for which the coefficients are determined by the extension (5.15) of Hebb's law. One has then

$$E(x) = - \sum_{|J|=d} w_J x_J, \qquad w_J = \sum_{k=1}^{p} \xi_J^{(k)}. \tag{5.48}$$

We shall also assume that the components $\xi_i^{(k)}$ of the prototype vectors are independent random variables taking the values $+1$ and -1 with equal probability. The network is initialized with a vector x at Hamming distance ρn from prototype $\xi^{(1)}$ and an upper bound on the number p of prototypes is sought which ensures direct attraction of x to $\xi^{(1)}$. This bound is essentially the result established by Peretto and Niez in reference [Peretto and Niez 86] and which is also cited by Baldi and Venkatesh [Baldi and Venkatesh 87]. We shall give here a simplified derivation in the spirit of the heuristic approach followed in Subsection 3.3.1. Replacing the energy by its expression (5.48), the dynamic equation (5.4) becomes

$$x_i(t+1) = \mathrm{Sgn} \left[\sum_{|J_i|=d-1} w_{i,J_i} x_{J_i} \right], \quad i = 1, 2, \ldots, n, \tag{5.49}$$

with

$$w_{i,J_i} = \sum_{k=1}^{p} \xi_i^{(k)} \xi_{J_i}^{(k)}. \tag{5.50}$$

The initial vector is directly attracted by $\xi^{(1)}$ if the right hand side of equation (5.49) has the same sign as $\xi_i^{(1)}$ or, in view of expression (5.50), if

$$S_i = \sum_{k=1}^{p} \sum_{|J_i|=d-1} \xi_i^{(1)} \xi_i^{(k)} \xi_{J_i}^{(k)} x_{J_i} > 0, \quad i = 1, 2, \ldots, n. \tag{5.51}$$

If we now separate the term $k = 1$, the quantity S_i can be rewritten as

$$S_i = s_i + z_i. \tag{5.52}$$

In the latter expression,

$$s_i = \sum_{|J_i|=d-1} \xi^{(1)}_{J_i} \, x_{J_i} \,, \tag{5.53}$$

is considered as a "signal" term because, if x is not too different from $\xi^{(1)}$, it brings a positive contribution to S_i. Similarly, z_i is a "noise" term given by

$$z_i = \sum_{k=2}^{p} \sum_{|J_i|=d-1} \xi^{(1)}_i \, \xi^{(k)}_i \, \xi^{(k)}_{J_i} \, x_{J_i} \,. \tag{5.54}$$

In order to estimate s_i, one observes that, if $x = \xi^{(1)}$ (or equivalently if $\rho = 0$), then $x_{J_i} = \xi^{(1)}_{J_i}$ and thus $s_i = \binom{n-1}{d-1}$ since this is the number of $(d-1)$-tuples in $\mathcal{N}_i$. If ρn components of x are altered, then ρ can be interpreted as the probability that a given component of x is in error. In other words,

$$\Pr(x_j = \xi^{(1)}_j) = 1 - \rho\,, \qquad \Pr(x_j = -\xi^{(1)}_j) = \rho. \tag{5.55}$$

Consequently, $\mathcal{E}(x_j) = (1 - 2\rho)\,\xi^{(1)}_j$ and, assuming that the components of x are independent random variables, one obtains then

$$\mathcal{E}(x_{J_i}) = (1 - 2\rho)^{d-1}\,\xi^1_{J_i}\,. \tag{5.56}$$

If we use these mean values to estimate the signal term s_i, we get

$$s_i = \binom{n-1}{d-1}(1 - 2\rho)^{d-1}. \tag{5.57}$$

For the estimation of the noise term z_i, one observes that it consists in a sum of $(p-1)\binom{n-1}{d-1}$ independent random variables with zero mean and unit variance. As a consequence of the central limit theorem [Cramér 57], the distribution of z_i tends for large values of n to a Gaussian distribution with zero mean and variance $\sigma^2 = (p-1)\binom{n-1}{d-1}$. The probability that, after one iteration, x_i coincides with $\xi^{(1)}_i$ is then given by

$$\begin{aligned} 1 - \Pr(S_i < 0) &= 1 - \Pr(z_i < -s_i), \\ &= 1 - Q\left(s_i / \sqrt{(p-1)\binom{n-1}{d-1}}\right), \end{aligned} \tag{5.58}$$

where the function Q is defined in (3.46). This expression holds for a *single* component of a *single* prototype vector. We shall assume here that the probability of direct attraction for the n components of the p prototypes is simply given by

$$R = \left[1 - Q\left(s_i / \sqrt{(p-1)\binom{n-1}{d-1}} \right) \right]^{np}, \tag{5.59}$$

as if these events were all independent. If we require that R should tend to unity when $n \to \infty$, then the following condition should hold:

$$\lim_{n \to \infty} np \, Q\left(s_i / \sqrt{(p-1)\binom{n-1}{d-1}} \right) = 0, \tag{5.60}$$

which is similar to condition (3.51) established in Subsection 3.3.1. Making use of the asymptotic approximation (3.49) for Q and taking into account expression (5.57) of s_i, this condition can be rewritten as

$$\lim_{n \to \infty} \left[\log n + \frac{3}{2} \log p - \frac{1}{2} \log\binom{n-1}{d-1} - (d-1)\log(1-2\rho) \right.$$
$$\left. - \frac{\binom{n-1}{d-1}(1-2\rho)^{2(d-1)}}{2(p-1)} \right] = 0. \tag{5.61}$$

Since, on the other hand,

$$\lim_{n \to \infty} \binom{n-1}{d-1} = \lim_{n \to \infty} n^{d-1}/(d-1)!, \tag{5.62}$$

one observes that relation (5.61) will be satisfied provided p is smaller than the upper bound given in the theorem below.

Theorem 5.7 *If, in a network of order $d \geq 2$, the number p of prototypes satisfies the inequality*

$$p < \frac{(1-2\rho)^{2(d-1)}\, n^{d-1}}{2\, d! \, \log n}, \tag{5.63}$$

then the probability that each prototype has a radius of direct attraction equal to ρn, tends to unity as $n \to \infty$.

Remarks • For $d = 2$, one recovers the result of Theorem 3.10. On the other hand, in the framework of Hebb's law, other expressions than (5.48) can be considered for the energy as, for example, a complete multilinear form (5.8) or expression (5.16) proposed in reference [Lee et al. 86]. In these cases, the energy can be expressed as a sum of homogeneous forms of the type (5.48) and, for the evaluation of the signal and noise terms, the homogeneous form of highest degree will dominate. Consequently, the capacity for these cases is still bounded by an expression of the type $n^{d-1}/2d! \log n$.

• In principle, recursive networks are "completely connected" in the sense that each unit is linked to all other units. Peretto and Niez examine how the capacity of a network could be increased by dividing it into disjoint subnetworks [Peretto and Niez 86]. According to this approach, a prototype is stored as a concatenation of λ partial prototypes of dimension $\nu = n/\lambda$. If we denote by $p(\nu)$ the storage capacity of a subnetwork of dimension ν, then the capacity resulting from the combination of λ subnetworks can, in principle, be as large as

$$p^* = [p(\nu)]^\lambda. \tag{5.64}$$

Peretto and Niez draw the attention to the fact that this last expression rests on the rather unrealistic assumption that *all* concatenations of partial prototypes are meaningful. Let us also observe that this hypothesis is even less realistic if one considers the basins of attraction around the partial prototypes and the resulting domains of attraction produced by concatenation. It is nevertheless interesting to estimate the potential gain which could be obtained by this type of architecture. In order to find the optimal size ν for the subnetworks, the derivative of expression (5.64) with respect to ν is set equal to zero, taking into account that $\lambda = n/\nu$. This yields the equation for ν

$$\log p(\nu) = \nu \, p'(\nu)/p(\nu), \tag{5.65}$$

where $p'(\nu)$ denotes the derivative of $p(\nu)$. Note that this equation is independent of n and thus that the optimal size of the subnetworks is independent of the dimension n of the complete network. In Theorem 5.7 we have seen that the maximum capacity of a network of dimension ν is proportional to $\nu^{d-1}/2d! \log \nu$ in the case of direct attraction. The denominator of this expression increases only slowly with ν when compared to the numerator and for simplicity one assumes that

$$p(\nu) \simeq \nu^{d-1}/K_d, \tag{5.66}$$

where K_d is a constant. With this approximation for $p(\nu)$, the solution of (5.65) yields the following expression

$$\nu = e \, K_d^{1/(d-1)}, \tag{5.67}$$

for the optimal size of the subnetwork, where e is the base of the natural logarithm. If ν is now replaced by this optimal value in (5.66) and (5.64), one finds for the global capacity p^* the expression

$$\log p^* = \frac{n(d-1)}{e \, K^{1/(d-1)}}. \tag{5.68}$$

Comparison of this result with the capacity limit of an unfragmented network of the same degree d, namely

$$\log p = (d-1) \log n - \log K_d, \tag{5.69}$$

leads to the conclusion that subdivision of a network may indeed considerably increase its capacity and that the gain, on a logarithmic scale, is of the order of $n/\log n$.

5.5 Long-term attraction

For higher order networks in asynchronous mode, Newman has investigated the possibility of obtaining a storage capacity p proportional to n^{d-1} [Newman 88]. As in Subsection 3.3.3, these results are based on the existence of an energy barrier around each prototype, provided the scaling factor $\alpha = p/n^{d-1}$ is sufficiently small. We take here the generalization of Hebb's law which leads to the expression (5.16) for the energy. In order to bring the notation closer to that used in Subsection 3.3.3, we shall here denote the energy associated with a state vector x by $H(x)$ and its expression is given by

$$H(x) = - \sum_{k=1}^{p} (x^T \xi^{(k)})^d. \tag{5.70}$$

Newman's main theorem [Newman 88], reproduced below, gives the conditions under which energy barriers are guaranteed to exist around each prototype. It generalizes the simplified statement given in Theorem 3.15 for the particular case $d = 2$.

Theorem 5.8 *There exists a strictly positive $\alpha_c(d)$ such that, if $\alpha = p/n^{d-1} < \alpha_c(d)$ then, with probability approaching unity, there exists around each prototype $\xi^{(k)}$, $(k = 1, 2, \ldots, p)$, a sphere $S(\xi^{(k)}, \rho)$ with $0 \le \rho < 1/2$ such that*

$$H(y) > H(\xi^{(k)}) + \epsilon n^d, \quad \forall y \in S(\xi^{(k)}, \rho), \quad k = 1, 2, \ldots, p, \tag{5.71}$$

for some $\epsilon > 0$. The parameters ρ and ϵ are functions of α and the probability of event (5.71) tends exponentially fast to unity when $n \to \infty$.

Proof We shall here simply indicate the modifications with respect to the arguments given in Theorem 3.15. The energies corresponding to a prototype $\xi^{(1)}$ and a vector y which disagrees with $\xi^{(1)}$ in the first ρn components, are respectively expressed as

$$H(\xi^{(1)}) = -n^d - \sum_{k=2}^{p} (V_n^{(k)} - \tilde{V}_n^{(k)})^d, \tag{5.72}$$

$$H(y) = -[n(1 - 2\rho)]^d - \sum_{k=2}^{p} (V_n^{(k)} + \tilde{V}_n^{(k)})^d, \tag{5.73}$$

where $V_n^{(k)}$ and $\tilde{V}_n^{(k)}$ are given by formula (3.102). Denoting by A the event (5.71), one has

$$1 - \Pr(A) \leq p \begin{pmatrix} n \\ \rho n \end{pmatrix} \Pr\left(H(\xi^{(1)}) - H(y) > -\epsilon\, n^d\right), \tag{5.74}$$

which, in view of (5.72) and (5.73), can also be rewritten in the form

$$1 - \Pr(A) \leq p \begin{pmatrix} n \\ \rho n \end{pmatrix} \Pr\left(\frac{1}{p}\sum_{k=2}^{p} W_n^{(k)} \geq \right.$$

$$\left. \left[1 - (1 - 2\rho)^d - \epsilon\right] \frac{n^{d/2}}{p}\right), \tag{5.75}$$

with

$$W_n^{(k)} = \left(\frac{V_n^{(k)} + \tilde{V}_n^{(k)}}{n^{1/2}}\right)^d - \left(\frac{V_n^{(k)} - \tilde{V}_n^{(k)}}{n^{1/2}}\right)^d. \tag{5.76}$$

The right hand side of (5.75) decreases exponentially fast in n if one can show that asymptotically

$$\Pr\left(\frac{1}{p}\sum_{k=2}^{p} W_n^{(k)} \geq \gamma\, p^{-(d-2)/2d-2}\right) \leq e^{-K\, p^{1/(d-1)}}, \tag{5.77}$$

for a certain $K = K(\gamma, \rho)$ where

$$\gamma = \frac{1 - (1 - 2\rho)^d - \epsilon}{\alpha^{d/2(d-1)}}. \tag{5.78}$$

By means of expressions (5.77) and (3.108), one obtains for the right hand side of inequality (5.75) the following bound

$$p \begin{pmatrix} n \\ \rho n \end{pmatrix} \Pr\left(\frac{1}{p}\sum_{k=2}^{p} W_n^{(k)} \geq \gamma\, p^{-(d-2)/(2d-2)}\right)$$

$$\leq e^{nh(\rho) - K p^{1/(d-1)}}. \tag{5.79}$$

Reference [Newman 88] shows then that, for α smaller than some critical value $\alpha_c(d)$, one can find $0 \leq \rho < 1/2$ and $K(\gamma, \rho)$ such that

$$K\, p^{1/(d-1)} > n\, h(\rho) \tag{5.80}$$

and this completes the main argument of the proof. □

Remark • The proof of the existence of a constant $K(\gamma, \rho)$ satisfying the inequality (5.80), also provides a lower bound for the constant $\alpha_c(d)$ as well as an upper bound for the residual error rate $\rho(\alpha)$ after convergence. One obtains in this way the results of Table 5.3 where the values, already derived in Chapter 3 for $d = 2$, are included for easier comparison [Newman 88].

$d = 2$	$\alpha_c > 0.056$	$\rho(\alpha) < 0.0012$
$d = 3$	$\alpha_c > 0.037$	$\rho(\alpha) < 0.063$
$d = 4$	$\alpha_c > 0.0067$	$\rho(\alpha) < 0.063$

Table 5.3 : The capacity factor α_c and residual error rate $\rho(\alpha)$
as a function of the degree d.

Thus, for $d = 3$, the number of prototypes which can be stored, grows asymptotically as $0.037n^2$ and the residual error rate is at most equal to 0.063. One can expect that these estimates are rather pessimistic since it is known from both experiments and other theoretical approaches that $\alpha_c \sim 0.14$ for networks of order $d = 2$.

We have seen in Subsection 3.3.3, that the residual error rate $\rho(\alpha)$ decreases approximately as $\exp(-1/2\alpha)$ when $\alpha \to 0$. The following theorem generalizes this result for higher order networks [Newman 88].

Theorem 5.9 *In a network of order d where the number of stored prototypes grows as $p = \alpha\, n^{d-1}$, the asymptotic order of magnitude of the residual error rate after convergence is given by the relation*

$$\lim_{\alpha \to 0} \rho(\alpha) = O\left(\exp\left(-\frac{B_d}{\alpha}\right)\right),$$ (5.81)

where

$$B_d = 2^{d-2}\,(d-1)!/(2d-2)!\,.$$ (5.82)

Conversely, for a given residual error rate ρ, an asymptotic bound on α is given by

$$\alpha(\rho) = O\left(\frac{B_d}{\log \rho^{-1}}\right) \qquad for \quad \rho \to 0.$$ (5.83)

As already mentioned in Subsection 3.3.4, it remains true, also for higher order networks, that energy barriers exist around each point of the domain $\{-1, 1\}^n$ which is a linear combination of prototypes according to the general formula

$$\eta = \text{Sgn}\left(\sum_{k=1}^{p} \nu_k\, \xi^{(k)}\right),$$ (5.84)

where $\nu = [\nu_1, \nu_2, \ldots, \nu_p]^T$ is a real vector with $|\nu_k| \leq 1$. This type of *parasitic fixed point* is a generalization of the *mixed solutions* considered in Chapter 4 in the framework of the mean field theory for networks of order $d = 2$. In order for this property to hold true, the coefficients ν_k should satisfy the following conditions :

i) ν has a finite number of nonzero components,

ii) $\sum_{k=1}^{p} a_k \nu_k \neq 0$ where the coefficients a_k can take values ± 1.

Examples of ν vectors satisfying these conditions are those in which there are an odd number of equal nonzero components, such as $(\frac{1}{2}, \frac{1}{2}, \frac{1}{2}, 0, \ldots)$ or those with unequal nonzero components, such as $(\frac{1}{2}, \frac{1}{2}, \frac{1}{4}, \frac{1}{4}, \frac{1}{4}, 0, \ldots)$. The existence of an energy barrier around η is guaranteed by the theorem below [Newman 88], whose proof is similar to that for Theorem 5.8.

Theorem 5.10 *For any vector ν satisfying conditions (i) and (ii) above, there exists a strictly positive $\alpha_c(d, \nu)$ such that, for any $\alpha = p/n^{d-1} < \alpha_c(d, \nu)$, one can find $0 \leq \rho < 1/2$ and $\epsilon > 0$ for which the probability*

$$\Pr\left(H(y) > H(\eta) + \epsilon\, n^d \right), \qquad \forall y \in \mathcal{S}(\eta, \rho), \tag{5.85}$$

tends to unity exponentially fast in n when $n \to \infty$.

One can also obtain asymptotic results, similar to those of Theorem 5.9, and which extend, for linear combinations (5.84), the relationship existing between α and the radius ρn of the energy barrier [Newman 88].

Theorem 5.11 *In a network of order d, where the number of prototypes grows as $p = \alpha\, n^{d-1}$, an asymptotic bound on the radius of the energy barriers around the mixed solutions (5.84) is given by*

$$\lim_{\alpha \to 0} \rho(\alpha) = O\left(\exp\left(-\frac{B_d\, \pi^2(\nu)}{\alpha} \right) \right), \tag{5.86}$$

with B_d defined by formula (5.82) and with

$$\pi(\nu) = \text{Min} \left\{ | \pm \nu_1 \pm \nu_2 \pm \cdots | \right\}, \tag{5.87}$$

where the minimum is taken over all possible choices of $\pm$ signs.

5.6 Thermodynamic extension

We close this chapter by sketching mean field theory for higher order networks. We assume, as in Chapter 4, that the probability of observing a state x follows a Gibbs distribution (4.6) but where the Hamiltonian $H(x)$ is now a multilinear form of degree d. A mean field theory, similar to that presented in Subsection 4.2.1, has to deal here with the additional difficulty that the Hamiltonian is no longer a quadratic form with the consequence that the Gaussian transformation (4.27) cannot be applied for the computation of the partition function. In contrast, the alternative approach, based on a property of the Dirac function and described in equations (4.40)–(4.45), can successfully be applied here to the extension (5.16) of Hebb's law and in the simple case where the number of prototypes is finite. Indeed, if we take as Hamiltonian the expression

$$H(x) = -\frac{1}{d\,n^{d-1}} \sum_{k=1}^{p} (x^T \xi^{(k)})^d, \tag{5.88}$$

then the partition function (4.8) can be written as

$$Z = \mathrm{Tr}_x \exp\left[\frac{\beta}{d\,n^{d-1}} \sum_{k=1}^{p} [g_k(x)]^d \right], \tag{5.89}$$

where $g_k(x)$ is defined by (4.28). Introducing the Dirac function δ, one obtains the equivalent expression

$$Z = \mathrm{Tr}_x \int \prod dm_k \exp\left[\frac{\beta n}{d} \sum_{k=1}^{p} m_k^d \right] \delta(m - n^{-1} g(x)), \tag{5.90}$$

where m and $g(x)$ are p-vectors whose components are respectively m_k and $g_k(x)$, $(k = 1, 2, \ldots, p)$. Replacing next the Dirac function by its inverse transform (4.41), one obtains

$$Z = \left(\frac{n\beta}{2\pi i}\right)^p \mathrm{Tr}_x \int \prod dm_k \prod ds_\ell \exp\left[\frac{\beta n}{d} \sum_{k=1}^{p} m_k^d \right.$$
$$\left. -\beta n \sum_{k=1}^{p} s_k m_k + \beta \sum_{k=1}^{p} s_k g_k(x) \right]. \tag{5.91}$$

Comparison of (5.89) and (5.91) shows that, via the computational trick with the Dirac function, the partition function is now expressed in terms of an exponential of a linear form in x. This allows the use of identity (4.33) and, after permutation of the trace and integration operators, one has

$$Z = \left(\frac{n\beta}{2\pi i}\right)^p \int \prod dm_k \prod ds_\ell \exp\left[\frac{\beta n}{d} \sum_{k=1}^{p} m_k^d - \beta n \sum_{k=1}^{p} s_k m_k \right.$$
$$\left. + \sum_{i=1}^{n} \log 2\cosh\beta \sum_{k=1}^{p} s_k \xi_i^{(k)} \right]. \tag{5.92}$$

Finally, the saddle point integration method of Lemma 4.1 is applied. Equating thus to zero the partial derivatives of the exponent in (5.92) with respect to the integration variables m_k and s_ℓ, one finds the mean field equations

$$\overline{m}_k = \frac{1}{n} \sum_{i=1}^{n} \xi_i^{(k)} \tanh \beta \sum_{\ell=1}^{p} \xi_i^{(\ell)} \overline{m}_\ell^{d-1} \quad (k = 1, 2, \ldots, p), \tag{5.93}$$

$$f(\overline{m}, \beta) = \frac{d-1}{d} \sum_{k=1}^{p} \overline{m}_k^d - \frac{1}{\beta n} \sum_{i=1}^{n} \log 2 \cosh \beta \sum_{k=1}^{p} \xi_i^{(k)} \overline{m}_k^{d-1}. \tag{5.94}$$

When the temperature $T = 1/\beta$ tends to zero, one easily verifies that the mean field equations (5.93) tend to the fixed point equations derived from (5.4). Indeed, replacing in the dynamic equations (5.4) the energy by its expression (5.16), one obtains

$$x_i = \mathrm{Sgn} \left[\sum_{\ell=1}^{p} \xi_i^{(\ell)} \left(\sum_{i=1}^{n} x_i \xi_i^{(\ell)} \right)^{d-1} \right] \tag{5.95}$$

and putting $m_k = n^{-1} \sum_{i=1}^{n} x_i \xi_i^{(k)}$, this gives

$$m_k = \frac{1}{n} \sum_{i=1}^{n} \xi_i^{(k)} \mathrm{Sgn} \left[\sum_{\ell=1}^{p} \xi_i^{(\ell)} m_\ell^{d-1} \right]. \tag{5.96}$$

For $d \to \infty$, Gross and Mézard [Gross and Mézard 84] compute the partition function by the replica method and use a technique developed by Parisi [Parisi 80] for replica symmetry breaking. On the other hand, the alternative solution proposed by Derrida for the asymptotic case $d \to \infty$, does not resort to replica methods and therefore avoids the difficulties which are inherent to this approach [Derrida 80].

Chapter 6

Network design

6.1 Introduction

The preceding chapters have been devoted to the investigation of the properties of recursive networks when the structure, and in particular the synaptic matrix, are specified as data of the problem. In this last chapter, the point of view will be reversed and the problem posed will be that of determining the synaptic matrix in such a way that the resulting network achieves some required performance. The central requirement is to store a number of patterns as fixed points of the system, each of them surrounded by a prescribed basin of long-term attraction. It has been emphasized above that it is difficult to take into account the evolution of the state vector during successive iterations of the dynamic equations of the network. As a consequence, one has in practice to be content when the basins of direct attraction have the required size. The problem can then be stated as follows : given p prototype vectors $\xi^{(1)}, \xi^{(2)}, \ldots, \xi^{(p)}$, and the corresponding basins of direct attraction, $B_1(\xi^{(1)}), B_1(\xi^{(2)}), \ldots, B_1(\xi^{(p)})$, find a synaptic matrix W and a threshold vector θ such that

$$\text{Sgn}\,(W\boldsymbol{x} - \theta) = \xi^{(k)}, \quad \forall \boldsymbol{x} \in B_1(\xi^{(k)}), \quad k = 1, 2, \ldots, p. \tag{6.1}$$

In principle, this problem can be decomposed in n independent subproblems, one for each row w_i^T of matrix W, which leads to the equivalent formulation

$$\text{Sgn}\,(w_i^T \boldsymbol{x} - \theta_i) = \xi_i^{(k)}, \quad \forall \boldsymbol{x} \in B_1(\xi^{(k)}),$$
$$k = 1, 2, \ldots, p, \quad i = 1, 2, \ldots, n. \tag{6.2}$$

In other words, one has to find the parameters w_i, θ_i of n threshold functions in $n + 1$ variables of prescribed value at each point of the p basins $B_1(\xi^{(k)})$. This in turn raises two questions. The first one is the existence of a solution satisfying (6.2) and this topic will be discussed in Subsection 6.2.1. As we shall see there, the problem amounts to the separability of a set of vectors by means of affine hyperplanes in n-dimensional space. The second question is to design algorithms for actually computing a solution w_i, θ_i. Subsection 6.2.2 will show that the perceptron algorithm can be adapted to this purpose, provided that the separability problem is soluble. In particular, it will become

155

apparent that the solutions obtained by perceptron-like algorithms are close
to the Hebbian rule. This then provides an a posteriori justification for the
detailed consideration of this rule in the preceding chapters.

Section 6.3 examines how Hebb's rule can be adapted to meet some specific
requirements. It should be clear from the analysis performed so far that a
recursive network has only limited storage capacity and that its memory dramatically degrades beyond a certain upper bound for the number of stored
patterns. To avoid this phenomenon, it may be attractive to be able to store
and memorize new patterns continuously, at the price of progressively eras-
ing the older ones. This can be achieved via the introduction of a forgetting
factor, as shown in Subsection 6.3.1. On the other hand, one may wish to memorize cycles or sequences of patterns instead of isolated prototypes. Similarly,
for pattern recognition purposes, it is useful to retrieve patterns from rotated
or shifted copies and more generally from two-dimensional transformations of
the original patterns. In both cases, the problem consists in incorporating in
the synaptic matrix the correlations existing between successive vectors of a
sequence or between an object and its transformation. As we shall see, the
general conclusion is that Hebb's law is in fact an efficient and flexible learning tool, in spite of its simplistic outlook. Indeed, the perceptron learning
strategies are, in the end, just variations of the Hebbian rule, which, on the
other hand, can also be extended to more elaborate situations such as storing
sequences or cycles.

6.2   Direct attraction

6.2.1   Existence of threshold functions

As pointed out above, the design of recursive networks with prescribed fixed
points and basins of direct attraction, amounts to determining a set of threshold functions satisfying (6.2). In order to elucidate under which conditions a
solution to this problem actually exists, we first simplify notation by observing
that equation (6.2) is of the general form

$$\text{Sgn}\left\{a^T[y^{(1)}, y^{(2)}, \ldots, y^{(m)}]\right\} = [s_1, s_2, \ldots, s_m], \tag{6.3}$$

where s_k is equal to +1 or −1, $y^{(i)}$ is a binary ν-vector whose last component
is equal to +1 and where a is a real ν-vector which has to be determined
so as to satisfy (6.3). In this setting, one immediately obtains the following
characterization [Delsarte and Kamp 89].

Theorem 6.1 *The sign vector* $\sigma = [s_1, s_2, \ldots, s_m]^T$ *is realizable by means of
the* $\nu \times m$ *matrix* $Y = [y^{(1)}, y^{(2)}, \ldots, y^{(m)}]$ *if and only if the convex hull of the*

points $s_1 y^{(1)}, s_2 y^{(2)}, \ldots, s_m y^{(m)}$ in the Euclidean space $\mathbf{R}^\nu$ does not contain the origin.

Proof The sign realization problem as stated above is equivalent to finding under which conditions equations (6.3) possess a solution for a. Equations (6.3) can be rewritten in the form $a^T s_i y^{(i)} > 0$ for $i = 1, 2, \ldots, m$. By Gordan's transposition theorem [Schrijver 86], there exists a vector a satisfying these inequalities, if and only if there exists no nonzero m-tuple $(\lambda_1, \lambda_2, \ldots, \lambda_m)$ with real nonnegative λ_i such that

$$\sum_{i=1}^{m} \lambda_i s_i y^{(i)} = 0. \tag{6.4}$$

This result is exactly equivalent to the statement of the theorem. □

One can take advantage of the fact that the $y^{(i)}$ vectors have the particular form

$$y^{(i)} = \begin{bmatrix} \eta^{(i)} \\ 1 \end{bmatrix}, \tag{6.5}$$

in order to obtain a more precise characterization. Let I^+ and I^- denote the set of indices i for which respectively $s_i = 1$ and $s_i = -1$. This induces on the set $\mathcal{H} = \{\eta^{(1)}, \eta^{(2)}, \ldots, \eta^{(m)}\}$ a partition into two complementary subsets $\mathcal{H}^+$ and $\mathcal{H}^-$ defined by

$$\mathcal{H}^+ = \{\eta^{(i)} \in \mathcal{H} : i \in I^+\}, \quad \mathcal{H}^- = \{\eta^{(i)} \in \mathcal{H} : i \in I^-\}. \tag{6.6}$$

We are now in the position to state the following version of Theorem 6.1 [Delsarte and Kamp 89].

Theorem 6.2 *If vectors $y^{(i)}$ are of the form (6.5), there exists a real ν-vector a which produces the sign vector $\sigma = [s_1, s_2, \ldots, s_m]^T$ in equation (6.3) if and only if the convex hulls of the sets $\mathcal{H}^+$ and $\mathcal{H}^-$ defined in (6.6) are disjoint.*

Proof Assume first that the sign vector σ is not realizable, i.e., that no solution a exists for equation (6.3). By Theorem 6.1, there exists then a linear relation of the form

$$\sum_{i \in I^+} \lambda_i y^{(i)} = \sum_{i \in I^-} \lambda_i y^{(i)}, \tag{6.7}$$

with $\lambda_i \geq 0$ for $i = 1, 2, \ldots, m$ and $\lambda_i > 0$ for at least one index i. By equating the last coordinate on both sides of (6.7), one obtains in view of (6.5),

$$\sum_{i \in I^+} \lambda_i = \sum_{i \in I^-} \lambda_i. \tag{6.8}$$

If we now normalize the λ_i with respect to the common positive value of both sides in (6.8), we observe that (6.7) implies that the convex hulls of $\mathcal{H}^+$ and $\mathcal{H}^-$ have a common point in $\mathbf{R}^{\nu-1}$. Conversely, if the convex hulls of $\mathcal{H}^+$ and $\mathcal{H}^-$ are not disjoint, then the convex hulls of the m points $s_i y^{(i)}$ contain the origin of $\mathbf{R}^\nu$. According to Theorem 6.1, this means that the sign vector σ cannot be realized with matrix Y.   □

Remark • It will be noted that the proofs of Theorems 6.1 and 6.2 do not make use of the fact that the vectors $\eta^{(i)}$ are binary vectors. The significance of these theorems is thus wider than suggested by the specific context in which they were derived.

We shall denote by B the $\nu \times m$ matrix defined by

$$B = [s_1 y^{(1)}, s_2 y^{(2)}, \ldots, s_m y^{(m)}]. \tag{6.9}$$

We shall write $\lambda \geq 0$ to denote a vector whose elements are all nonnegative and $\lambda \neq 0$ for a vector which is not identically zero. Theorem 6.1 guarantees that the sign vector σ is realizable if there exists no vector $\lambda \geq 0, (\lambda \neq 0)$, such that $B\lambda = 0$. In order to check in practical applications whether a sign vector is realizable, one can make use of the following two practical rules [Singleton 62] based on Theorem 6.1.

Theorem 6.3 *If B has a row where the elements are all ≥ 0 (or all ≤ 0), then, in testing for solubility of (6.3), this row can be deleted as well as all columns of B where this row has nonzero elements.*

Proof Each nonzero element of such a row gives a nonnegative contribution to the product $B\lambda$ and this implies that the corresponding element in λ should be zero in order to satisfy $B\lambda = 0$. On the other hand, if an element of λ is zero, then the corresponding column of B can be deleted. Finally, one is left with a row of zeros in B which does not contribute to the product $B\lambda$ and the row can thus be suppressed altogether.   □

Theorem 6.4 *For a given matrix B, one can always find a permutation matrix P and a nonsingular matrix T such that*

$$TBP = \begin{bmatrix} I & A \\ 0 & 0 \end{bmatrix}. \tag{6.10}$$

The sign vector σ is realizable if there exists no vector $v \geq 0, (v \neq 0)$ such that $Av \leq 0$.

Example One can show that, for a network of dimension $n = 4$, the vectors $\xi^{(1)} = [1, 1, 1, 1]^T$ and $\xi^{(2)} = [-1, 1, -1, 1]^T$ cannot be stored as fixed points with direct attraction in their N_1 neighbourhood. Indeed, equations (6.2) for $i = 1$ become in this case

$$\text{Sgn}\left\{[w_1^T, -\theta_1]\right.$$

$$\times \begin{bmatrix} 1 & -1 & 1 & 1 & 1 & | & -1 & 1 & -1 & -1 & -1 \\ 1 & 1 & -1 & 1 & 1 & | & 1 & 1 & -1 & 1 & 1 \\ 1 & 1 & 1 & -1 & 1 & | & -1 & -1 & -1 & 1 & -1 \\ 1 & 1 & 1 & 1 & -1 & | & 1 & 1 & 1 & 1 & -1 \\ 1 & 1 & 1 & 1 & 1 & | & 1 & 1 & 1 & 1 & 1 \end{bmatrix}\right\} =$$

$$\begin{bmatrix} 1 & 1 & 1 & 1 & | & -1 & -1 & -1 & -1 & -1 \end{bmatrix} \tag{6.11}$$

and, according to (6.9), matrix B is then given by

$$B = \begin{bmatrix} 1 & -1 & 1 & 1 & 1 & | & 1 & -1 & 1 & 1 & 1 \\ 1 & 1 & -1 & 1 & 1 & | & -1 & -1 & 1 & -1 & -1 \\ 1 & 1 & 1 & -1 & 1 & | & 1 & 1 & 1 & -1 & 1 \\ 1 & 1 & 1 & 1 & -1 & | & -1 & -1 & -1 & -1 & 1 \\ 1 & 1 & 1 & 1 & 1 & | & -1 & -1 & -1 & -1 & -1 \end{bmatrix}. \tag{6.12}$$

Multiplying on the left by

$$T = \begin{bmatrix} 1 & 0 & 0 & 0 & 0 \\ 0 & 1 & 0 & 0 & 0 \\ 0 & 0 & 1 & 0 & 0 \\ 0 & 0 & 0 & 1 & 0 \\ -1 & -1 & -1 & -1 & 2 \end{bmatrix} \begin{bmatrix} -1 & 0 & 0 & 0 & 1 \\ 0 & -1 & 0 & 0 & 1 \\ 0 & 0 & -1 & 0 & 1 \\ 0 & 0 & 0 & -1 & 1 \\ 0 & 0 & 0 & 0 & 1 \end{bmatrix}, \tag{6.13}$$

we transform matrix B into

$$TB = 2 \begin{bmatrix} 0 & 1 & 0 & 0 & 0 & | & -1 & 0 & -1 & -1 & -1 \\ 0 & 0 & 1 & 0 & 0 & | & 0 & 0 & -1 & 0 & 0 \\ 0 & 0 & 0 & 1 & 0 & | & -1 & -1 & -1 & 0 & -1 \\ 0 & 0 & 0 & 0 & 1 & | & 0 & 0 & 0 & 0 & -1 \\ 1 & 0 & 0 & 0 & 0 & | & 1 & 0 & 2 & 0 & 2 \end{bmatrix}. \tag{6.14}$$

By applying Theorem 6.3 successively to rows 5,4 and 2, we reduce matrix TB to $[I_2 \ A]$ where I_2 is the unit matrix of order 2 and where A is given by

$$A = \begin{bmatrix} 0 & -1 \\ -1 & 0 \end{bmatrix}. \tag{6.15}$$

It is clear now that vector $v = [1,1]^T$ gives $Av \leq 0$ and, according to Theorem 6.4, the sign vector on the right hand side of (6.11) is thus not realizable.

6.2.2   Perceptron-type algorithms

For networks of large dimensions, i.e. for large values of n, the rules presented in the preceding subsection are in fact not very efficient for checking whether the sign realization problem (6.3) can be solved. Hence, a solution frequently adopted in practice, consists in taking the realizability for granted and to apply the perceptron algorithm to effectively compute a solution a satisfying (6.3). The weak point of these approaches is that the perceptron-type algorithms do not converge but keep oscillating indefinitely when the sign vector is not realizable. From this point of view, the least mean square algorithm [Tou and Gonzalez 74], also known as the Ho-Kashyap algorithm, offers the advantage of indicating, during execution, whether the problem is soluble or not. Unfortunately, the latter algorithm is also computationally more expensive. We shall rather pursue the perceptron approach, in view of its simplicity and of the fact that it is, in principle, close to the learning techniques used for neural networks and, in particular, strongly related to Hebb's law. Before entering upon the numerous variants and adaptations of the perceptron algorithm, it will prove useful to recall its basic version below.

An equivalent formulation of problem (6.3), is that one should find a real ν-vector a such that

$$a^T sy > 0, \tag{6.16}$$

for every element sy of the set $\mathcal{Y} = \{s_1 y^{(1)}, s_2 y^{(2)}, \ldots, s_m y^{(m)}\}$ where s_i is a scalar and $y^{(i)}$ a column vector. The following algorithm provides a solution for this problem [Minsky and Papert 69].

Theorem 6.5 *Starting from the initialization $a(0) = 0$, each element of $\mathcal{Y}$ is repeatedly presented to the learning algorithm. If sy is the element presented at stage ℓ, then the vector $a(\ell - 1)$ of the preceding step is modified according to the rule*

$$a(\ell) = a(\ell - 1) + \epsilon \, sy, \tag{6.17}$$

where

$$\epsilon = 1 \quad if \quad a^T(\ell)\, sy < 0,$$
$$= 0 \quad otherwise. \tag{6.18}$$

If a solution a^* exists satisfying (6.16) for all elements of $\mathcal{Y}$, then this algorithm converges in a finite number of steps to a solution of (6.16).

Proof Without loss of generality, vector a^* can be normalized such that $\|a^*\| = 1$. By hypothesis, there exists some strictly positive δ satisfying

$$a^{*T} sy \geq \delta > 0 \qquad \forall sy \in \mathcal{Y}. \tag{6.19}$$

Using the Schwarz inequality, one can see that, at each stage of the algorithm,

$$\frac{a^{*T} a(\ell)}{\| a(\ell) \|} \leq 1. \tag{6.20}$$

If the vector a has been modified at step ℓ, one has

$$a(\ell) = a(\ell - 1) + sy, \qquad sy \in \mathcal{Y}, \tag{6.21}$$

and thus, in view of (6.19),

$$a^{*T} a(\ell) \geq a^{*T} a(\ell - 1) + \delta. \tag{6.22}$$

Assuming that the algorithm has been initialized with $a(0) = 0$, a lower bound for the numerator of (6.20) is now obtained, namely

$$a^{*T} a(L) \geq L\delta, \tag{6.23}$$

where L stands for the total number of steps where vector a has effectively been corrected. On the other hand, from (6.21) one also derives the equality

$$\| a(\ell) \|^2 = \| a(\ell - 1) \|^2 + \| sy \|^2 + 2\, a^T(\ell - 1)\, sy. \tag{6.24}$$

Since vector a has indeed been corrected, one has, by assumption, $a^T(\ell-1)sy \leq 0$ and thus

$$\| a(\ell) \|^2 \leq \| a(\ell - 1) \|^2 + \nu, \tag{6.25}$$

where ν is the dimension of the binary vector sy. With the initialization $a(0) = 0$, one obtains in this way the following upper bound for the denominator of (6.20),

$$\| a(L) \|^2 \leq L\nu. \tag{6.26}$$

Taking (6.23) into account, the final conclusion is that

$$L \leq \nu/\delta^2, \tag{6.27}$$

which shows that the number of corrections for vector a is necessarily finite.
□

Remarks • In order to apply this perceptron algorithm to the determination
of a row w_i^T of the synaptic matrix, it is sufficient to notice that (6.2) can be
put in the form

$$(w_i^T x - \theta_i)\, \xi_i^{(k)} > 0, \quad \forall x \in B_1(\xi^{(k)}), \quad k = 1, 2, \ldots, p \tag{6.28}$$

and comparison of this inequality with (6.16) leads to the identification

$$a = \begin{bmatrix} w_i \\ -\theta_i \end{bmatrix}, \qquad sy = \begin{bmatrix} x \\ 1 \end{bmatrix} \xi_i^{(k)}. \tag{6.29}$$

One obtains in this way the learning strategy presented in reference [Gardner
et al. 88].

• When the algorithm is restricted to the fixed points only, then sy in (6.29)
reduces to

$$sy = \begin{bmatrix} \xi^{(k)} \\ 1 \end{bmatrix} \xi_i^{(k)} \tag{6.30}$$

and the modification of vector w_i performed by the algorithm according to rule
(6.17) becomes now

$$w_{ij}(\ell) = w_{ij}(\ell - 1) + \epsilon\, \xi_i^{(k)}\, \xi_j^{(k)}, \tag{6.31}$$

if $\xi^{(k)}$ is the vector presented at stage ℓ. This produces the incremental form
(1.24) of the Hebbian rule. The perceptron learning procedure provides thus
an algorithmic justification for Hebb's rule and comes as a complement to the
neuro-biological arguments used in this context (see the references given in
[Herz et al. 89]). As for the threshold θ_i, it is modified according to the rule
$\theta_i(\ell) = \theta_i(\ell - 1) - \xi_i^{(k)}$.

• Instead of imposing basins of direct attraction in an explicit way, as in
(6.28), one can try to generate these basins indirectly, by requiring that these
inequalities should be satisfied by the prototype vectors only, but with a given
margin Δ. This leads to the following formulation :

$$(w_i^T \xi^{(k)} - \theta_i)\xi_i^{(k)} \ge \Delta > 0, \quad k = 1, 2, \ldots, p, \quad i = 1, 2, \ldots, n, \tag{6.32}$$

which is precisely the solution proposed in references [Forrest 88] and
[Diederich and Opper 87]. The perceptron algorithm (6.17), remains unchanged, except for an obvious modification of (6.18) which now becomes

$$\epsilon \; = \; 1 \quad if \quad a^T(\ell)\,sy < \Delta,$$
$$= \; 0 \quad otherwise. \tag{6.33}$$

The reader will find in reference [Tou and Gonzalez 74] a convergence proof adapted to this particular situation.

• A consequence of the fact that the problem has been solved separately for different rows of the synaptic matrix is that this matrix will, in general, not be symmetric. We shall show below that, in the case of a zero threshold vector θ, a global version of the perceptron algorithm can be set up which guarantees the symmetry of the resulting synaptic matrix.

Theorem 6.6 *Starting with the initialization* $W(0) = O_n$, *the vectors* x *of* $B_1(\xi^{(k)})$ *for* $k = 1, 2, \ldots, p$ *are repeatedly presented. At stage* ℓ, *the matrix* $W(\ell - 1)$ *of the preceding step is modified according to the rule*

$$W(\ell) = W(\ell - 1) + E\,\xi^{(k)}\,x^T + x\,\xi^{(k)T}\,E\,, \tag{6.34}$$

where $E = \; diag\,(\epsilon_1, \epsilon_2, \ldots, \epsilon_n)$ *with*

$$\epsilon_i \; = \; 1 \quad if \quad w_i^T(\ell)\,x\,\xi_i^{(k)} < 0,$$
$$= \; 0 \quad otherwise. \tag{6.35}$$

If there exists a symmetric matrix W^*, *whose column vectors* w_i^* *satisfy the inequality*

$$w_i^{*T}\,x\,\xi_i^{(k)} \; > \; 0, \quad \forall x \in B_1(\xi^{(k)}),$$
$$k = 1, 2, \ldots, p, \quad i = 1, 2, \ldots, n, \tag{6.36}$$

then the algorithm (6.34), (6.35) converges in a finite number of steps.

Proof Without loss of generality, matrix W^* can be normalized such that $\|W^*\|^2 = \mathrm{Tr}(W^*W^{*T}) = 1$ and the Schwarz inequality yields then

$$\frac{\mathrm{Tr}(W^*W^T(\ell))}{\|\,W(\ell)\,\|} \leq 1. \tag{6.37}$$

By (6.34), one has

$$\mathrm{Tr}[W^*W^T(\ell)] = \mathrm{Tr}[W^*W^T(\ell - 1)] + 2\,\mathrm{Tr}[W^*x\,\xi^{(k)T}E], \tag{6.38}$$

by taking into account the fact that $\mathrm{Tr}(AB) = \mathrm{Tr}(BA)$ if matrix AB is square. On the other hand, one easily verifies the equality

$$\mathrm{Tr}[W^*\,x\,\xi^{(k)T}\,E] = \sum_{i=1}^{n} \epsilon_i\,w_i^{*T}\,x\,\xi_i^{(k)}. \tag{6.39}$$

If matrix W has been modified at stage ℓ, at least one among the ϵ_i is nonzero and, in view of hypothesis (6.36), there exists a $\delta > 0$ such that

$$w_i^{*T} x \, \xi_i^{(k)} \geq \delta, \qquad \forall x \in B_1(\xi^{(k)}),$$
$$k = 1, 2, \ldots, p, \quad i = 1, 2, \ldots, n. \tag{6.40}$$

Consequently, one derives from (6.38) the inequality

$$\text{Tr}[W^* W^T(\ell)] \geq \text{Tr}[W^* W^T(\ell - 1)] + 2\,\delta, \tag{6.41}$$

which, in view of the initialization $W(0) = O_n$, yields the following bound for the numerator in the left hand side of (6.37)

$$\text{Tr}\,[W^* W^T(\ell)] \geq 2\,L\,\delta. \tag{6.42}$$

Here L denotes the number of iterations where matrix W has been corrected. On the other hand, from (6.34) one also derives the following relation

$$\| W(\ell) \|^2 = \| W(\ell - 1) \|^2 \; + \; \| E\,\xi^{(k)} x^T + x\,\xi^{(k)T} E \|^2$$
$$+ \; 4\,\text{Tr}[W(\ell - 1) x\,\xi^{(k)T} E], \tag{6.43}$$

with

$$\| E\,\xi^{(k)} x^T + x\,\xi^{(k)T} E \|^2 \leq 4n^2 \tag{6.44}$$

and where

$$\text{Tr}[W(\ell - 1) x\,\xi^{(k)T} E] = \sum_{i=1}^{n} \epsilon_i\, w_i^T(\ell - 1)\, x\,\xi_i^{(k)} \tag{6.45}$$

is strictly negative, since, by assumption, W has been modified at stage ℓ. Consequently,

$$\| W(\ell) \|^2 \leq \| W(\ell - 1) \|^2 + 4\,n^2 \tag{6.46}$$

and, owing to the initialization $W(0) = O_n$, one obtains in this way the upper bound

$$\| W(\ell) \|^2 \leq 4\,L\,n^2. \tag{6.47}$$

Taking into account the inequalities (6.42) and (6.47) derived for the numerator and the denominator of (6.37), one finally concludes that the total number L of modifications of the synaptic matrix is bounded by

$$L \leq n^2/\delta^2, \tag{6.48}$$

which proves the desired result.   □

Instead of looking for a solution w_i, θ_i which satisfies the inequalities (6.32) with a fixed margin Δ, it would be preferable to seek the solution which provides the largest margin for a given normalization of the parameters w_i and θ_i. Assuming for simplicity a zero threshold vector, the problem can be stated as follows : maximize $\Delta \geq 0$ subject to the constraint that a vector w_i can be found satisfying the requirements

$$w_i^T \xi^{(k)} \xi_i^{(k)} \geq \Delta, \quad k = 1, 2, \ldots, p, \quad i = 1, 2, \ldots, n, \tag{6.49}$$

$$\| w_i \| = 1. \tag{6.50}$$

Assuming that this problem can be solved, let us denote the solution by Δ_{opt}. Krauth and Mézard suggest a suboptimal solution for this problem which they obtain by an iterative method, similar in spirit to the perceptron algorithm [Krauth and Mézard 87]. The prototype vectors $\xi^{(1)}, \xi^{(2)}, \ldots, \xi^{(p)}$ are presented repeatedly and at stage ℓ one selects prototype $\xi^{(m)}$ for which

$$w_i^T(\ell - 1)\, \xi^{(m)} = \text{Min}_{k=1,2,\ldots,p} \{w_i^T(\ell - 1)\, \xi^{(k)}\}. \tag{6.51}$$

If

$$w_i^T(\ell - 1)\, \xi^{(m)} < c, \tag{6.52}$$

where c is a fixed constant, then w_i is corrected as follows

$$w_i(\ell) = w_i(\ell - 1) + \frac{1}{n}\, \xi^{(m)}. \tag{6.53}$$

In the opposite case, the algorithm stops and the normalized margin is given by

$$\Delta_c = \frac{w_i^T(\ell)\xi^{(m)}}{\| w_i(\ell) \|} \geq \frac{c}{\| w_i(\ell) \|}. \tag{6.54}$$

The next theorem provides, on the one hand, a convergence proof for the algorithm and, on the other hand, an estimate for the quality of this suboptimal solution by means of the ratio Δ_c/Δ_{opt} [Krauth and Mézard 87] .

Theorem 6.7 *If the original problem admits a solution under the constraints (6.49) and (6.50), then the algorithm described by relations (6.51)-(6.53) converges in a finite number of steps. The quality of the solutions is bounded from below by the inequality*

$$\Delta_c \geq \frac{c}{1 + 2c}\, \Delta_{opt}. \tag{6.55}$$

Proof Without loss of generality, one can assume that $\xi_i^{(k)} = 1$ in (6.49) and, in order to simplify the notations, we will temporarily write w instead of w_i. By assumption, there exists thus a vector w^* with unit norm and such that

$$w^{*T}\xi^{(k)} \geq \Delta_{opt}. \tag{6.56}$$

The Schwarz inequality yields for each iteration ℓ of the learning procedure

$$\frac{w^{*T}w(\ell)}{\|w(\ell)\|} \leq 1. \tag{6.57}$$

With $w(0) = 0$, one has, in view of (6.53),

$$w(\ell) = \frac{1}{n}\sum_{k=1}^{p} r_k\,\xi^{(k)}, \tag{6.58}$$

where r_k is the number of times that prototype $\xi^{(k)}$ has been used in the correction rule (6.53) since the beginning of the algorithm. By definition, $\ell = \sum_k r_k$ and, taking (6.56) into account, one has thus

$$w^{*T}w(\ell) \geq \frac{\ell}{n}\Delta_{opt}. \tag{6.59}$$

Relation (6.53) yields, on the other hand,

$$\|w(\ell)\|^2 = \|w(\ell-1)\|^2 + \frac{2}{n}w^T(\ell-1)\xi^{(m)} + \frac{1}{n} \tag{6.60}$$

and, since it was assumed that a correction was applied at iteration ℓ of the algorithm, one has, in view of (6.52),

$$\|w(\ell)\|^2 < \|w(\ell-1)\|^2 + \frac{1+2c}{n}. \tag{6.61}$$

In view of the initialization $w(0) = 0$, one has thus

$$\|w(\ell)\|^2 < \frac{\ell(1+2c)}{n} \tag{6.62}$$

and, combining the latter inequality with (6.57) and (6.59), one finally obtains

$$\frac{\sqrt{\ell}}{\sqrt{n(1+2c)}}\Delta_{opt} \leq \frac{w^{*T}w(\ell)}{\|w(\ell)\|} \leq 1, \tag{6.63}$$

which concludes the convergence proof. On the other hand, from the inequalities (6.59) and (6.57) one derives

$$\frac{\ell\,\Delta_{opt}}{n\,\|w(\ell)\|} \leq 1 \tag{6.64}$$

and relation (6.54) provides then the inequality

$$\Delta_c \geq \frac{c\,\ell\,\Delta_{opt}}{n\,\|\,w(\ell)\,\|^2}.$$

(6.65)

Taking (6.62) into account, this then proves the estimate (6.55) of the theorem.
□

Remarks • The quality factor of the results, Δ_c/Δ_{opt}, depends on the constant c used for the correction rule (6.52). In fact, one can show the stronger result that $\Delta_c/\Delta_{opt} \to 1$ as $c \to \infty$ [Krauth and Mézard 87]. But the learning rules (6.51)-(6.53) show then that a large value of c may imply a large number of corrections and hence slow convergence.

• Instead of the normalization (6.50), one could also have used the constraint

$$-\frac{1}{\sqrt{n}} \leq w_{ij} \leq \frac{1}{\sqrt{n}}$$

(6.66)

and in this case the problem can be solved by linear programming [Krauth and Mézard 87].

• Peretto suggests solution of (6.49), (6.50), by minimization of a cost function G which is a continuous decreasing function of the quantities

$$S_i^{(k)} = w_i^T \xi^{(k)} \xi_i^{(k)}, \quad k = 1, 2, \ldots, p, \quad i = 1, 2, \ldots, n,$$

(6.67)

which appear in the left hand side of (6.49) [Peretto 88]. One should remember that perfect storage of the prototypes requires that all $S_i^{(k)}$ should be positive. For simplicity, it is assumed that G can be decomposed into a sum of identical decreasing functions g which depend only on a single $S_i^{(k)}$, i.e.

$$G = \sum_{k=1}^{p} \sum_{i=1}^{n} g(S_i^{(k)}).$$

(6.68)

For the minimization of G, Peretto proposes the following relaxation scheme

$$
\begin{aligned}
w_{ij}(\ell+1) &= w_{ij}(\ell) - \alpha \sum_{k=1}^{p} \frac{\partial g}{\partial w_{ij}}, \\
&= w_{ij}(\ell) - \alpha \sum_{k=1}^{p} \xi_i^{(k)} \xi_j^{(k)} \frac{\partial g}{\partial S_i^{(k)}},
\end{aligned}
$$

(6.69)

where α is a positive learning coefficient. In particular, if g is defined by

$$
\begin{aligned}
g(x) &= 0 \quad &&\text{for} \quad x > 0, \\
&= -x \quad &&\text{for} \quad x < 0,
\end{aligned}
$$

(6.70)

one recovers the perceptron algorithm (6.31). Ideally, however, function g should not only be decreasing but, in addition, bounded from below and convex in order for the relaxation procedure (6.69) to converge to a unique finite minimum. An appropriate choice for g in this sense is the exponential function $g(x) = \exp(-\beta x)$ with $\beta > 0$. Peretto observes that the asymptotic behaviour of the relaxation algorithm depends on whether the number of prototypes p is larger or smaller than the limit $2n$ established by Cover (Theorem 3.1). If $p < 2n$, then the relaxation algorithm converges to a fixed point at infinite range where the prototypes are correctly memorized but where the synaptic weights diverge. Indeed, if there exists a set of weights w_{ij} such that the $S_i^{(k)}$ are positive, then the cost function (6.68) can be reduced even further, simply by multiplying all weights by the same positive constant. For $p > 2n$, the algorithm converges to a point at finite range and experiments show that, for finite n, the number of frustrated inequalities $S_i^{(k)} > 0$ increases as p tends to the limit value $2n$. Similarly, the number of iterations, required to insure proper storage of the prototypes, diverges when $p = 2n$ [Peretto 88].

6.3   Extensions of Hebb's law

6.3.1   Short-term memory

The low memory capacity of recursive networks has been emphasized in Chapters 3 and 4. Even when some residual error rate is tolerated after the network has settled down, the number of prototypes which can be stored is still limited to $0.14n$ and, beyond this point, the retrieval performance degrades abruptly. It is thus natural to look for techniques which would allow continuous acquisition of new prototypes, at the expense of progressively forgetting the older ones. The introduction to this effect of a forgetting factor in the learning procedure had already been proposed by Kohonen [Kohonen 84] and, less explicitly, by Hopfield [Hopfield 82]. Here, we will develop the solution proposed by Mézard, Nadal and their coauthors in the framework of Hebb's rule [Mézard et al. 86], [Nadal et al. 86].

In this subsection we will denote by $\xi^{(1)}$ the most *recent* prototype, by $\xi^{(2)}$ the preceding one and so on. The values of the synaptic weights after registration of the last prototype are given by

$$w_{ij} = \frac{1}{n} \sum_{k \geq 1} \Lambda(k/n)\, \xi_i^{(k)}\, \xi_j^{(k)}, \qquad i, j = 1, 2, \ldots, n, \tag{6.71}$$

where the forgetting factor $\Lambda(k/n)$ is a positive valued decreasing function of the registration index k. The synaptic intensities are normalized by the condition

$$\int_0^\infty \Lambda^2(\alpha)\,d\alpha = 1.$$ (6.72)

Here, we shall mainly concentrate on the *marginalist scheme* defined by

$$\Lambda_\mu(\alpha) = \epsilon\,e^{-\epsilon^2\alpha/2}.$$ (6.73)

For the most recent prototypes, $\alpha = k/n$ is close to zero and the patterns are thus learned with intensity ϵ. For the oldest prototypes, k/n is large and the forgetting factor is then close to zero.

In order to investigate the behaviour of a network, the parameters of which are defined by (6.71), one can apply the mean field theory developed in Chapter 4, provided one takes into account the forgetting factor $\Lambda(k/n)$ associated with prototype $\xi^{(k)}$ for the construction of the synaptic matrix. Thus, expression (4.21) of the partition function becomes now

$$Z = \mathrm{Tr}_x \exp\left[\frac{\beta}{2n}\sum_{k\geq 1}\Lambda(k/n)(\sum_{i=1}^n x_i\,\xi_i^{(k)})^2 - \frac{\beta p}{2}\right].$$ (6.74)

As in Section 4.4 we shall restrict the analysis to those state vectors which have macroscopic overlap with a finite number ν of prototypes (so called main prototypes). By analogy with (4.138), we introduce the ν overlaps

$$\overline{m}_{k_t} = \frac{1}{n}\sum_{i=1}^n \xi_i^{(k_t)}\,\overline{x}_i, \qquad (t = 1, 2, \ldots, \nu),$$ (6.75)

where $\overline{x} = [\overline{x}_1, \overline{x}_2, \ldots, \overline{x}_n]^T$ is the mean state vector with respect to the Gibbs distribution (4.6). Similarly, the variable r, which in (4.140) represents the contribution of the overlaps with the secondary prototypes, is now redefined as

$$r = \sum_{v\neq k_t}\Lambda^2(v/n)\,\overline{m}_v^2.$$ (6.76)

Parameter q, however, keeps its former definition (4.142). With these modifications, the mean field equations (4.144)-(4.146) now become [Mézard et al. 86]

$$\overline{m}_{k_\ell} = \ll \xi_i^{(k_t)}\tanh\beta\left[\sqrt{r}\,z + \sum_{t=1}^\nu \xi_i^{(k_t)}\,\Lambda(k_t/n)\overline{m}_{k_t}\right]\gg,$$

$$\ell = 1, 2, \ldots, \nu,$$ (6.77)

$$r = \int_0^\infty \frac{q\,\Lambda^2(u)}{[1 - \beta(1-q)\,\Lambda(u)]^2}\,du,$$ (6.78)

$$q = \ll \tanh^2\beta\left[\sqrt{r}\,z + \sum_{t=1}^\nu \xi_i^{(k_t)}\,\Lambda(k_t/n)\,\overline{m}_{k_t}\right]\gg,$$ (6.79)

with $\beta = T^{-1}$ and where $\ll . \gg$ stands for a combined average over the distribution of the $\xi_i^{(k_t)}$, $(t = 1, 2, \ldots, \nu)$ and over the Gaussian noise z. Here, we are of course mainly interested in the possibility of retrieving a prototype at distance $k = \alpha n$ in the past and, consequently, we seek a solution such that

$$
\begin{aligned}
\overline{m}_{k_t} &= m \qquad \text{if} \qquad k_t = \alpha\, n, \\
&= 0 \qquad \text{otherwise}.
\end{aligned}
\tag{6.80}
$$

This problem will now be considered in the zero temperature limit. For the values (6.80) of the overlaps, and for $T \to 0$, equations (6.77)-(6.79) yield

$$
m = \sqrt{\frac{2}{\pi}} \int_0^{m\,\Lambda(\alpha)/\sqrt{r}} e^{-z^2/2}\, dz,
\tag{6.81}
$$

$$
r = \int_0^\infty \frac{\Lambda^2(u)}{[1 - C\,\Lambda(u)]^2}\, du,
\tag{6.82}
$$

where

$$
C = \sqrt{\frac{2}{\pi r}}\, \exp\left[-\frac{m^2\Lambda^2(\alpha)}{2r}\right].
\tag{6.83}
$$

This forms a system of three equations in the unknowns m, r and C which can be solved numerically once the forgetting factor $\Lambda(\alpha)$ has been specified.

For the marginalist scheme, Λ_μ, the following conclusions are obtained [Mézard et al. 86]. A solution $m \neq 0$ exists only if the learning intensity ϵ is larger than a minimum threshold value $\epsilon_c = 2.465$. In addition, even for $\epsilon > \epsilon_c$, the parameter α has to be small enough, i.e. $\alpha < \alpha_c(\epsilon)$, which means that retrieval is possible only for prototypes which are not too far away in the past. Figure 6.1 shows that the curve $\alpha_c(\epsilon)$ goes through a maximum $\alpha_{opt} = 0.04895$

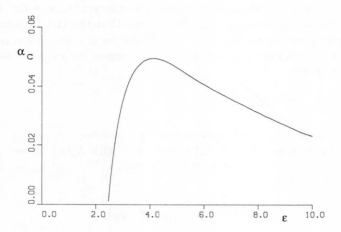

Figure 6.1 : Capacity factor α_c as a function of the learning intensity ϵ
for short-term memories.
(Reprinted by permission of Les Editions de Physique, Orsay ©1986)

which is much lower than the critical value $\alpha_c = 0.14$ obtained for the classical
Hebbian rule. This capacity reduction represents the price to be paid for
preserving the possibility of continuously acquiring new prototypes.

It is interesting to have a closer look at equation (6.81) in the neighbourhood
of $m = 1$, which corresponds to a small error rate in the retrieval of the
prototype. For a given learning intensity $\epsilon > \epsilon_c$, one can compute via (6.81)
the oldest prototype which can be retrieved with a prescribed overlap value
m. Equation (6.81) shows indeed that m will be close to unity if the upper
integration limit tends to infinity. This, in turn, implies via (6.83) that $C \to 0$
and, in view of (6.82) and (6.72), that $r \to 1$. When m tends to unity, the
asymptotic expression of (6.81) becomes

$$m = 1 - \sqrt{\frac{2}{\pi}} \frac{1}{\Lambda_\mu(\alpha)} \exp\left[-\frac{\Lambda_\mu^2(\alpha)}{2}\right]. \tag{6.84}$$

Let $y = \Lambda_\mu(\alpha)$ denote the solution of this equation for a given value of m.
From (6.73) one derives then the value of α as

$$\alpha = \frac{2}{\epsilon^2} \log\left(\frac{\epsilon}{y}\right), \tag{6.85}$$

whence finally

$$k_t = \frac{2n}{\epsilon^2} \log\left(\frac{\epsilon}{y}\right). \tag{6.86}$$

Another simple illustration of short-term memory effects is the repeated learning of the same prototype. Let us assume that the last presentation of this prototype occurred at time $k = \alpha n$. If the same prototype was learned in the past with periodicity gn, then it will appear in the modified Hebb rule (6.71) with a weight

$$\Lambda_g(\alpha) = \sum_{\ell \geq 0} \Lambda\left(\alpha + \ell g\right). \tag{6.87}$$

If one is interested in the state vectors having a macroscopic overlap with this prototype, the same equation (6.81) applies, but with $\Lambda_g(\alpha)$ instead of $\Lambda(\alpha)$. Since $\Lambda_g(\alpha) > \Lambda(\alpha)$, it is clear that the overlap will indeed be larger in the case of periodic learning.

6.3.2   Storage of cycles

We shall here consider only the synchronous mode and it may be useful to recall that, for this mode, the *existence* of cycles requires synaptic matrices which are not positive definite (see Theorem 2.4). This necessary condition, however, is not enough to solve the problem of memorizing cycles.

Herz and his coauthors take as starting point that, in order to store and retrieve cycles of patterns, one must incorporate the temporal relations between elements of the cycle, both in the dynamic equations of the network and in the structure of the synaptic matrix [Herz et al. 88], [Herz et al. 89]. A straightforward implementation of this idea at the level of the dynamic equations consists in making the state vector $x(t)$ depend, not only on the immediately preceding state $x(t-1)$, but also on $x(t-2), \ldots, x(t - \tau_{\max})$. The interaction with the past states is performed via a separate synaptic matrix for each value of the delay. According to this design rule, the vector of synaptic potentials is then given by

$$h(t) = \sum_{\tau=1}^{\tau_{\max}} W(\tau)\, x(t - \tau), \tag{6.88}$$

from which the current state vector is computed via the usual relation

$$x(t) = \text{Sgn}\left[h(t)\right]. \tag{6.89}$$

This approach is supported by the biological observation that the information transport between neurons is performed both by fast and by slower axons, and that the synaptic potential is the resultant of these contributions over a rather broad time window [Herz et al. 89].

In order to explain how the matrices $W(\tau)$ are determined, we shall consider the simple situation where the largest delay coincides with the length of the cycle $\xi^{(0)}, \xi^{(1)}, \ldots, \xi^{(q-1)}$ to be stored. One has thus $\tau_{\max} = q$. The usual Hebbian rule, which we write here as

$$w_{ij} = \frac{1}{n} \sum_{k=0}^{q-1} \xi_i^{(k)} \xi_j^{(k)}, \tag{6.90}$$

captures the correlation between the activity levels of neurons i and j at the same instant of time and, in the case at hand, for the same prototype. For cycles however, one should, in addition, also memorize the correlations between the activities of these neurons, but at different time instants. More precisely, one should code in the synaptic weights the fact that, if a state vector is $\xi^{(k)}$ at some given time, it should be $\xi^{(k+1)}$ at the next instant, $\xi^{(k+2)}$ after two clock periods and so on. This leads to the generalized Hebb rule

$$w_{ij}(\tau) = \frac{\epsilon}{n} \sum_{k=0}^{q-1} \xi_i^{((k+\tau)\bmod q)} \xi_j^{(k)}, \quad (\tau = 1, 2, \ldots, \tau_{\max} = q). \tag{6.91}$$

We shall denote by $X^{(0)}$ the matrix of the prototypes forming the cycle

$$X^{(0)} = \left[\xi^{(0)}, \xi^{(1)}, \ldots, \xi^{(q-1)} \right] \tag{6.92}$$

and by $X^{(k)}$ the matrix of the same prototypes but shifted by k positions in the cycle, namely,

$$X^{(k)} = \left[\xi^{(k)}, \xi^{(k+1)}, \ldots, \xi^{(q-1)}, \xi^{(0)}, \ldots, \xi^{(k-1)} \right]. \tag{6.93}$$

Based on (6.91), the synaptic matrix corresponding to delay τ is then given by

$$W(\tau) = \frac{\epsilon}{n} X^{(\tau)} X^{(0)T} \quad (\tau = 1, 2, \ldots, \tau_{\max} = q). \tag{6.94}$$

With these definitions, we shall see from a simple example of length $q = 4$ how robust retrieval of the correct cycle can be insured, even if some errors are present in the initial values. In view of (6.88) and (6.89), the network is a dynamic system with $\tau_{\max}$ delays and we have thus to specify the initial conditions $x(-1), \ldots, x(-\tau_{\max})$. We begin by assuming that the network is initialized at time $t = 0$ with a correct cycle, for instance,

$$x(-4) = \xi^{(1)}, \quad x(-3) = \xi^{(2)}, \quad x(-2) = \xi^{(3)}, \quad x(-1) = \xi^{(0)}. \tag{6.95}$$

To simplify the computations, we assume that the prototypes are orthogonal. Thus $\xi^{(k)T} \xi^{(\ell)} = n\, \delta_{k,\ell}$, whence we derive

$$
\begin{aligned}
X^{(0)T} x(-1) &= n[1,0,0,0]^T, & X^{(0)T} x(-2) &= n[0,0,0,1]^T, \\
X^{(0)T} x(-3) &= n[0,0,1,0]^T, & X^{(0)T} x(-4) &= n[0,1,0,0]^T,
\end{aligned}
\tag{6.96}
$$

Applying next (6.94) and (6.88), we find $h(0) = 4 \epsilon \xi^{(1)}$ and thus $x(0) = \xi^{(1)}$. The initial values for time $t = 1$ become then

$$x(-3) = \xi^{(2)}, \ x(-2) = \xi^{(3)}, \ x(-1) = \xi^{(0)}, \ x(0) = \xi^{(1)}, \qquad (6.97)$$

which gives $x(1) = \xi^{(2)}$ and, in the same way, one finds successively $x(2) = \xi^{(3)}$, $x(3) = \xi^{(0)}$, $x(4) = \xi^{(1)}$ etc. In other words, the network reproduces faithfully the cycle $\xi^{(0)}, \xi^{(1)}, \xi^{(2)}, \xi^{(3)}$.

If the initialization sequence at time $t = 0$ contains an error, for example,

$$x(-4) = \xi^{(1)}, \ x(-3) = x(-2) = \xi^{(2)}, \ x(-1) = \xi^{(0)}, \qquad (6.98)$$

then it will automatically be corrected. Indeed, in contrast to (6.96) we have now $X^{(0)T} x(-2) = n[0, 0, 1, 0]^T$, and this gives via relations (6.94) and (6.88)

$$h(0) = \epsilon (3 \xi^{(1)} + \xi^{(0)}). \qquad (6.99)$$

Nevertheless, one recovers the correct value $x(0) = \xi^{(1)}$ and hence the correct cycle $x(1) = \xi^{(2)}$ etc. It should be noticed that the network generates the correct cycle even if the initialization is limited to a single vector of the sequence, as for example,

$$x(-4) = x(-3) = x(-2) = 0; \quad x(-1) = \xi^{(0)}. \qquad (6.100)$$

Remarks • The approach presented here incorporates the *complete* temporal structure of the cycle via dedicated synaptic matrices for each of the delay values $\tau = 1, 2, \ldots, \tau_{\max}$. This is essentially the reason why such a system is robust against corrupted initializations. Indeed, much simpler cycle generators are conceivable, such as networks where the synaptic potential is defined by

$$h(t) = W(q - 1) x(t - q + 1), \qquad (6.101)$$

which amounts to keeping just a single term in (6.88). One easily verifies on the example considered above that the network produces a correct cycle for the exact initialization (6.95). However, there will be no correction if the initialization contains errors as in (6.98). One finds indeed the correct value $x(0) = \xi^{(1)}$ since (6.101) gives $h(0) = W(3) x(-3) = W(3) \xi^{(2)} = \epsilon \xi^{(1)}$; but for $t = 1$, the initial conditions are

$$x(-3) = \xi^{(2)}, \ x(-2) = \xi^{(2)}, \ x(-1) = \xi^{(0)}, \ x(0) = \xi^{(1)}, \qquad (6.102)$$

which gives $h(1) = h(0)$ and thus $x(1) = \xi^{(1)}$, with the consequence that the correct cycle is never restored.

• In order to store isolated prototypes, one can keep the same rule (6.94) for the construction of the synaptic matrix. It suffices to consider the degenerate cycle obtained by repeating the same vector. In that case, all matrices $W(\tau)$ are identical.

- If the maximum delay $\tau_{\max}$ of the network exceeds the length q of the cycle, then the construction rule (6.94) remains essentially unchanged, except for the fact that $W(\tau) = W \ (\tau \bmod q)$. This is equivalent to the assumption that, during the training phase, the basic cycle $\xi^{(0)} \ldots \xi^{(q-1)}$ is periodically repeated.

- The solution summarized in relations (6.88) and (6.94) is not the only one which permits the retrieval of cycles starting from a degraded version. Alternative solutions are examined in [Herz et al. 89] but fall beyond the scope of this work.

6.3.3 Invariant pattern recognition

For vision and image processing applications, it is important to recognize patterns independently of certain transformations such as translation, rotation or scaling. Different approaches have been suggested to solve this problem of "invariant pattern recognition".

A first group of solutions takes as starting point that the invariant property to recognize is a pattern of *relations* between image points. In this setting, images are essentially represented by relational graphs. Kree and Zippelius propose a two level architecture which first transforms the relational graph of the input data and next retrieves the prototype graph [Kree and Zippelius 88]. For Bienenstock and von der Malsburg, on the other hand, an image is represented by a feature distribution (grey levels, local edge orientations, etc) on the nodes of a graph and the links connecting the nodes represent the vicinity relationship of the local features [Bienenstock and von der Malsburg 87], [von der Malsburg and Bienenstock 87]. The strength of the links between nodes are the dynamic variables of the recursive network used to retrieve the pattern.

A second group of solutions does not make use of image representations in terms of relational graphs. Instead, Dotsenko introduces explicitly the parameters of translation, rotation and scaling as additional dynamic variables which are optimized in a first stage, followed next by a classical retrieval step [Dotsenko 88]. It is shown that this two stage scheme can in fact be integrated into a single model by using the degrees of freedom provided by the threshold vector. Hereunder, we discuss in somewhat more detail the solution of Coolen and Kuijk which is closer to the techniques we have discussed so far [Coolen and Kuijk 89].

Let T be a transformation of the domain $\{-1, 1\}^n$ into itself. The main problem considered by Coolen and Kuijk is to store this transformation in a recursive network in such a way that the state vectors are successively $T(x)$,

$T^2(x), \ldots$ etc, where x denotes the initialization vector. To achieve invariant pattern recognition, one should code in the synaptic matrix, on the one hand, the fixed patterns (which can be achieved by the usual Hebbian rule), and, on the other hand, the transformation operator T. It is essentially this last problem which will be discussed below in the simple case of zero threshold vector.

Since $\mathrm{Sgn}(W\,x)$ should, for all x, be as close as possible to $T(x)$, it seems natural to measure the extent to which transformation T has been memorized by the quality factor

$$Q = \frac{1}{n} \sum_{i=1}^{n} \ll (T(x))_i \; \mathrm{Sgn}\Big(\sum_{j=1}^{n} w_{ij}\,x_j\Big) \gg, \tag{6.103}$$

where $\ll \cdot \gg$ stands for the statistical mean over the distribution of the state vectors x. Ideally, Q should of course be close to unity. Since $T(x)$ is by definition an element of $\{-1, 1\}^n$, we can rewrite (6.103) under the form

$$Q = \frac{1}{n} \sum_{i=1}^{n} \ll \mathrm{Sgn}\, y_i \gg = \frac{1}{n} \sum_{i=1}^{n} [2\,\mathrm{Pr}(y_i > 0) - 1], \tag{6.104}$$

where y_i is defined as

$$y_i = \left[(T(x))_i \sum_{j=1}^{n} w_{ij}\,x_j \right], \quad (i = 1, 2, \ldots, n). \tag{6.105}$$

For simplicity we will assume that y_i has a Gaussian distribution and we obtain then for the quality factor Q the following expression

$$Q = \frac{1}{n} \sum_{i=1}^{n} \sqrt{\frac{2}{\pi}} \int_0^{\mu_i/\sigma_i} e^{-z^2/2}\, dz, \tag{6.106}$$

where μ_i and σ_i are respectively the mean and variance of the random variable y_i.

On the other hand, we assume that transformation T is coded in the synaptic matrix by the following extension of Hebb's rule

$$w_{ij} = \frac{1}{n} \ll (T(\eta))_i \; \eta_j \gg, \tag{6.107}$$

where η is a binary learning vector, drawn from the same distribution as the vectors x which serve to estimate the quality factor Q. Taking (6.107) into account, we see that the mean value of y_i is given as

$$\mu_i = \frac{1}{n} \sum_{j=1}^{n} \ll (T(x))_i \; x_j \gg^2, \quad i = 1, 2, \ldots, n \tag{6.108}$$

and the variance can be computed by

$$\sigma_i^2 = \ll y_i^2 \gg -\mu_i^2 = \ll \left(\sum_{j=1}^{n} w_{ij} x_j \right)^2 \gg -\mu_i^2 ,$$

$$= \frac{1}{n^2} \sum_{j=1}^{n} \sum_{k=1}^{n} \ll (T(\eta))_i \eta_j \gg \ll x_j x_k \gg \ll (T(\eta))_i \eta_k \gg -\mu_i^2 . \tag{6.109}$$

If we assume that the distribution of the state vectors is such that their components are independent random variables taking on the values $+1$ and -1 with equal probability, then we obtain finally

$$\sigma_i^2 = \mu_i(1 - \mu_i), \qquad i = 1, 2, \ldots, n. \tag{6.110}$$

Returning to the expression (6.106) of Q, one concludes that the network will faithfully reproduce $T(x)$ as soon as a sufficient number of μ_i's are of the order of unity. Taking the mean value (6.108) into account, this condition can be rewritten as

$$\frac{1}{n^2} \sum_{i=1}^{n} \sum_{j=1}^{n} \ll (T(x))_i x_j \gg^2 = O(1), \tag{6.111}$$

since, by (6.110), all μ_i belong to the interval $[0,1]$. Coolen and Kuijk consider more particularly those transformations which are permutations of the elements of the state vector, i.e. $T(x) = Px$ with $(Px)_i = x_{\pi(i)}$ where π is a permutation of the indices $\{1, 2, \ldots, n\}$. In this case, relation (6.107) gives the following expression for the synaptic weights

$$w_{ij} = \frac{1}{n} \ll \eta_{\pi(i)} \eta_j \gg = \frac{1}{n} \delta_{\pi(i),j} , \tag{6.112}$$

with the consequence that $W = n^{-1}P$ and $Q = 1$ in view of definition (6.103). If, in addition, the prototypes $\xi^{(1)}, \xi^{(2)}, \ldots, \xi^{(p)}$ have been stored by the classical Hebbian rule, the complete synaptic matrix is given by

$$W = P + \frac{\epsilon}{n} \sum_{k=1}^{p} \xi^{(k)} \xi^{(k)T} , \tag{6.113}$$

where ϵ is a positive weighting coefficient which should insure adequate balance between the learning of isolated prototypes and learning of transformations. Assuming that the initial state vector is a permutation P^m of prototype $\xi^{(1)}$ and that ϵ is set to an adequate value, the network will successively generate via (6.113) the permutations $P^{m+1} \xi^{(1)}$, $P^{m+2} \xi^{(1)}, \ldots$, etc until, for $P^{m+\ell} = I$ one recovers prototype $\xi^{(1)}$ as fixed point. It is not a priori obvious that there exists a value of ϵ which achieves this adequate balance between convergence to a prototype and repeated application of the transformation : if ϵ is too small, the network will keep applying the transformation, while, if ϵ is too large, the transformation is forgotten and the network will evolve to the nearest prototype. Experiments on translations, rotations and scaling of binary images tend to show that in most cases an adequate value lies around $\epsilon = 2$ [Coolen and Kuijk 89].

Remark • The approaches described in the last two subsections are in principle closely connected in that they both rely on the incorporation in the synaptic matrix of the correlations between vectors which are related either through some delay or by some transformation. They differ however on the following point. In the solution proposed by Coolen and Kuijk, the synaptic matrix learns the temporal relation resulting from *one* application of the transformation to the set of *all* state vectors. For Herz and his coauthors, learning concerns only the prototypes but covers *all* the relations induced by the different values of the delay.

Bibliography

[Aarts and Korst 88] E. Aarts and J. Korst. *Simulated annealing and Boltzmann machines.* J. Wiley & Sons, New York, 1988.

[Abu-Mostafa and St. Jacques 85] Y. Abu-Mostafa and J. St. Jacques. Information capacity of the Hopfield network. *IEEE Trans. on Information Theory*, vol. IT-31:pp. 461–464, 1985.

[Amari 71] S. Amari. Characteristics of randomly connected threshold-element networks and network systems. *Proc. IEEE*, vol. 59:pp. 35–47, 1971.

[Amari 72] S. Amari. Learning patterns and pattern sequences by self-organizing nets of threshold elements. *IEEE Trans. on Computers*, vol. C-21:pp. 1197–1206, 1972.

[Amari 74] S. Amari. A method of statistical neurodynamics. *Kybernetik*, vol. 14:pp. 201–215, 1974.

[Amari 77] S. Amari. Neural theory of association and concept formation. *Biological Cybernetics*, vol. 26:pp. 175–185, 1977.

[Amari and Maginu 88] S. Amari and K. Maginu. Statistical neurodynamics of associative memory. *Neural Networks*, vol. 1:pp. 63–73, 1988.

[Amit 87] D. Amit. The properties of models of simple neural networks. In J. van Hemmen and I. Morgenstern, editors, *Heidelberg Colloquium on glassy dynamics 1986*, pages 430–484, Springer Verlag, Berlin, 1987.

[Amit et al. 85a] D. Amit, H. Gutfreund, and H. Sompolinsky. Spin-glass models of neural networks. *Physical Review A*, vol. 32:pp. 1007–1018, 1985.

[Amit et al. 85b] D. Amit, H. Gutfreund, and H. Sompolinsky. Storing infinite number of patterns in a spin-glass model of neural networks. *Physical Review Letters*, vol. 55:pp. 1530–1533, 1985.

[Amit et al. 87a] D. Amit, H. Gutfreund, and H. Sompolinsky. Information storage in neural networks with low levels of activity. *Physical Review A*, vol. 35:pp. 2293–2303, 1987.

[Amit et al. 87b] D. Amit, H. Gutfreund, and H. Sompolinsky. Statistical mechanics of neural networks near saturation. *Annals of Physics*, vol. 173:pp. 30–67, 1987.

[Anderson and Hinton 81] J. Anderson and G. Hinton. Models of information processing in the brain. In G. Hinton and J. Anderson, editors, *Parallel models of associative memory*, pages 9–48, Lawrence Erlbaum Ass., Hillsdale (NJ), 1981.

[Baldi 88a] P. Baldi. Neural networks, acyclic orientations of the hypercube and sets of orthogonal vectors. *SIAM J. Disc. Math.*, vol. 1:pp. 1–13, 1988.

[Baldi 88b] P. Baldi. Neural networks, orientations of the hypercube and algebraic threshold functions. *IEEE Trans. on Information Theory*, vol. IT-34:pp. 523–530, 1988.

[Baldi and Venkatesh 87] P. Baldi and S. Venkatesh. Number of stable points for spin-glasses and neural networks of higher order. *Physical Review Letters*, vol. 58:pp. 913–916, 1987.

[Barnett and Storey 70] S. Barnett and C. Storey. *Matrix methods in stability theory*. Th. Nelson & Sons, London, 1970.

[Belevitch 68] V. Belevitch. *Classical network theory*. Holden Day, San Francisco, 1968.

[Bienenstock and von der Malsburg 87] E. Bienenstock and C. von der Malsburg. A neural network for invariant pattern recognition. *Europhysics Letters*, vol. 4:pp. 121–126, 1987.

[Bruck and Goodman 88] J. Bruck and J. Goodman. A generalized convergence theorem for neural networks. *IEEE Trans. on Information Theory*, vol. IT-34:pp. 1089–1092, 1988.

[Bruck and Roychowdhury 90] J. Bruck and V. Roychowdhury. On the number of spurious memories in the Hopfield model. *IEEE Trans. on Information Theory*, vol. IT-36:pp. 393–397, 1990.

[Chua and Lin 88] L. Chua and L. Lin. A neural network approach to transform image coding. *International Journal of Circuit Theory and its Applications*, vol. 16:pp. 317–324, 1988.

[Collobert and Maruani 89] D. Collobert and A. Maruani. Connexionisme, calcul, reconnaissance des formes et intelligence artificielle. *Annales des Télécommunications*, vol. 44:pp. 331–341, 1989.

[Coolen and Kuijk 89] A. Coolen and F. Kuijk. A learning mechanism for invariant pattern recognition in neural networks. *Neural Networks*, vol. 2:pp. 495–506, 1989.

[Cover 65] T. Cover. Geometrical and statistical properties of systems of linear inequalities with applications in pattern recognition. *IEEE Trans. on Electronic Computers*, vol. EC-14:pp. 326–334, 1965.

[Cramér 57] H. Cramér. *Mathematical methods of statistics.* Princeton University Press, Princeton (NJ), 1957.

[Crisanti and Sompolinsky 88] A. Crisanti and H. Sompolinsky. Dynamics of spin systems with randomly asymmetric bonds: Ising spins and Glauber dynamics. *Physical Review A*, vol. 37:pp. 4865–4874, 1988.

[Crisanti et al. 86] A. Crisanti, D. Amit, and H. Gutfreund. Saturation level of the Hopfield model of neural network. *Europhysics. Lett.*, vol. 2:pp. 337–341, 1986.

[de Bruijn 58] N. de Bruijn. *Asymptotic methods in analysis.* Northholland, Amsterdam, 1958.

[Delsarte and Kamp 89] P. Delsarte and Y. Kamp. Low rank matrices with a given sign pattern. *SIAM J. Disc. Math.*, vol. 2:pp. 51–63, 1989.

[Dembo 89] A. Dembo. On the capacity of associative memories with linear threshold functions. *IEEE Trans. on Information Theory*, vol. IT-35:pp. 709–720, 1989.

[Derrida 80] B. Derrida. Random energy model: limit of a family of disordered models. *Physical Review Letters*, vol. 45:pp. 79–82, 1980.

[Derrida 81] B. Derrida. Random energy model: an exactly solvable model of disordered systems. *Physical Review B*, vol. 24:pp. 2613–2626, 1981.

[Dertouzos 65] M. Dertouzos. *Threshold logic: a synthesis approach.* MIT Press, Cambridge (MA), 1965.

[Diederich and Opper 87] S. Diederich and M. Opper. Learning of correlated patterns in spin-glass networks by local learning rules. *Physical Review Letters*, vol. 58:pp. 949–952, 1987.

[Dotsenko 88] V. Dotsenko. Neural networks : translation-, rotation- and scale-invariant pattern recognition. *J. Phys. A : Math. Gen.*, vol. 21:pp. 783–787, 1988.

[Duda and Hart 73] R. Duda and P. Hart. *Pattern classification and scene analysis.* J. Wiley & Sons, New York, 1973.

[Eccles 77] J. Eccles. *The understanding of the brain.* McGraw-Hill, New York, 1977.

[Edwards and Anderson 75] S. Edwards and P. Anderson. Theory of spin glasses. *J. Phys. F : Metal. Phys.*, vol. 5:pp. 965–974, 1975.

[Feller 66] W. Feller. *An introduction to probability theory and its applications.* Volume 1, J. Wiley & Sons, New York, 1966.

[Fogelman-Soulie and Weisbuch 87] F. Fogelman-Soulie and G. Weisbuch. Random iterations of threshold networks and associative memory. *SIAM J. Computing*, vol. 16:pp. 203–220, 1987.

[Fogelman-Soulie et al. 83] F. Fogelman-Soulie, E. Goles, and G. Weisbuch. Transient length in sequential iteration of threshold functions. *Discrete Applied Mathematics*, vol. 6:pp. 95–98, 1983.

[Forrest 88] B. Forrest. Content-addressability and learning in neural networks. *J. Phys. A : Math. Gen.*, vol. 21:pp. 245–255, 1988.

[Fukanaga 72] K. Fukanaga. *Introduction to statistical pattern recognition.* Academic Press, New York, 1972.

[Gantmacher 60] F. Gantmacher. *The theory of matrices.* Chelsea Publ. Cy, New York, 1960.

[Gardner et al. 88] E. Gardner, N. Stroud, and D. Wallace. Training with noise: application to word and text storage. In R. Eckmiller and C. v.d. Malsburg, editors, *Neural Computers*, pages 251–260, Springer Verlag, Berlin, 1988.

[Glauber 63] R. Glauber. Time-dependent statistics of the Ising model. *J. Math. Phys.*, vol. 4:pp. 294–307, 1963.

[Goles 82] E. Goles. Fixed point behaviour of threshold functions on a finite set. *SIAM J. Alg. Disc. Meth.*, vol. 3:pp. 529–531, 1982.

[Goles and Olivos 81] E. Goles and J. Olivos. Comportement périodique des fonctions à seuil binaires et applications. *Discrete Applied Mathematics*, vol. 3:pp. 93–105, 1981.

[Goles et al. 85] E. Goles, F. Fogelman-Soulie, and D. Pellegrin. Decreasing energy functions as a tool for studying threshold networks. *Discrete Applied Mathematics*, vol. 12:pp. 261–277, 1985.

[Golub and Van Loan 83] G. Golub and C. Van Loan. *Matrix computations*. North Oxford Academic, Oxford, 1983.

[Greville 60] T. Greville. Some applications of the pseudo-inverse of a matrix. *SIAM Rev.*, vol. 2:pp. 15–22, 1960.

[Gross and Mézard 84] D. Gross and J. Mézard. The simplest spin-glass. *Nuclear Physics*, vol. B240:pp. 431–452, 1984.

[Guyon et al. 88a] I. Guyon, L. Personnaz, and G. Dreyfus. Of points and loops. In R. Eckmiller and C. v.d. Malsburg, editors, *Neural Computers*, pages 261–269, Springer Verlag, Berlin, 1988.

[Guyon et al. 88b] I. Guyon, L. Personnaz, J. Nadal, and G. Dreyfus. High order neural networks for efficient associative memory design. In D. Anderson, editor, *Proceedings of the IEEE Conference on Neural Information Processing Systems Denver 1987*, pages 233–241, American Institute of Physics, New York, 1988.

[Hall 67] M. Hall. *Combinatorial theory*. Blaisdell, London, 1967.

[Hebb 49] D. Hebb. *The organization of behavior*. J. Wiley & Sons, New York, 1949.

[Herz et al. 88] A. Herz, B. Sulzer, R. Kühn, and J. van Hemmen. The Hebb rule: storing static and dynamic objects in an associative neural network. *Europhysics Letters*, vol. 7:pp. 663–669, 1988.

[Herz et al. 89] A. Herz, B. Sulzer, R. Kühn, and J. van Hemmen. Hebbian learning reconsidered: representation of static and dynamic objects in associative neural nets. *Biological Cybernetics*, vol. 60:pp. 457–467, 1989.

[Hinton and Sejnowski 86] G. Hinton and T. Sejnowski. Learning and relearning in Boltzmann machines. In D. Rumelhart, J. McClelland, and the PDP Research Group, editors, *Parallel and distributed processing, Volume 1: Foundations*, pages 282–317, MIT Press, Cambridge (MA), 1986.

[Hopfield 82] J. Hopfield. Neural networks and physical systems with emergent collective computational abilities. *Proc. Ntl. Acad. Sci. USA*, vol. 79:pp. 2554–2558, 1982.

[Hopfield 84] J. Hopfield. Neurons with graded response have collective computational properties like those of two-state neurons. *Proc. Ntl. Acad. Sci. USA*, vol. 81:pp. 3088–3092, 1984.

[Hopfield and Tank 85] J. Hopfield and D. Tank. Neural computation of de-
cisions in optimization problems. *Biological Cybernetics*, vol. 52:pp. 141–
152, 1985.

[Jacyna and Malaret 89] G. Jacyna and E. Malaret. Classification performance of a Hopfield neural network based on a Hebbian-like learning rule.
IEEE Trans. on Information Theory, vol. IT-35:pp. 263–280, 1989.

[Kanter and Sompolinsky 87] I. Kanter and H. Sompolinsky. Associative recall of memory without errors. *Physical Review A*, vol. 35:pp. 380–392,
1987.

[Keeler 86] J. Keeler. Basins of attraction of neural network models. In
J. Denker, editor, *Neural Networks for Computing, AIP Conference Proceedings*, pages 259–264, American Institute of Physics, New York, 1986.

[Kendall and Stuart 63] M. Kendall and A. Stuart. *The advanced theory of
statistics, vol 1: Distribution theory*. Griffin, London, 1963.

[Kinzel 85] W. Kinzel. Learning and pattern recognition in spin glass models.
Z. Phys. B-Condensed Matter, vol. 60:pp. 205–213, 1985.

[Kirkpatrick and Sherrington 78] S. Kirkpatrick and D. Sherrington. Infinite-
ranged models of spin-glasses. *Physical Review B*, vol. 17:pp. 4384–4403,
1978.

[Kleinfeld and Pendergraft 87] D. Kleinfeld and D. Pendergraft. Unlearning
increases the storage capacity of content addressable memories. *J. Biophysics*, vol. 51:pp. 47–53, 1987.

[Kohonen 77] T. Kohonen. *Associative memory*. Springer Verlag, Berlin,
1977.

[Kohonen 84] T. Kohonen. *Self-organization and associative memory*.
Springer Verlag, Berlin, 1984.

[Kohonen and Ruohonen 73] T. Kohonen and M. Ruohonen. Representation
of associated data by matrix operators. *IEEE Trans. on Computers*, vol.
C-22:pp. 701–702, 1973.

[Komlós and Paturi 88] J. Komlós and R. Paturi. Convergence results in an
associative memory model. *Neural Networks*, vol. 1:pp. 239–250, 1988.

[Krauth and Mézard 87] W. Krauth and M. Mézard. Learning algorithms
with optimal stability in neural networks. *J. Phys. A : Math. Gen.*, vol.
20:pp. L745–L752, 1987.

[Kree and Zippelius 88] R. Kree and A. Zippelius. Recognition of topological features of grahs and images in neural networks. *J. Phys. A : Math. Gen.*, vol. 21:pp. 813–818, 1988.

[Kuffler et al. 84] S. Kuffler, J. Nicholls, and A. Martin. *From neuron to brain.* Sinauer, Massachusetts, 1984.

[Kuh and Dickinson 89] A. Kuh and B. Dickinson. Information capacity of associative memories. *IEEE Trans. on Information Theory*, vol. IT-35:pp. 59–68, 1989.

[Lee et al. 86] Y. Lee, G. Doolen, H. Chen, G. Sun, T. Maxwell, H. Lee, and C. Giles. Machine learning using a higher order correlation network. *Physica*, vol. 22D:pp. 276–306, 1986.

[Lippmann 87] R. Lippmann. An introduction to computing with neural nets. *IEEE ASSP Magazine*, vol. 4:pp. 4–22, 1987.

[Little 74] W. Little. The existence of persistent states in the brain. *Math. Biosc.*, vol. 19:pp. 101–120, 1974.

[Maćkowiak 82] J. Maćkowiak. On the mean field description of systems of point particles in equilibrium. *Physica*, vol. 110 A:pp. 302–320, 1982.

[Mattis 76] D. Mattis. Solvable spin systems with random interactions. *Phys. Lett.*, vol. 56 A:pp. 421–422, 1976.

[McCulloch and Pitts 43] W. McCulloch and W. Pitts. A logical calculus of the ideas immanent in nervous activity. *Bulletin of Mathematical Biophysics*, vol. 5:pp. 115–133, 1943.

[McEliece et al. 87] R. McEliece, E. Posner, E. Rodemich, and S. Venkatesh. The capacity of the Hopfield associative memory. *IEEE Trans. on Information Theory*, vol. IT-33:pp. 461–482, 1987.

[Mézard et al. 86] M. Mézard, J. Nadal, and G. Toulouse. Solvable models of working memories. *J. Physique*, vol. 47:pp. 1457–1462, 1986.

[Minsky and Papert 69] M. Minsky and S. Papert. *Perceptrons - An introduction to computational geometry.* MIT Press, Cambridge (MA), 1969.

[Moore 84] M. Moore. Random systems in condensed matter physics. In K. Bouwler and A. McKane, editors, *Statistical and particle physics: common problems and techniques*, pages 303–357, SUSSP Publications, University of Edinburgh, Edinburgh, 1984.

[Nadal et al. 86] J. Nadal, G. Toulouse, J. Changeux, and S. Dehaene. Networks of formal neurons and memory palimpsests. *Europhysics Letters*, vol. 1:pp. 535–542, 1986.

[Newman 88] C. Newman. Memory capacity in neural network models: rigorous lower bounds. *Neural Networks*, vol. 1:pp. 223–238, 1988.

[Parisi 80] G. Parisi. Magnetic properties of spin glasses in a new mean field theory. *J. Phys. A : Math. Gen.*, vol. 13:pp. 1887–1895, 1980.

[Pearson and Lippmann 88] J. Pearson and R. P. Lippmann. Adaptive knowledge processing. In The DARPA neural network study steering committee, editor, *The DARPA neural network study (part 2)*, pages pp. 79–202, AFCEA Int. Press, Fairfax (VA), 1988.

[Penrose 56] R. Penrose. On best approximate solutions of linear matrix equations. *Proc. Cambridge Philos. Soc.*, vol. 52:pp. 17–19, 1956.

[Peretto 84] P. Peretto. Collective properties of neural networks: a statistical physics approach. *Biological Cybernetics*, vol. 50:pp. 51–62, 1984.

[Peretto 88] P. Peretto. On the dynamics of memorization processes. *Neural Networks*, vol. 1:pp. 309–322, 1988.

[Peretto and Niez 86] P. Peretto and J. Niez. Long term memory storage capacity of multiconnected neural networks. *Biological Cybernetics*, vol. 54:pp. 53–63, 1986.

[Personnaz et al. 85] L. Personnaz, I. Guyon, and G. Dreyfus. Information storage and retrieval in spin-glass like neural networks. *J. Phys. Lett.*, vol. 46:pp. 359–365, 1985.

[Personnaz et al. 86] L. Personnaz, I. Guyon, and G. Dreyfus. Collective computational properties of neural networks: new learning mechanism. *Physical Review A*, vol. 34:pp. 4217–4228, 1986.

[Personnaz et al. 87a] L. Personnaz, I. Guyon, and G. Dreyfus. High-order neural networks: information storage without error. *Europhysics Letters*, vol. 4:pp. 863–867, 1987.

[Personnaz et al. 87b] L. Personnaz, I. Guyon, and G. Dreyfus. Neural networks for associative memory design. In H. Haken, editor, *Computational systems–natural and artificial*, pages 142–151, Springer Verlag, Berlin, 1987.

[Pierce and Posner 80] J. Pierce and E. Posner. *Introduction to communication science and systems*. Plenum, New York, 1980.

[Piret 88] P. Piret. Analysis of a modified Hebbian rule. 1988. Manuscript M280, Philips Research Laboratory, Brussels.

[Provost and Vallee 83] J. Provost and G. Vallee. Ergodicity of the coupling constants and the symmetric n-replicas trick for a class of mean-field spin-glass models. *Physical Review Letters.*, vol. 50:pp. 598–600, 1983.

[Robert 86] F. Robert. *Discrete iterations*. Springer Verlag, Berlin, 1986.

[Rozonoer 69a] L. Rozonoer. Random logical nets I. *Automat. Telemekh.*, vol. 5:pp. 137–147, 1969.

[Rozonoer 69b] L. Rozonoer. Random logical nets II. *Automat. Telemekh.*, vol. 6:pp. 99–109, 1969.

[Rozonoer 69c] L. Rozonoer. Random logical nets III. *Automat. Telemekh.*, vol. 7:pp. 127–136, 1969.

[Schrijver 86] A. Schrijver. *Theory of linear and integer programming*. J. Wiley & Sons, New York, 1986.

[Singleton 62] R. Singleton. A test for linear separability as applied to self-organizing machines. In M. Yovits, G. Jacobi, and G. Goldstein, editors, *Self-organizing systems*, pages 503–524, Spartan Books, Washington (DC), 1962.

[Sompolinsky 86] H. Sompolinsky. Neural networks with nonlinear synapses and a static noise. *Physical Review A*, vol. 34:pp. 2571–2574, 1986.

[Sompolinsky 87] H. Sompolinsky. The theory of neural networks: the Hebb rule and beyond. In J. van Hemmen and I. Morgenstern, editors, *Heidelberg Colloquium on glassy dynamics 1986*, pages 485–527, Springer Verlag, Berlin, 1987.

[Stanley 71] H. Stanley. *Introduction to phase transitions and critical phenomena*. Clarendon Press, Oxford, 1971.

[Stephen 83] M. Stephen. Lectures on disordered systems. In F. Hahne, editor, *Critical phenomena*, pages 259–300, Springer Verlag, Berlin, 1983.

[Sussmann 89] H. Sussmann. On the number of memories that can be perfectly stored in a neural net with Hebb weights. *IEEE Trans. on Information Theory*, vol. IT-35:pp. 174–178, 1989.

[Tanaka and Edwards 80] F. Tanaka and S. Edwards. Analytic theory of the ground state properties of a spin glass: I. Ising spin glass. *J. Phys. F : Metal. Phys.*, vol. 10:pp. 2769–2778, 1980.

[Tank and Hopfield 86] D. Tank and J. Hopfield. Simple neural optimization networks: an a/d converter, signal decision circuit, and a linear programming circuit. *IEEE Trans. on Circuits and Systems*, vol. CAS-33:pp. 533–541, 1986.

[Thouless et al. 77] D. Thouless, P. Anderson, and R. Palmer. Solution of solvable model of a spin glass. *Philosophical Magazine*, vol. 35:pp. 593–601, 1977.

[Tou and Gonzalez 74] J. Tou and R. Gonzalez. *Pattern recognition principles.* Addison-Wesley, Reading, 1974.

[van Hemmen 82] J. van Hemmen. Classical spin-glass models. *Physical Review Letters*, vol. 49:pp. 409–412, 1982.

[van Hemmen 87] J. van Hemmen. Nonlinear neural networks: efficient storage and retrieval of information. In J. van Hemmen and I. Morgenstern, editors, *Heidelberg Colloquium on glassy dynamics 1986*, pages 547–568, Springer Verlag, Berlin, 1987.

[van Hemmen and Kühn 86] J. van Hemmen and R. Kühn. Nonlinear neural networks. *Physical Review Letters*, vol. 57:pp. 913–916, 1986.

[van Laarhoven and Aarts 87] P. van Laarhoven and E. Aarts. *Simulated annealing: theory and applications.* D. Reidel, Dordrecht, 1987.

[Venkatesh 86] S. Venkatesh. Epsilon capacity of neural networks. In J. Denker, editor, *Neural Networks for Computing, AIP Conference Proceedings*, pages pp. 440–445, American Institute of Physics, New York, 1986.

[Venkatesh and Psaltis 89] S. Venkatesh and D. Psaltis. Linear and logarithmic capacities in associative neural networks. *IEEE Trans. on Information Theory*, vol. IT-35:pp. 558–568, 1989.

[von der Malsburg and Bienenstock 87] C. von der Malsburg and E. Bienenstock. A neural network for the retrieval of superimposed connection patterns. *Europhysics Letters*, vol. 3:pp. 1243–1249, 1987.

[Weisbuch and d'Humières 86] G. Weisbuch and D. d'Humières. Determining the dynamic landscape of Hopfield networks. In Nato Advanced

Studies Institute, editor, *Disordered systems and biological organization*, pages 187–191, Springer Verlag, Berlin, 1986.

[Weisbuch and Fogelman-Soulie 85] G. Weisbuch and F. Fogelman-Soulie. Scaling laws for the attractors of Hopfield networks. *J. Physique Lett.*, vol. 46:pp. 623–630, 1985.

Index

A
Activity level 55
Acyclic orientation 136
Algorithm
  least mean square $\sim$ 160
  perceptron $\sim$ 17, 160
Analysis 14
Aperiodic process 108
Approach
  deterministic $\sim$ 18
  statistical $\sim$ 19
Asynchronous operation 4, 24,
  68, 82
Attraction
  direct $\sim$ 16, 70, 76
  long-term $\sim$ 81
Autoassociation 5

B
Balance
  detailed $\sim$ principle 108
Barrier
  energy $\sim$ 84, 87, 149, 152
Basin
  of attraction of order k 7
  of direct attraction 6, 78,
    79, 147
  of long-term attraction 7
Bath
  heat $\sim$ 97
Block-sequential operation 4, 33

C
Capacity 15, 35, 68
Convex hull 156
Cycle 5

in asynchronous operation
  24, 25, 136
in block-sequential operation
  34
in Little model 117
in synchronous operation 29,
  30, 138
storage of $\sim$ 142, 172

D
Degree of monomial 134
Deterministic approach 18
Difference vector 45
Diluted network 132
Dimension of network 1
Dirac function 105, 110, 153
Direct attraction 16, 70, 76
Discrete derivative 46
Distance
  Hamming $\sim$ 6
Domain of direct attraction 6
Dynamic equation 1, 134, 139

E
Energy
  barrier 84, 87, 149, 152
  free $\sim$ 97
  function 18, 23, 100, 134
  internal $\sim$ 96
Entropy 81, 96
Equation
  dynamic $\sim$ 1, 134, 139
  evolution $\sim$ 54, 61
  mean field $\sim$ 21, 95, 154
Error rate 62
  residual $\sim$ 65, 82, 87, 151

191

U   unit step function 3, 74

V   Variable
    extensive ~ 96
    intensive ~ 96
    macroscopic ~ 20, 54

Vector
  difference ~ 45
  of synaptic potentials 2
  prototype ~ 5
  state ~ 1
  threshold ~ 2

W   Weight
    synaptic ~ 2